Passionate Revolutions

Ohio University Research in International Studies

This series of publications on Africa, Latin America, Southeast Asia, and Global and Comparative Studies is designed to present significant research, translation, and opinion to area specialists and to a wide community of persons interested in world affairs. The series is distributed worldwide. For more information, consult the Ohio University Press website, ohioswallow.com.

Books in the Ohio University Research in International Studies series are published by Ohio University Press in association with the Center for International Studies. The views expressed in individual volumes are those of the authors and should not be considered to represent the policies or beliefs of the Center for International Studies, Ohio University Press, or Ohio University.

Executive editor:
Gillian Berchowitz

Southeast Asia Series consultants:
Elizabeth F. Collins and William H. Frederick

Passionate Revolutions

The Media and the Rise and Fall of the Marcos Regime

Talitha Espiritu

OHIO UNIVERSITY RESEARCH IN INTERNATIONAL STUDIES
SOUTHEAST ASIA SERIES NO. 132
OHIO UNIVERSITY PRESS
ATHENS

To obtain permission to quote, reprint, or otherwise reproduce or distribute
material from Ohio University Press publications, please contact our rights and
permissions department at (740) 593-1154 or (740) 593-4536 (fax).

Printed in the United States of America
The books in the Ohio University Research in International Studies Series are
printed on acid-free paper ⊚ ™

27 26 25 24 23 22 21 20 19 18 17   5 4 3 2 1

Library of Congress Cataloging-in-Publication Data
Names: Espiritu, Talitha, author.
Title: Passionate revolutions : the media and the rise and fall of the Marcos
regime / Talitha Espiritu.
Description: Athens : Ohio University Press, [2017] I Series: Ohio University
research in international studies. Southeast Asia series ; no. 132 I
Includes bibliographical references and index.
Identifiers: LCCN 2017000722I ISBN 9780896803121 (pb : alk. paper) I ISBN
9780896803114 (hc : alk. paper) I ISBN 9780896804982 (pdf)
Subjects: LCSH: Philippines—Politics and government—1973–1986. I
Philippines—History—Revolution, 1986. I Mass media—Political
aspects—Philippines. I Politics and culture—Philippines. I Mass media
and culture—Philippines.
Classification: LCC DS686.5 .E87 2017 I DDC 959.904/6—dc23
LC record available at https://lccn.loc.gov/2017000722

To my parents,

Christian and Gliceria Espiritu,

and to my husband,

Kevin Durr

Contents

Introduction

THE POWER OF POLITICAL EMOTIONS

The dictatorship of Ferdinand Marcos came to an ignominious end on February 25, 1986. After twenty-one years in power, Marcos fled the Philippines following a four-day popular revolt dubbed people power. The euphoria in the streets was televised live around the globe. With the force of national allegory, these televised images conveyed a seemingly incontrovertible message: here is visible evidence that a people's democratic aspirations can triumph over authoritarianism; here is proof of the utopian possibilities of political emotions.

The political spectacle of people power conjoins two stories, each one pivoting on the activation of emotion in the political sphere. On the one hand, there is the melodramatic story of how Marcos rose to power by creating a national family, a political fantasy that was both seductive and treacherous in its claims to transform the nation into a postcolonial utopia via a dictatorship of love. On the other hand, there is the story of how a sentimental culture of protest grew in close proximity to the "official" political sphere, an intimate public laboriously channeling the moral outrage of a people pained by the egregious excesses of the Marcos regime. The media figured prominently in both these stories. Marcos, after all, was a master of the political spectacle, and melodrama was both the mode and modus operandi of his statecraft. After the assassination of Marcos's arch political rival, Benigno Aquino, Jr., in August 1983, however, the "freest press in Asia" came alive after a decade of state repression, galvanizing a "new politics" premised on affective displays of collective grief and concomitant demands for social justice. Meanwhile, the politicized auteurs of the so-called New Philippine Cinema engaged in unprecedented cultural activism both onscreen and in the streets. Combining melodrama's proclivities for hyperemotionality with sentimentality's faith in emotion as a direct conduit to affective truth, these forms of publicity were vital supports to the drama of emotional contestation that climaxed in people power.[1]

Marcos's rise to power and the 1986 popular revolt bring into relief a problem perennially addressed in the "affective turn" in the field of social movement studies: the deeply entrenched fear of mass action as the irrational exercise of mob psychology.[2] This fear turns on the normative split between the private and public spheres and the corollary pitting of feeling against thought. Emotions, according to this classic paradigm, belong in the intimate sphere. Their containment therein guarantees that the rule of reason will remain inviolate in the public sphere, understood as a scene of abstract debate. That these two "passionate revolutions" trafficked in ethico-emotional spectacles drawing heavily on melodramatic and the sentimental codes, points to what Lauren Berlant has described as the ascendance of a political culture of true feeling.[3]

Berlant sees an affective public taking the place of the mythical rational public imagined at the center of classic accounts of U.S. citizenship. Challenging the Enlightenment view of rationality as the distinguishing trait of the human subject, the culture of true feeling holds that what makes us human is our ability to empathize with the suffering of others. Elevating compassion to a civic duty, the culture of true feeling is premised on the notion that subjects are "emotionally identical in their pain and suffering and therefore imaginable by each other." As the glue that holds an affective public together, an emotional humanism presumes that "to feel emotion x in response to injustice" morally authorizes one to participate in the political sphere. Paradoxically, however, this brand of visceral politics locates political agency in private emotional acts.

It transforms citizenship into a form of spectatorship, in which the "citizen is moved rather than moving." The culture of true feeling thus keys us to the consequences of a political epistemology that sees emotion as the "best material from which determinations about justice are made."[4]

Berlant's concept of "true feeling" is a productive starting point for thinking about the power—as well as the pitfalls—of political emotions in the two stories that I trace in this book. These stories are due for a critical reappraisal in light of a renewed interest in affect and emotion in the study of political cultures. Recent work on the Marcos dictatorship has indeed begun to explore the affective and emotional dynamics of political repression and dissent. Joyce Arriola's work on print culture and Rolando Tolentino's prolific writings on the cinema similarly see the conflict between Marcos and his critics in terms of a binary struggle between "official" and "popular" forms of nationalism, eliciting hegemonic and abject political feelings, respectively.[5] With a much broader purview that explores the relations between Philippine visuality and the visual economy of an emergent world media system, Jonathan Beller's analysis of the protest aesthetic of anti-Marcos filmmakers draws attention to the revolutionary potential of a social realism based on emotional excess.[6] And engaging the cultural legacy of the Marcos regime from the perspective of queer cultural politics, Bobby Benedicto's study of Marcos-era architecture productively highlights how the physical ruins of the regime's film culture constitute an affective environment that articulates a "lost sense of progress, optimism and globalism," while simultaneously bringing to light the indeterminacy of national identity.[7] *Passionate Revolutions* builds on these important developments in the field. As a focused study of the role of the press and the cinema in the rise and fall of the Marcos regime, it seeks to explain how political emotions operate in official and popular forms of nationalism, and how these two affective realms intersect in the interfaces between national allegory, melodramatic politics and sentimental publicity.

National Allegory, Melodrama, and Popular Struggle

What is the relationship between nationalist movements and their symbolic forms? Berlant has coined the term "national symbolic" to refer to the range of discursive resources—icons, rituals, metaphors, and narratives—that constitute a culture's shared language for constructing a collective consciousness.[8] The national symbolic is what gives "official" nationalism its "heart"—and in the postcolonial world, its importance cannot be understated. In *The Wretched of the Earth,* Frantz Fanon emphasizes the psychoaffective dimensions of this process that hinges on using national culture to "make the *totality of the nation* a reality to each citizen" and to "make the history of the nation part of the *personal experience* of each of its citizens."[9] The national symbolic, in other words, activates public subjectivity in the realm of fantasy. Here, the fractured and depersonalized colonized subject is restored to state of wholeness by an affective act of identification with an imagined national body.

Marcos's many tracts on national culture echo Fanon's polemic in *Wretched of the Earth.* Like Fanon, Marcos saw the importance of addressing the psychic wounds of the colonized subject, whose self-worth can be restored only via a program of cultural rehabilitation. This basic precept was the animus behind the regime's cultural policy (see chapter 2). Let me signpost the affective dimensions of this policy here. Briefly put, it is not enough to have a cultivated mind; the task of national regeneration requires the citizen to have a reeducated heart. It is up to the state, then, to create a national culture that would provide a space of emotional contact, recognition, and reflection for its citizens. As a dramaturgical mirror designed to reflect back to the citizen an image of her best self, this national culture will transform the citizen into a subject of feeling: someone with affective commitments to the regime and its fantasy of a national family.

It has become a truism that Ferdinand and Imelda Marcos ruled the nation via a conjugal dictatorship that drew on the family form to secure its legitimacy.[10] But much work still remains to be done to explain the complex relationship between the Marcos romance—the love plot that organizes the regime's national symbolic—and the political and economic realities subtending the conjugal dictatorship. Two separate spheres, the intimate and the public, appear to be at work here, calling to mind related dichotomies: emotion vs. reason, representation vs. politics, and melodrama vs. documentary realism. On the face of things, these dichotomies appear to correspond with our habituated ways of organizing the disparate materials in the Marcos archive: films, literary works, and the ephemera of everyday life (what we in the humanities call texts) are studied with the interpretive approaches appropriate to the humanities, while the "hard facts" of state policy, political economy, and social movements are left up to social scientists to collect and narrate using the empirical methods of the social sciences. But if we were to take seriously the salience of "true feeling" in the political sphere, and if we were to take just as seriously the ways in which political-economic structures impinge on the national symbolic, we would see the necessity of rejecting these dichotomies in favor of a more interdisciplinary approach that blends fact and interpretation. Considering the Marcos romance as a national allegory is an important first step.

As a critical concept and political methodology, national allegory has become a prominent fixture in postcolonial discourse, particularly in Latin America. Ismail Xavier's pathbreaking study of Brazilian cinema fruitfully traces the rise of national allegory as a militant cultural practice in the 1960s and 1970s, a time "when the movement in world history seemed to elect the so-called Third World as the epicenter of change." In Brazil, this convulsive moment resulted in films that sought to "present a totalizing view of the country," with a clear "preference for allegory."[11] As both a "source of knowledge" and the "embodiment of a critical view of history," national allegory encapsulated an aesthetic and political predisposition toward creating social texts with a totalizing rhetoric anchored in a specific ideological-political conjuncture—one in which "the issues of class, race and gender were subordinate to the national question," and the notion of "underdevelopment was the nucleus of national thinking."[12] National allegory, in other words, became the medium for analyzing—and intervening in—the postcolonial condition and the failure of the national dream.

The notion of underdevelopment resonated in the Philippines in the early 1970s, when Marcos and his critics were locked in a power struggle that culminated in his declaration of martial law, in September 1972. At the time, the dominant framework for apprehending the "national question" in the Philippines was the neocolonial, or dependency, model.[13] Leftist nationalists argued that the economic practices of transnational corporations instantiated the indirect colonial rule of the United States over the Philippines, which was reinforced by the military pacts between the two countries. The nation's dependent status vis-à-vis an external military and economic power consigned it to a condition of underdevelopment that could be corrected only by radical social transformation.

When Marcos became dictator, he assumed the position of the nation's "official writer," as Arriola puts it, "mix[ing] state policy with ideology and propaganda to rally the people toward a 'nation.'"[14] Marcos went so far as to "author" *Tadhana: The History of the Filipino People,* a multivolume series that was touted to be the definitive history of the Philippines. In it, Marcos answered his critics' gloomy prognosis with a self-affirming narrative of a postcolonial nation overcoming all odds.[15] *Tadhana*'s "official history" resonated with Ferdinand and Imelda Marcos's own biographies, which were meant to be read as autobiographies of collective experience. Complementing *Tadhana*'s affirmative narrative, they present Ferdinand and Imelda's dreams, struggles and triumphs as allegories of the nation's colonial past, unstable present and optimistic future. They present the couple's intimate union and political partnership as a rule of love, the social solution to the nation's condition of underdevelopment.

In the Marcos regime's political lexicon, *love* is a euphemism for modes of social control secured in and through cultural policy. It bears noting that cultural policy straddles the intimate and public spheres: insofar as it is primarily concerned with the normalization of tastes and the regimentation of social conduct, cultural policy requires the alignment of the intimate sphere of domesticity with the public culture of the state. The two spheres are assumed to work in tandem, inculcating a drive toward self-improvement in the cultural citizen. And as Jürgen Habermas reminds us, it is in the domestic sphere where citizens are prepared for their critical social function in the public sphere, where the public's role as critic is guided and made possible by the ideal of collective intimacy.[16] Cultural policy indeed turns on what Berlant, after Habermas, calls "the migration of intimacy expectations between the public and the domestic."[17] Simply put, it assumes that the cultivation of good taste in the intimate sphere leads to good citizenship in the public sphere. What is striking about the cultural policy of the Marcos regime is its allegorization of this classic model of the ethico-aesthetic in the person of Imelda Marcos, who, as "mother of the Filipino people," was the primary civilizing agent of the national family. This book unpacks Imelda's complex and highly ambivalent role as the melodramatic heroine of the Marcos romance whose desire for the good life encapsulates the melodramatic imaginary of the regime's cultural policy.

Melodrama is a constitutive feature of the allegorical impulse to narrate "the truth" of a nation. Indeed, the overlap between national allegory and melodrama is of central concern to my project, and a brief explication of their mutually reinforcing dynamic is in order.

As a critical concept, melodrama is a notoriously slippery term. Since the 1960s and 1970s, when melodrama emerged as a major topic in film studies, scholars have tried to pin down its essential qualities. But so many inconsistencies abound in the usage of the term, and so many mutations have surfaced in its cross-media adaptations that no consensus has been reached on whether melodrama constitutes a coherent genre or a more elusive "mode" of expression.[18] Recent scholarship has shifted the terms of debate from what melodrama is to what it does.[19] Whether scholars approach it as a specific genre, or engage it as a pervasive mode of popular culture narrative, all agree that it is particularly responsive to experiences of dislocation and trauma.[20] All agree, furthermore, that its key features—strong pathos, moral legibility, and sensational expressionism—resonate with subaltern audiences, or those among us whose material vulnerability and experiences of social marginalization have been most acute.

Emerging in the wake of the Enlightenment, melodrama, Peter Brooks argues, seeks above all to make moral principles legible in a secular world, where "the traditional patterns of moral order no longer provide the necessary social glue." It has long been the job of melodrama to serve a compensatory, quasi-religious function, defusing social anxieties with stories enacting the "eventual victory of virtue."[21] But as Linda Williams has more recently argued, the force of melodrama's ameliorative function rests not so much on a drama of the defeat of evil by good but on the "all important recognition of a good or evil that was previously obscure." Indeed, what melodrama really does is to allow us to see "a previously unrecognized problem or contradiction within modernity" and to "generate outrage against realities that could and should be changed."[22]

These insights allow us to apprehend melodrama as a discursive practice that is also mode of social activism: it is a means of "[making] truth and justice legible by demanding a clear binary between right and wrong."[23] Melodrama does not simply reflect a mode of consciousness in a postsacred world; it *acts upon* that consciousness by supplying a "dominant language on the modern conduct of public life and politics."[24] This book contends that melodrama fundamentally structures the key operation at the heart of all national allegories: the impetus to reveal the "truth" of the nation in a mode that appeals to the affective reason of the citizen.

Discussions of melodrama's aesthetic force often turn on the notion of excess. In melodrama, exaggerated emotionality and a predilection for spectacle combine to produce an overwrought drama that "produces and foments psychic energies and emotions."[25]

Ultimately, melodramatic excess constitutes a sensational economy that activates a complex process of psychological identification for the viewer.

Central to the discursive practice of melodrama is the presentation of victimization. Almost without exception, moral virtue is signified by pathos and suffering. Melodrama's sensational economy triggers two interrelated processes: a heightened perception of moral injustice (against an undeserving victim) and the cathartic transformation of raw emotions (of distress and moral outrage). The audience feels strong pathos, "a sort of pain at an evident evil of a destructive or painful kind . . . the evil being one which we imagine to happen to ourselves."[26] The pathos that accompanies melodramatic identification, in short, is a form of self-pity.

The psychoaffective processes of melodrama have a powerful ideological effect. As many critics have noted, melodrama has a conservative social vision: the suffering of the victim must be vindicated through acts of redemptive violence, which then restores a community to its lost "space of innocence."[27] But as Matthew Buckley has recently pointed out, the critical tendency to privilege melodrama's redemptive social vision obscures the genre's complicated affective conditioning. Melodrama, he reminds us, initially invites sympathetic attachment to victimized heroes and heroines. However, opposing emotions of hatred and fear ultimately supersede feelings of sympathy, as negative affects are "projected or 'dumped' outward . . . upon some clear other, through angry and often violent action."[28] A radical disconnect thus emerges between the consoling vision of melodrama's moral structure and the violent projections of its affective structure. The latter, to borrow Buckley's terms, encourages "infantile processes of defensive withdrawal," substituting "the passive consumption of sensational fantasy for the more complex and demanding performance of collective identification and communal action and identity."[29]

A fundamental tension exists, then, between melodrama's two core operations: the imperative to move audiences to feel moral outrage against social contradictions, and the validation of traditional figures of political authority, who ultimately emerge as the real agents of moral retribution. While the former registers melodrama's implicit drive toward social activism, the latter speaks to melodrama's opposing tendency to reduce political action to the spectatorial pleasures of mass entertainment. The push-pull between these two melodramatic operations was amply in evidence in Marcos's rise to power and in the 1986 popular revolt.

This book unpacks the melodramatic politics inhering in the national allegories created by Marcos and his critics. It locates these allegories in press reports, magazine features, campaign biographies, propaganda films, biopics, and studio films that serve as melodramatic transcripts of the rise and fall of the Marcos regime. These allegories bring to the fore the continuing salience of a fundamental question, first broached by Ana Lopez, that continues to inform studies of melodrama in non-Western contexts: "Is it possible that this form, the product and instrument of the dominant classes and the servant of dominant ideologies, can be utilized and read as a *positive* force for socio-cultural change in dependent societies?"[30]

Media scholars and practitioners have routinely attacked melodrama as a retrograde cultural form, "helping to produce the 'perfect' subject of political and economic dependence in the Third World." But as Lopez cogently argues, these naysayers are blindsided by melodrama's special affinity with the popular classes. Exactly how these melodramas "meet the real desires and needs of real people" is the crux of the problem.[31] Uncover that and we might begin to analyze melodrama's critical potential as a site of resistance in Third World societies. More recently, Sheetal Majithia has problematized the implicit privileging of reason over emotion, the secular over the sacred and the West over the non-West in melodrama studies. Postcolonial melodramas, Majithia argues, show how powerful political attachments are formed through the affective reason activated by melodrama: the way it illuminates "our power to affect the world around us and our power to be affected by it."[32] Susan Dever also sees the democratic potential of melodramas, which may "provide a means for newly-enfranchised subjects to reflect—both cognitively and affectively—on the significance of their participation in nation-states whose sacred legitimacy revolution has called into question."[33] Building on these insights, this book examines how melodrama can channel the desires of disempowered groups to articulate a popular democratic politics in resistance to the elitist and paternalistic discourses that dominate "Philippine-style" democracy.

As Reynaldo Ileto argues, the history of political struggle in the Philippines has been characterized by the coexistence of two competing notions of politics: *pulitika,* the deficient formal democracy of the elite, and the more "meaningful politics" of the oppressed. Dismissed by elites as mere "emotional outpourings," the latter produced numerous popular uprisings galvanized by such concepts as *awa* (pity) and *damay* (empathy) for an aggrieved person or community.[34] Popular forces, in short, have understood political struggle as melodrama. And here, the social and the political become legible only "as they touch on the moral identities and relationships of individuals."[35] As I demonstrate in this book, the national allegories of the oppositional media engaged the audience's visceral capacity to recognize the pain of the popular forces as proof of virtue. They denigrated the civic ardor of those still invested in pulitika as the chicanery of a debased democracy. Such denigration of "official" politics is a clear indicator of the sentimental ethos animating the anti-Marcos movement. But despite its concerted efforts to distance itself from Marcos, the movement shared with the dictator an unwavering faith in the logic of true feeling. As we shall see, a sentimental politics based on compassion is not qualitatively different from Marcos's own claim to govern the nation with love.

National Sentimentality: Once More, with Feeling

What is the place of painful feeling in the making of political worlds? Berlant's work on "national sentimentality" centers on this question, which resonates in my reading of the national allegories documented in this book. Let me briefly outline the central premises of the concept and explain how they inform my methodology. Berlant describes national sentimentality as a mode of political rhetoric that makes a captivating promise to its public. Simply put, it promises that the social injustices fracturing a nation will be put to right through the power of empathy and identification. This promise comes out of the long-standing contest between two models of citizenship that roughly correspond to the above description of pulitika and the "meaningful" politics of the oppressed. On the one hand, there is the classic model of citizenship that sees the value of each citizen to lie in their juridical status as an abstract person before the law. On the other hand, there is a sentimental model of citizenship that Berlant traces back to the labor, feminist, and antiracist struggles in the United States in the nineteenth century. These social movements imagined a nation peopled not by abstract persons but by "suffering citizens and noncitizens" structurally excluded from the "American dreamscape."[36] Lest we forget, the U.S. Constitution constructed the person as the unit of political membership in the American nation, but in practice, this privilege really only belonged to white, property-owning males. The notion of national identity thus serves to protect the implied whiteness and maleness of the original American citizen, whose privilege it was "to appear to be without notable qualities." Indeed, the notion of abstract personhood so dear to the classic model of citizenship presupposes a white male body as the relay to legitimation. And the power to suppress this body becomes the measure of one's authority in the public sphere.[37]

Sentimental politics turns the classic model of citizenship on its head, positing the pain of subaltern subjects—those who have never had the privilege to suppress the event of the body—as the true core of national collectivity. It insists that a utopian society can be achieved by identification with their pain. Note, however, that a power imbalance supports this transaction of pain and recognition, which is focalized from the perspective of the culturally privileged.

The pain of African-Americans, women, and the poor "burns into the conscience of classically privileged national subjects, such that they feel the pain of flawed or denied citizenship as their pain."[38] Sentimentality, in short, assumes that structural social change is possible, provided that a bond of compassion—"an affective and redemptive linkage"—can be forged "between the privileged and the socially abject."[39]

What creates the bond of compassion? The short answer: sentimental publicity. Sentimental citizenship abhors the "official" institutions of politics. It locates its interventions not in the political domain but "near it, against it, above it," in the "juxtapolitical" space of everyday life, whenever and wherever an intimate public forms around scenes and stories of social injustice. Books, newspapers, films, TV, and all other forms of popular narrative are the diverse media of sentimental publicity. They provide the material infrastructure for circulating sentimental narratives and for gathering an intimate public together—whether physically, as in the case of the gregarious communitas of cinema spectatorship, or imaginatively, as in the case of the solitary reader/viewer who imagines a shared horizon of experience with other readers/viewers of sentimental texts.

But it is a sentimental aesthetic that allows sentimental narratives and their representations of social wrongs to gain political traction within this intimate public. And this aesthetic is defined by the use of personal suffering to "express or exemplify conflicts in national life." In sentimental narratives, stereotypes and clichés imbue a "local drama of compassionate attachment with a sense of import beyond the scene of its animation." The struggle of an individual thereby takes on the expansive and totalizing logic of national allegory. And when crises of the heart are resolved, the "emotional justice achieved on the small scale figures its resolution on the larger."[40]

The sentimental aesthetic seeks to transform its privileged public. It elevates reading to a powerful act of compassionate cosmopolitanism: to read a sentimental text is to enter a space of dis-interpellation insofar as one is compelled to identify with someone else's pain. Identification with suffering is indeed the only ethical response to a sentimental plot. Liberal empathy—the idea that you will never be the same—is thus the "radical threat and great promise" of the sentimental aesthetic. It embodies the ethico-aesthetic project of cultural policy writ large: the idea that "proper reading will lead to more virtuous, compassionate feeling and therefore to a better self."[41]

Again: sentimental publicity locates compassionate citizenship in the transactions of pain and recognition that bind the members of an intimate public. But resting primarily on an aesthetic activity, sentimental publicity generates a mode of citizenship that does not easily map onto the political sphere, if we understand the latter as a "place of acts oriented towards publicness." What we get instead is a "world of private thoughts" projected outward. This, in essence, is what a sentimental public is: "private individuals inhabiting their own affective changes."[42] This brings us to the "unfinished business" of national sentimentality as Berlant sees it: how do changes in feeling, even on a mass scale, bring about structural social change?

This book seeks to weigh in on this question from the postcolonial perspective of the Philippines during the historically significant period of the Marcos dictatorship. A critical feature of my methodology is to draw attention to the process of rough translation that has accompanied the transplantation of U.S. models of democracy and cultural policy to the former colony. These rough translations attest to what Majithia describes as the "coeval but uneven conditions that characterize postcolonial and global conditions."[43] Taking a relational perspective indeed allows one to appreciate how the sentimental political culture described by Berlant also inheres in a nation-state conceived in the image of the United States. It allows us to see how political attachments in these two distinct—but profoundly interconnected—national contexts often "derive from visceral and inchoate fears, resentments, anxieties, desires, aspirations, senses of belonging or non-belonging that an individual (or an ideal, or an organization) somehow stirs up and addresses." It also allows us to see how the structurally oppressed and the socially abject in both countries "often have strongly conflicted sentiments about themselves and the society that has made them 'other.'"[44]

This ambivalence was certainly a concern for Marcos, who often referred to the shame and self-hatred of the colonized subject. But he was also wont to invoke the rage of the oppressed, stressing how this protorevolutionary emotion could have dire consequences for the republic. The containment of this terrible rage was indeed Marcos's pretext for declaring martial law. Meanwhile, there were limits to the anti-Marcos movement's sentimental will to correct social wrongs. From the earliest days of the dictatorship, the various "pain alliances" that comprised the anti-Marcos coalition were internally torn between those who sought radical social change and those seeking the more moderate solution of a regime change. These factions, however, stood united—however briefly and tenuously—in the belief that a compassionate public feeling was a necessary first step toward social transformation. But the deciding factor was the popular classes: Marcos and his critics routinely invoked their rage and pain and sought to control it. Both sides sought to create a sentimental bargain with the popular classes. To borrow Berlant's terms, this involved "substituting for representations of pain and violence representations of its sublime self-overcoming."[45] Both sides however, evinced a profound lack of knowledge—distrust, even—of the popular classes. In recreating the story of Marcos's rise and fall, I emphasize the double representation of the popular classes—as simultaneously abject and politically volatile—as a case study of how, as Deborah Gould puts it, the ambivalence of the abject and the marginalized "shapes a sense of political (im)possibilities," and can have "tremendous influence on political action and inaction."[46]

The above discussion of sentimental publicity makes clear the importance of engaging the aesthetic dimension of sentimental texts. The sentimental ideal of liberal empathy indeed grounds the various national allegories that I analyze in this book. I explicate how these texts imagine social transformation not as a structural event, but as an emotional one: how the ability to feel for the subordinate other is presented as something that progressively grows into a desire for the emancipation of that person, and by extension, the community. However, as Berlant warns, an overinvestment in the emotional event of the reader's psychological transformation, at the expense of tracking what is needed for structural change, confines sentimental politics to the business of "delivering virtue to the privileged."[47] It thus behooves us to analyze these sentimental texts alongside the "official texts" of government (presidential decrees, congressional speeches, white papers, conference proceedings, etc.), and to place them in their proper historical and social contexts. For indeed, the "pain politics" of sentimental culture "falsely promises a sharp picture of structural violence."[48] It is necessary, therefore, to bring the political economy of the regime to bear on our discussion of the sentimental politics of the anti-Marcos movement. Lest we forget, feeling is a powerful but unreliable measure of justice.

With a historical sweep that spans twenty-one years of the Marcos era, this book presents the stories of two "passionate revolutions." Chapters 1 through 3 examine Marcos's so-called "democratic revolution," while chapters 4 through 6 trace the story of people power. Chapter 1 examines the protest culture of the Philippines on the eve of martial law. I reconstruct the volatile political climate generated by the so-called First Quarter Storm, the violent street protests that rocked the nation in early 1970. I read the national allegories on display in these protests, as memorialized in Jose F. Lacaba's *Days of Disquiet, Nights of Rage.* Consisting of Lacaba's first-person accounts of the protests for the *Philippines Free Press,* the iconic text captures the visceral performance of moral clarity at the heart of sentimental politics.[49] But the sentimental publicity that enabled Marcos's critics to become an intimate public finds a counterpart in his command of political spectacle. I examine a rare propaganda film, *The Threat—Communism,* which draws on the U.S. tradition of "political demonology" to contain the revolutionary sentiments then sweeping the nation. The film is a perfect illustration of the affective conditioning that constitutes melodrama's negative pole, and constitutes a hermeneutic key for making sense of Marcos's pivotal declaration of martial law, in 1972.

Chapter 2 examines the cultural policy of the Marcos regime. I tease out how Marcos's cultural liberation program mimicked the paternalistic rhetoric of the colonial policy of benevolent assimilation: both decreed the ethico-aesthetic training of cultural subjects as a prerequisite to the exercise of the rights and duties of citizenship. But Marcos's cultural liberation program also echoed Fanon's theorization of cultural rehabilitation in *The Wretched of the Earth:* the cultural imperative to correct the "self-contempt, resignation and abjuration" of the colonized and thereby effect the psychoaffective creation of "new men."[50] Marcos's New Society was indeed an ambitious cultural-policy endeavor that sought to create the New Filipino by synthesizing the paternalist, U.S.-centric and neocolonialist discourse of modernization with the populist, nationalist, and anticolonial cultural politics of an emergent Third World consciousness. The chapter revisits the Marcos romance, showing how this love plot underpins the regime's national symbolic and its double-speaking cultural policy.

Chapter 3 examines the impact of the regime's cultural policy directives on the cinema, beginning with a "national sexuality" campaign against a *bomba* (sex-and-violence) film culture that mirrored the irrational and libidinous excesses of Philippine politics in the late 1960s and early 1970s. I trace how a dual policy of strict censorship and artistic promotion—and Imelda's "internationalist" aspirations for the cinema—would ironically lead to the consolidation of a cinema vanguard committed to raising awareness of political repression in the New Society among a world audience. Their antiauthoritarian cultural politics bore a striking affinity with the protest culture of the First Quarter Storm. I tease out the resonances of the First Quarter Storm and the bomba film culture in Lino Brocka's *Tinimbang ka ngunit kulang* (Weighed and found wanting, 1974), a sentimental text that allegorizes social cleansing in the New Society.

Chapter 4 traces the various fronts of the anti-Marcos struggle from the earliest days of martial law to just before the Aquino assassination. I situate the movement's pain alliances against the political-economic backdrop of the Marcos regime's disastrous development initiatives. I read Behn Cervantes's *Sakada* (1976) as a sentimental text that self-reflexively reveals the paternalism of both radical and moderate factions of the anti-Marcos movement toward the oppressed groups in whose name the struggle against dictatorship was being waged. The film begs to be read against the real-world activism of the popular classes. I thus examine two cases instantiating "democracy from below" in the New Society: the struggle of the Kalinga and Bontoc mountain peoples against militarization and the struggle of urban squatters against their forced displacement from Imelda's so-called City of Man. With only the New Cinema, the Catholic media, and a handful of defiant journalists in the controlled media to publicize their causes, these communities fought at a disadvantage for the very ideals that Nathan Gilbert Quimpo identifies as the salient goals of democracy from below: "popular empowerment, a more equitable distribution of wealth, and a more participatory democracy."[51]

Chapter 5 examines the "quiet revolt" of the establishment press, the return of the bomba film, and the sentimental publicity occasioned by the Aquino assassination, in 1983. Marcos's failing health and a succession struggle within the national family had emboldened journalists within the controlled press to expose the military's human-rights abuses. Meanwhile, the sensation stirred by the screening of pornographic films at the 1983 Manila International Film Festival brought into relief the growing fault lines in Marcos's "household" and propelled cultural workers to organize against the regime. I reconstruct the Aquino assassination as the melodramatic event that compelled the various factions of the anti-Marcos struggle to close ranks. I show how national grief transformed the elite politician into the martyr of a new sentimental politics.

Chapter 6 examines the dramatic escalation of protest activity after the assassination. I show how the melodramatic mass-action strategies of the movement hinged on stoking the class hostilities of the popular classes—and, crucially, transforming mass anger into a politically viable expression of resistance. I examine the activism of New Cinema filmmaker Lino Brocka and present a close reading of *Bayan ko: Kapit sa patalim* (My country: Seize the blade, 1985), his homage to the new politics. As a bellwether of the 1986 popular revolt, this national allegory offers valuable insights into the often-overlooked role of the popular forces in the unfolding of people power.

Contrary to the dominant interpretation of the 1986 revolt as a middle-class phenomenon, people power was in fact the culmination of the long popular struggle against the regime. Various grass-roots struggles from the earliest days of martial law created both a melodramatic imaginary and an infrastructure of resistance that allowed millions of disempowered Filipinos to stage an awesome public drama bearing the full force of twenty-one years of resistance against a repressive and corrupt regime. The mobilizing efforts of an alternative press and the New Cinema were crucial supports in this drama. But at bottom it was the overwhelming presence of the popular classes and their melodramatic performances of their democratic aspirations that were on display. It was, in short, the force of national allegory that toppled the dictator.

Chapter 1

THE FIRST
QUARTER STORM

When Ferdinand Marcos declared martial law in the Philippines on September 21, 1972, the country was on the cusp of a revolutionary upheaval. The economy was in crisis, exacerbating class divisions in a nation where 50 percent of the national wealth was concentrated in the hands of 5 percent of the population.[1] On the political front, the nation was still reeling from the staggering violence and fraud that attended the November 1969 elections, which saw Marcos reelected to an unprecedented second term. Meanwhile, a "special relationship" with the United States guaranteed Philippine support for America's war in Vietnam and the country's wholesale capitulation to the International Monetary Fund's oppressive demands for drastic cuts in social expenditures. Against this dire political and economic backdrop, waves of strikes and demonstrations swept the nation's capital, escalating to dramatically violent confrontations between the military and dissident groups during the first three months of 1970. Collectively dubbed the First Quarter Storm, these public dramatizations of urban unrest closely followed the steady advance of an underground guerrilla insurgency movement in the countryside. These two fronts of militant dissident action—one highly visible, the other covert—were mutually reinforcing features of an ascendant cult of revolutionism that Marcos ostensibly aimed to defuse by declaring martial law.

In his martial law declaration, Marcos alleged that "lawless elements" presented a "clear, present and grave" danger to the republic, threatening to undermine the government with acts of "rebellion and armed insurrection." The Communist Party of the Philippines (CPP) and its military arm, the New People's Army (NPA), were specifically targeted as the principal instigators of the conflict. In the face of the enemy's "well-trained, well-armed, highly indoctrinated and greatly expanded revolutionary force," martial law was deemed a necessary corrective to the nation's "state of political, social, psychological and economic instability."[2]

Even as he condemned the upsurge of radical militant action in the nation as the immediate justification for establishing authoritarian rule, Marcos was deeply enamored of the cult of revolutionism generated by this militancy. Shortly before assuming his dictatorship, Marcos would write, "We live in a revolutionary era. It is an era of swift, violent and often disruptive change, and rather than lament this vainly, we have to decide whether we are the masters or victims of change."[3] The statement, issued in his 1971 political tract "Today's Revolution: Democracy," demonstrates Marcos's readiness to appropriate the revolutionary feeling buoying his critics.[4] As the *New York Times* reported in March 1970, the word *revolution* was becoming a byword for an ever-widening spectrum of oppositional groups in the country, including "workers, peasants, middle-class intellectuals, clergy, moderate students as well as radical revolutionary students."[5] "Today's Revolution" paradoxically parrots the broad-based opposition's calls for social reforms, even trying to outdo the populist bent of the opposition's reformist agenda by demanding nothing less than radical social transformation.

In the Philippines, Marcos writes, "revolution is inevitable."[6] This inevitability is subtended by the utter failure of social reform in the face of a debased democracy. Marcos is quick to enumerate the symptomatic features of such a democracy: the unchecked political and economic power of the oligarchy, the sensational practices of the media, the rampant corruption in the public and private sectors, and the existence of private armies and political warlords.[7] Reflecting a fundamentally flawed social contract, the nation's flailing democracy demands that society itself must be radically transformed. Otherwise, Marcos argues, those to whom reforms are a necessity "have no other recourse but violent revolution."[8]

For Marcos, what the nation needed was a *democratic* revolution: "The process we need—and want—is thus a revolution by democratic means, the only method of cleansing society and rescuing it from its ills."[9] What would make such social cleansing "democratic" was that the martial law declaration that occasioned it was perfectly legal, based on a constitutional provision guaranteeing the executive's special powers under times of war. Marcos coined the phrase "constitutional authoritarianism" to describe his new dictatorial powers, which he claimed to be using in radical ways.[10] By turns a reactionary and revolutionary concept, constitutional authoritarianism promised to create a working fit between two otherwise contradictory systems—dictatorial rule and democracy—with an eye to generating a more perfect society and, consequently, a purer social contract. But for this social experiment to be legitimate, at least on paper, the onus lay on Marcos to prove that the nation was in fact in a state of war, so much so that martial law had become a necessary and exigent measure.

The spectacular nature of the First Quarter Storm, aided in large part by sensational media coverage of the demonstrations, ironically worked to strengthen Marcos's position regarding martial law. This was indeed significant because the president and the oligarchy-controlled media had been at loggerheads, at least since Marcos's much-disputed reelection in 1969. In the months following his reelection, the media launched a de facto anti-Marcos campaign, feeding the public with a daily diet of anti-Marcos announcements from both the political right and left. Both ends of the political spectrum had charged the newly incumbent president with "seeking to perpetuate his power" and failing to "curb corruption, the private armies of warlord-politicians, and an obstructive Congress."[11] During the fateful First Quarter Storm, oligarchs hostile to Marcos (most notably the Lopez family, who owned and controlled the powerful ABS-CBN television network and the national daily *Manila Chronicle*) used their vast media holdings to publicize the demonstrations, thus inadvertently aiding the leftist dissidents in their efforts to bring down the government through violent confrontation.

Marcos was quick to transform what would ordinarily amount to a political deficit into a golden opportunity. The First Quarter Storm, which had taken him by surprise in 1970, had taught him the invaluable lesson that the revolution was fundamentally governed by the dynamics of spectacle. But while his opponents labored to spectacularize national discontent in the hopes of discrediting his administration, Marcos, in an act of classic one-upmanship, would translate these spectacles of social disorder into a public drama justifying authoritarian social control. To fully understand this critical shift in the revolutionary momentum of the nation on the eve of martial law, we need to revisit the public drama that was the First Quarter Storm.

The January 26 Riot

The First Quarter Storm began on January 26, 1970, when fifty thousand students, workers, and peasants convened outside the Congress Building in downtown Manila. Carefully timed to coincide with the opening of Congress, the rally was a provocative parody of the official proceedings simultaneously taking place. Fiery speeches delivered by dissident leaders excoriated the government for the country's social ills, which were traced back to three essential sources: imperialism, feudalism, and fascism. Blatantly referencing critical concepts in the ideology of the CPP, the speakers flouted the country's 1950 Anti-Subversion Law (Republic Act no. 1700), which had declared communism illegal in the Philippines. And, as if to deliver communism from its shadowy existence underground, the streets were aflame with red banners bearing the taboo slogans Revolt Is Necessary and Welcome to the NPA.

The demonstrators and the public officials secreted in the building behind locked doors constituted two parallel congresses—one illicit, the other official. A one-way public address system allowed the demonstrators to hear the official proceedings, though their attention was riveted to the speakers among their ranks whom they could see.[12] Four hours into the demonstration, the president, unseen by the demonstrators, took to the microphone to deliver his state of the nation address. It was at this point that the two parallel congresses may be said to intersect. While Marcos delivered his speech, "National Discipline: The Key to Our Future," the demonstrators became increasingly rowdy, as if to mock the president's calls for sobriety and self-restraint. When the First Couple emerged from the Congress Building, the protestors burned three effigies in full view of the president: a coffin, to represent the death of democracy (an allusion to the violence of the last election); a crocodile, to represent the corrupt Congress; and a cardboard likeness of the president himself.[13] The demonstrators hurled the flaming effigies at the visibly shaken couple, and then proceeded to pelt them with rocks and soda bottles. Within seconds, military police charged at the crowd, scattering the demonstrators with truncheons.

The majority of the demonstrators were forced to flee the rally grounds along Burgos Drive, but two thousand protestors stood their ground. As they proceeded to sing the communist anthem "Internationale," the stragglers became marked men. Linking arms, the exposed communists openly defied the police and the riot squad, chanting a new slogan: "*Makibaka! Huwag Matakot!*" (Fight and fear not). A full battle then ensued between the police and the radical dissidents, who could no longer claim to belong to the more moderate political organizations present at the rally.

It must be remembered that all this time, news cameras were capturing the events for the television audience. The presence of the media seemed to invite dramatic acts of defiance from the dissidents, as when three lone students, facing an advancing contingent of police, silently held aloft a banner bearing the name Kabataang Makabayan, or Nationalist Youth (KM). The youth organization, by far the most radical in the country, was anathema to the police, who held back nothing in their frontal attack of the three students. *Philippines Free Press* reporter Jose Lacaba describes the alarming violence of the scene:

> In full view of the horrified crowd, [the police] flailed away at the three. . . . The two kids holding the side poles [of the banner] either managed to flee or were hauled off to the legislative building to join everybody else who had the misfortune of being caught. The boy in the center crumpled to the ground and stayed there cringing, bundled up like a foetus. . . . The cops made a small tight circle around him, and then all that could be seen were the rattan sticks moving up and down and from side to side in seeming rhythm. When they were through, the cops walked away nonchalantly, leaving the boy on the ground. One cop, before leaving, gave one last aimless swing of his stick as a parting shot, hitting his target in the knees.[14]

The three students had raised the KM banner for the rest of the nation to see. The symbolic gesture created a spectacle with a veritable allegorical register. The ensuing actions of the police dramatized the failure of the rule of law in the country, and the presence of the media worked to make this and other spectacles of student dissidence and police brutality indelible in the public mind.

The battle of Burgos Drive, as the January 26 riot later came to be known, ended at eight o'clock that evening, a full seven hours after the demonstration had started. Rumors circulated that the dissidents, who had retreated or were chased into the walled city of Intramuros, were regrouping for an armed reprisal. The next day, the authorities and some concerned citizens made several public statements to account for the shocking turn of events.

In the words of Deputy Chief James Barbers of the Metropolitan Police Department, "the police acted swiftly at a particular time when the life of the President of the Republic—and that of the First Lady—was being endangered by the vicious and unscrupulous elements among student demonstrators." Manila Mayor Antonio J. Villegas corroborated the statement, commending the police for their "exemplary behavior and courage." For their part, the faculty of the University of the Philippines issued a joint statement denouncing "the use of brutal force by state authorities against the student demonstrators," and supporting "unqualifiedly the students' exercise of democratic rights in their struggle for revolutionary change."[15]

Despite their political differences, all those commenting on the explosive events of January 26 shared the view that the resulting spectacle bore grave portent for the future of the nation. As the faculty of the Lyceum put it in their position statement:

> Above the sadism and the inhumanity of the action of the police, we fear that the brutal treatment of the idealistic students has done irreparable harm to our society. For it is true that the skirmish was won by the policemen and riot soldiers. *But if we view the battle in the correct perspective of the struggle for the hearts and minds of our youth,* we cannot help but realize that the senseless, brutal, and uncalled-for acts of the police have forever alienated many of our young people from society. The police will have to realize that in winning the battles, they are losing the war for our society.[16]

The statement demands an *allegorical reading* of the January 26 riot as a Cold War drama. The struggle for "hearts and minds," a clear reference to the ideological battle between the "free" and communist worlds, is the hermeneutic key for interpreting the emblematic actions of the students and the police in this national allegory. The statement must be seen in relation to what, for many middle-class Filipinos, was an alarming phenomenon: the dramatic upsurge of a radical youth movement in Manila's college campuses, where more and more of the student population—numbering over half a million—were "discovering" Marxist ideology.[17]

The Diliman campus of the University of the Philippines was the epicenter of the radical student movement. At the time of the First Quarter Storm, student activism on campus focused on two key issues: the U.S. military bases in the country and the government's neocolonial relations with the United States. International events like the ongoing Vietnam War and the rise of the Sukarno government in Indonesia radicalized students even more. For many, the leap from nationalism to Marxism was a natural progression.

University of the Philippines instructor Jose Maria Sison founded the KM (Nationalist Youth) in 1964. Under the pen name Amado Guerrero (Beloved Warrior), he wrote "Philippine Society and Revolution," a comprehensive Marxist analysis of Philippine history and society widely circulated in mimeographed form. Sison's account argued for the necessity of a revolution along the lines of Mao Zedong's Cultural Revolution. A clandestine meeting of a coterie of his brightest followers in an obscure barrio in Pangasinan Province resulted in the formation of the CPP, on December 26, 1968. The avowed purpose of this secret organization was the "overthrow of U.S. imperialism, feudalism, and bureaucratic capitalism," and the "seizure of political power and its consolidation."[18] The NPA was created specifically for this purpose on March 29, 1969, when the CPP struck a decisive alliance with a group of peasant guerrillas under the leadership of "Commander Dante" (Bernabe Buscayno). Commander Dante was a Huk—a rebel fighter for the moribund Hukbong Magpalaya ng Bayan (People's Liberation Army), the peasant-based guerrilla movement that threatened to seize state power in the early 1950s, but that, by the 1960s, had devolved into a gangster and racketeering organization.[19]

For those in the political mainstream, the recently consolidated CPP-NPA represented the "dark side" of the left. That the students at the January 26 demonstration could be irrevocably drawn to this dark side or, worse, be active agents carrying out its orders, was cause for alarm. The *Philippine Collegian* had in fact published Sison's influential essay entitled "Student Power?" just days before the rally. The essay was a call to arms, exhorting student activists to enfold peasants and laborers into their movement.[20] The political inclusiveness of the demonstration and the ideological substance of many of the speeches and the slogans chanted that day would seem to indicate that Sison, who had been in hiding since 1969, was present at least in spirit at the demonstration. Rumors quickly spread that for his part, Commander Dante, who had a price of 90,000 pesos on his head, had managed to infiltrate enemy lines to personally attend the rally.[21] Suffice it to say that in light of these developments, the January 26 demonstration represented a critical juncture for the radical Left. As clashes between the NPA and the Philippine Constabulary began to multiply in the hills and flatlands of Luzon, radical students had, it seemed, begun to take a new tack: provoking violent confrontation in the streets.[22]

The students at the January 26 rally used mass action, or the threat of it, as their political weapon against the government. Theirs was a performative mode of politics that pivoted on the affective presentation of a collective identity—one based on their values and lifestyle *as youths.* Such a form of "identity politics" was colored by the politically calculated performance of nonnormative or abject identities. Consider the students' slogans and shibboleths: "Their slogan was "Fight! Fear Not!" and they made a powerful incantation of it: Maki-BAKA! Huwag ma-TAKOT! They marched with arms linked together, baiting [the police], taunting them. *"Pulis, pulis, titi mong matulis!"* (Pigs, pigs, uncircumcised dicks!) . . . *Baka magreyp pa kayo, lima-lima na ang asawa ninyo!"* (You might be thinking of raping someone, you already have so many wives!), *"Mano-mano lang, o!"* (Let's have it out, one on one!)."[23]

The students, it must be pointed out, chose to stage the rally in Tagalog. It was a way of distancing their public sphere from the official business of Congress (carried out, as per political custom, in English). Their acts of defiance, though reminiscent of child play, aimed to transform the terms of political contestation in the nation. Vicente Rafael's focus on the linguistic dimensions of the affective style of youth politics is instructive: "Rather than acknowledge authority as the giver of gifts, the language of the demonstrators negated the conventions of [official politics]. Taunts replaced respect, opening a gap between the language of the state and that of the students."[24] As we shall see in a moment, however, the students' tendentious language and performance of nonnormative conduct came at a price.

The January 30 Revolt

Student agitation resumed with a vengeance on January 30. Of the even more spectacular violence that erupted that day, a police officer would comment, "This is no longer a riot. This is an insurrection." President Marcos, final arbiter on these matters, would call it a *revolt*—"a revolt by local Maoist Communists."[25]

The January 30 "revolt" began with simultaneous demonstrations held in front of the Congress Building and Malacañang, the presidential palace. By early evening, the two demonstrations merged. Exactly what triggered the battle that spread to other parts of the city and lasted till dawn the next day may never be known. Lacaba gives the following account:

> The students who came in from Congress claim that, as they were approaching J. P. Laurel Street, they heard something that sounded like firecrackers going off. When they got to Malacañang, the crowd was getting to be unruly. It was growing dark, and the lamps on the Malacañang gates had not been turned on. There was a shout of *Sindihin ang ilaw!* *Sindihin ang ilaw!* (Turn on the lights! Turn on the lights!) Malacañang obliged, the lights went on, and then *crash!* a rock blasted out one of the lamps. One by one, the lights were put out by stones or sticks.[26]

Lacaba's report provides us with a highly symbolic incipit—or narrative opening—for the volatile events that would follow. The insistent demand for light, which, upon provision is immediately put out by persons unknown, paradoxically sets the stage for the most spectacular public drama to emerge out of the First Quarter Storm. It is indeed ironic that the January 30 "revolt" begins under the cover of darkness. It creates a gaping hole—an enigma—around exactly who or what precipitated the ensuing battle between the military and the dissidents. Despite this enigma—or maybe even because of it—the events of January 30 were highly sensationalized by the media, which followed the drama until its denouement the next day.

According to Lacaba's report, chaos almost instantaneously erupted after the lights went out. Holding aloft CPP banners and crying "Dante for president," hundreds of demonstrators surged into the palace grounds, lobbing homemade bombs at buildings and vehicles in the vicinity. The Presidential Guards Battalion came out to meet them in full force, firing bullets into the air. When the demonstrators refused to desist, they fired tear gas bombs at the charging crowd.

Reinforcements from the constabulary soon arrived. By 9:00 p.m., the students and the military had secured their own strongholds, each side "capturing" major city streets extending deep into the heart of Manila's so-called university belt. The battle would reach its climax when constabulary troopers guarding the Mendiola Bridge faced two advancing "armies" of students. They opened fire on the students.

Immortalized by the media soon after as the battle of Mendiola Bridge, the incident performs a mythological function in the public record of the First Quarter Storm. Now designated by military terms (*combatants, armies*) the students have ceased to be activists, and have crossed the bridge—so to speak—into the war zone of the NPA insurgents. Profusely captured in print, radio, and television accounts, the legendary confrontation at the bridge created a spectacle in which two previously discrete phenomena—the recent wave of student agitation and the underground insurgency—appeared to overlap. The mythological quality of the resulting spectacle hinged on the instantaneous collapsibility of the two phenomena, a substitution that suddenly appeared natural and irrefutable. Buried in that spectacle was the seemingly irrelevant detail that authorities were shooting at unarmed civilians, most of whom were just teenagers.

Many spectators found they could no longer passively watch the volatile turn of events. As Lacaba points out, students "found doors being opened to them, or people at second-floor windows warning them with gestures about the presence of soldiers in alleys."[27] The lines separating spectacle and spectator had effectively collapsed. The phenomenon was a microcosm of the revolutionary feeling gripping the nation at large. In Lacaba's words:

> In many a middle-class home, parents could only shake their heads in sorrow and bewilderment, no my child was not a part of it, my child was an innocent bystander, my child was never an activist. But that night of January 30 no one who did not belong to the camp of the enemy could remain a bystander; anyone who was not a minion of the state became instantly an activist, even if only for a moment. Every soul who had ever experienced poverty and oppression found himself linked to his neighbor in those hours of turmoil, welded tightly by a shared fate. . . . A spirit was abroad that night, and the streets spoke of it in whispers: *the revolution has arrived* . . . . And indeed, the revolution was on everybody's mind, *before everybody's eyes.* Mothers and fathers and brothers and sisters and friends sat by the radio throughout that sleepless night, all on edge, thinking of the revolution.[28]

Media coverage of the revolt allowed spectators to see themselves as actors in a public drama. Their lack of political indoctrination notwithstanding, subaltern groups, who rose to the occasion by aiding dissidents, became temporary "activists." Meanwhile, Manila's most powerful families, certain that their homes would be "set afire by an avenging people," made ghost towns of the city's wealthiest neighborhoods. The next day, the nation took stock of the night's events. Four students were reported killed. Untold numbers sustained injuries. Almost 300 were arrested and detained at Camp Crame. As it turned out, the revolution had not yet arrived. The public drama of the January 30 revolt was nonetheless a foretaste of that crucial threshold where spectacle ends, and where the revolution might begin. It was an object lesson for Marcos, who would appropriate that spectacle in order to begin foisting a revolution of his own.

In the aftermath of the January 30 "revolt," Marcos appeared on national television to mythologize the identities of the so-called rebels in a manner that would suit his political interests. The mob that attacked Malacañang, he said, was not a mob of students. Performing an allegorical reading of the media spectacles of the night before, he identified the key visual and auditory cues indicating that the perpetrators of the palace bombings were communist subversives. These mysterious men, he said, waved red banners, carried the Philippine flag with the red field up,[29] called the streets they occupied "liberated areas," and chanted "Dante for president." These cues proved that the perpetrators were not a group of rowdy youths but a highly organized army acting with the clear intent of seizing state power. Marcos statement was tantamount to a public erasure of the student demonstrators from the January 30 revolt. The spontaneous eruption of mob violence, which was captured by the news media, was thus transformed into a carefully orchestrated attack by urban guerrillas.

Marcos proceeded to defend the brutal actions of the police and the military: "The nonparticipants of that tragic night (read: spectators) could easily accuse the military and the police of 'fascist' and 'repressive' methods, but what was apparent to the participants was the beginning of a 'revolutionary' confrontation *stage-managed* by a determined minority."[30] Likening the night's events to a stage play, Marcos would describe the melodramatic logic of its mise-en-scène:

> The cries of "revolution" . . . indicated that [the demonstrations] were experiments in . . . overthrowing a duly

constituted regime. . . . The strategy of the nihilist radicals and leftists should . . . be clear. By provoking the military and police authorities into acts of violence, they hoped to show before society—before all people—that the government is "fascistic" and undemocratic. This is the reason behind the repetitious charges of "fascism" against the duly constituted authority: to deprive it of its legitimacy.[31]

The president's public statements produced a true transfer of power, as responsibility for the public drama of January 30 shifted from the student demonstrators—whose presence was vividly captured by the media—to the backstage "Maoist Communists" who had presumably masterminded the conflict. This mystification, which relied on red-scare tactics to conjure an invisible threat to society, paradoxically played a critical role in Marcos's efforts to demystify the spectacle of January 30. In effect warning the public not to believe its own eyes, Marcos would deflate the spectacle of the January 30 by asking his public to believe in what it could not see. And, keenly aware of the surprisingly sophisticated use the demonstrators had made of the media during the First Quarter Storm, Marcos would launch his own "revolution" by playing a role—that of the heroic leader—for the national audience.

Heroic Leadership and Political-Image Building

Marcos's self-presentation as heroic leader necessitated the recuperation of his political image, which had since been tarnished by the 1969 elections. I shall analyze the stigma of the 1969 elections in greater detail in chapter 3, but for now, it behooves us to note that no other president before Marcos—and none since—had as commanding a presence before the camera. In fact, Marcos's overwhelming popularity during his first presidential run, in 1965, was a part of the melodramatic theatricality of his political career, which was closely followed by the print, film, and broadcast media.

Ferdinand Marcos first entered the public consciousness as a defendant charged with murdering his father's rival in their home province of Ilocos Norte just after the 1935 legislative elections. He had turned eighteen nine days before the proclaimed winner, Julio Nalundasan, was shot dead by an unknown assailant on the night of September 20, 1935. In December 1938 authorities arrested Ferdinand, who at the time was a law student at the University of the Philippines, about to graduate as class valedictorian. After a much-publicized trial, the twenty-one-year-old Marcos was found guilty and was sentenced to seventeen years in prison. He managed to top the bar exams while under state custody and later served as his own counsel when his case went to the Supreme Court. Displaying the oratorical skills that would come to define his political style, he persuaded the court to reverse the conviction. The stunning reversal led the *Philippines Free Press* to put his photo on the cover and declare him a public hero.[32]

If Marcos's charisma and oratorical style had saved him from a crisis at the beginning of his career, there was no reason to suspect that they would fail him now. Particularly in crises, the media-savvy Marcos had proven himself time and again to be adept at political-image building. His polished public image, which combined equal parts glamour and crisis mongering, seemed to have been carefully modeled after the U.S. president who had singularly captured the symbiotic relationship between the two—John F. Kennedy. Like Kennedy before him, Marcos was most in his element in front of the camera. Like Kennedy, he had a beautiful "aristocratic" wife who would charm the public and function as the essential ornament to his political career. But above all, like Kennedy, he was a political leader much of whose power derived from being both seen and heard.

Marcos's inauguration, on December 30, 1965, was reported as the "coming of Camelot to the Philippines." His inaugural speech, "A Mandate for Greatness," made representatives of the U.S. media experience a "[flash back] to JFK's inaugural a few years earlier."[33] Interrupted nineteen times by applause (the loudest when he declared that he had been given a "mandate of greatness"), Marcos's speech so impressed Jack Valenti, future president of the Motion Picture Association of America, that his memorandum to President Lyndon B. Johnson described Marcos as "one of the most magnetic speakers you have ever heard." The speech, Valenti wrote, was "perfectly timed, ingeniously shaped, in a voice that must tritely be compared only to an organ." Aside from being "enormously intelligent," Marcos was "tough," and "had guts," Valenti wrote.[34]

Valenti's comments cast Marcos as a composite of the Hollywood leading man—one who combined the civility of the cosmopolitan easterner with the rugged individualism of the western hero. Such observations meshed with the U.S. endorsement of "heroic leadership" in the Third World during this period. As formulated by Kennedy adviser Arthur Schlesinger in his essay "On Heroic Leadership and the Dilemma of Strong Men and Weak People," the doctrine of heroic leadership postulated that the political grooming of strong leaders in the Third World was the "most effective means of charging semi-literate people with a sense of national and social purpose."[35] Thus hitched to the Cold War project of inculcating Third World peoples with the culture and values of the United States, heroic leadership, as Hoberman points out, was defined in particular by the culture and values disseminated by Hollywood.[36]

Marcos's transfiguration as heroic leader was experienced as a national ceremony—a feat made all the more remarkable by the absence of the necessary communications infrastructure for "wiring the nation." With approximately 600,000 radio receivers (at 19 sets per 1,000 people), 120,000 television sets (3.8 sets per 1,000 people) and 776 cinema screens (2.6 seats per 100 people), the Philippines in 1965 was not nearly as internally colonized by the media as the United States was.[37] Indeed, Marcos would hold the "modernization" of the media to be among the New Society's top priorities. The dictator would ostensibly make good this promise with the importation of satellite and computer-based technologies by the late 1970s.[38] In anticipation of this dramatic media expansion, however, Marcos had enlisted the country's available media resources, however modest, to mold himself as the "Philippine JFK." The Kennedy campaign was a tough act to follow. But follow Marcos did, releasing a biography, inspiring a feature film, and having his every move on the campaign trail followed by the press.

That Marcos's role as heroic leader could piggyback on the one created a few years earlier by Kennedy points to the global spread of what Daniel Boorstin, in 1962, termed the pseudo-event: a mass-mediated public drama that functions as a "press release writ large."[39] In the U.S. context, the pseudo-event was characterized by a tendency to proliferate, becoming increasingly self-reflexive and self-conscious. In Boorstin's words, "One interview comments on another; one television show spoofs another; novel, television show, radio program, movie, comic book, and the way we think of ourselves, all become merged into mutual reflections."[40]

Boorstin's observations anticipated Jean Baudrillard's theorization of simulation and simulacra as distinctively postmodern phenomena. No longer representations of an objective reality, the simulations produced by the media do not refer to anything other than the intertextual relations underpinning them. A media text, according to this view, "has no relation to reality whatsoever; it is its own pure simulacrum."[41]

For Hoberman, the pseudo-event and the discursive continuum extending it were part and parcel of the nation's "dream life," in which "images themselves were shadows cast by shadows and mirrors of mirrors." The purpose of this image-driven totality, as Hoberman puts it, was to sell an ideal image of American identity back to America.[42] This "dream life" acquired a particular urgency within the atmosphere of heightened anxiety attending Kennedy's management of the Cold War. If at the beginning of his presidency, Marcos inspired "flashbacks" to Kennedy, it could very well have been because Americans desired a Third World simulacrum of Kennedy, or at the very least, a congenial image of heroic leadership that the United States could disseminate as a symbolic weapon against communist incursion in the Third World.

Cold War Western:
The United States and Third World Nationalism

For a United States struggling to preserve its post–World War II position as the world's greatest economic and military power, so much was perceived to be at stake in Marcos's bailiwick—the so-called Third World. This blanket term for the numerous "new states" engendered by the collapse of European empires at the end of World War II underscored the precarious balance of power opened up by decolonization.[43] U.S. strategists feared that the political and economic instability engendered by decolonization could not but lead to the spread of revolutionary movements linking Marxism with the force of nationalist aspirations. At issue was the apparent clash between Third World nationalism and what was then coming to the fore as a *defensive* U.S. nationalism.

On the occasion of his first televised State of the Union address, on January 30, 1961, the newly elected Kennedy conjured the specters of the Cuban revolution, Ngo Dinh Diem's faltering hold over South Vietnam and the escalating war in the Congo. "Today, the crises multiply," he warned. "Each day, their solution grows more difficult. Each day, we draw nearer the hour of maximum danger."[44] The alarmist tones of Kennedy's speech exemplified the crisis mongering that would come to define his administration's foreign policy. Simply put, the public had to be conditioned to support America's war on communism—for what was at stake, as political theorist Walt Whitman Rostow put it, was nothing less than the survival of the nation and its defining values.[45]

The Truman administration's famous military document, NSC-68, presciently expressed Kennedy's posture of a defensive nationalism when it warned that the United States might be "crippled by internal weakness at the moment of its greatest strength."[46] In the intervening years the worry that the American public would not support the nation's postwar economic and security roles was a persistent one, and the permanent mobilization of the population (to support foreign aid and military interventions in the decolonizing world) posed chronic problems.

The specter of public apathy found a powerful solution in the covert military operation, which was closely intertwined with public anticommunist mobilizations.[47] In the early Cold War years, the former served the interests of military elites while the latter engaged the masses. The lines separating the two became increasingly hazy with Kennedy, for whom the "theory and practice of foreign interventions served less to preserve imperial interests than to demonstrate the firmness of American will."[48]

With the New Frontier as his campaign signature, Kennedy had at his disposal a powerful set of symbols to "summon the nation as a whole to undertake (or at least support) a *heroic* engagement in the 'long twilight struggle' against Communism."[49] In particular, he resurrected the frontiersman whose rugged individualism, self-sacrifice, and constant vigilance had figured prominently in the nation's expansionist history. Kennedy's New Frontier glamorized this violent history, and it did so by making covert military operations in the Third World function as spectacle.

In Kennedy's time the hero of the frontier myth metamorphosed into the covert operator, also known as the freedom fighter. This new and improved icon of the nation's expansionist-cum-anticommunist foreign policy was invoked—literally or metaphorically—in a series of media spectaculars, most notably the Bay of Pigs invasion (Operation Zapata; April 14, 1961) and the Cuban Missile Crisis (October 16–28, 1962). As Hoberman points out, these pseudo-events began as top-secret happenings, "scripted, produced and directed by the CIA" with the full participation of the president.[50] Whether by design or by happenstance, these events were thrust into the nation's living rooms and daily papers. This development pointed to the increasingly permeable border between public spectacle and covert operations; a phenomenon that, Rogin points out, has since become a characteristic feature of the "postmodern American empire."[51]

Rogin convincingly argues that covert military interventions derive from the imperatives of spectacle. Furthermore, they owe

their invisibility not to secrecy but to something else entirely—
political amnesia. As a form of "motivated forgetting," political
amnesia is the phenomenon whereby "that which is insistently represented becomes, by being normalized to invisibility, absent and
disappeared." In the covert spectacle, the freedom fighter enacts a
"countersubversive" fantasy. Like the frontiersman of the western
myth, he "enters racially alien ground, regresses to primitivism in
order to destroy the subversive and appropriate his power."[52] Political amnesia, then, constitutes a "cultural structure of motivated
disavowal." It implicates the audience, whose desire to experience
the violence of the countersubversive scenario is matched by an
equally powerful desire not to retain it in memory.

The specular form of the covert spectacle is crucial in this regard.
In contrast to the subject-centered story of narrative, spectacles are
"superficial, sensately intensified, short-lived and repeatable." Spectacle, then, is the cultural form of amnesiac representation. It produces a sensory overstimulation that "disconnects from their objects
and severs from memory those intensified, detailed shots of destruction, wholesaled on populations and retailed on body parts."[53] In the
fragmented jumble of "interchangeable individuals, products and
body parts" displayed in the covert spectacle, centrifugal threats—
threats to the subject and threats to the state—are depicted in a
manner conducive to containing as well as enjoying them.

But what is displayed and forgotten in the covert spectacle is
the "historical content of American political demonology." As
Rogin has convincingly shown elsewhere, the covert spectacle may
be traced back to an almost pathological fear of subversion subtending the nation's political culture.[54] This "countersubversive"
tradition has historically played on fears of secret penetration and
social contamination presented by an imagined alien power. Political demonology has been a concomitant feature of this tradition.
It begins as a "rigid insistence on difference" that extends to "the
inflation, stigmatization and dehumanization of political foes."[55]
Such demonology provides the performative space within which
the countersubversive might be allowed to indulge in forbidden

desires. Or to put it another way, political demonology is what enables the countersubversive, in the name of battling the subversive, to imitate its enemy.

The covert spectacle constituted a form of symbolic recovery: their significance lay less in stopping the spread of communism than in convincing the public that the United States had the power to direct world events. In Rogin's words,

> Individual covert operations may serve specific corporate or national security-clique interests, and the operations themselves are often (like Iran/Contra) hidden from domestic subjects who might hold them to political account. But even where the particular operation is supposed to remain secret, the government wants it known it has the power, secretly to intervene. The payoff for many covert operations is their intended demonstration effect.[56]

The Cold War, it must be remembered, was fought mainly with symbols and surrogates—in the visible military buildup of weapons that function more as "symbols of intentions in war games rather than evidence of war-fighting capabilities; and in the invasion of private and public space by the fiction-making visual media."[57] Even the two fronts of Cold War military action—the nuclear-weapons race and the "low-intensity" anti-insurgency campaigns in the Third World—were aimed at demonstrating U.S. resolution without incurring substantial risks at home. They consigned foreign policy to pseudo-events staged for public consumption, but with one important caveat. The symbols thus produced for consumption at home and abroad "have all too much substance for the victims of those symbols, the participant-observers on the ground in the Third World."[58]

It bears emphasizing that, to U.S. security strategists, the Philippines was an important outpost of the New Frontier. Indeed, it was here where the United States had first fought a counterinsurgency war in the name of defeating communism. In anticipation of the specular foreign policy inaugurated by the Kennedy era, Washington sent Edward G. Lansdale to crush the aforementioned Huks.[59] Combining paramilitary operations, psychological warfare and the manipulation of electoral politics, Lansdale's anti-Huk campaign would in fact serve as the blueprint for U.S. anticommunist counterinsurgency operations elsewhere—in Colombia, Venezuela, and Vietnam.

Because of his "pro-Western" stance, the CIA endorsed Marcos in the 1965 elections. He was touted as "Washington's man in Asia," not only because of his avowed anticommunist beliefs but also because he fit the mold of the "freedom fighter." I return now to Marcos's crisis management of the First Quarter Storm, which clearly echoed the crisis mongering and political demonology of Kennedy's interventionist policies. But as we shall see in a moment, Marcos's red-scare tactics were hardly subservient to Washington's interests.

Marcos's Countersubversive Performance

On his September 1966 state visit to the United States, Marcos spoke boldly about the need to stanch the communist threat in Vietnam. Ever mindful of the unpopularity of the war at home, however, he demurred when President Johnson requested more Filipino troops in Vietnam.[60] A May 1969 report by the U.S. magazine *New Republic* cogently interpreted Marcos's vacillation:

> The president is judged by his own people according to the number of benefits and concessions he succeeds in wheedling from Washington, and by the extent to which he dares defy what may appear from time to time to be Washington's wishes. On the first count, President Marcos got some favors from President Johnson by posing as LBJ's "right hand in Asia." . . . On the second count, President Marcos has sternly warned the United States that if it reduces its forces

in Asia (meaning, if Washington cuts its military spending), he will feel compelled in prudence to seek a *modus vivendi* with Communist China. The warning can scarcely have frightened Washington and in any event was intended for domestic consumption.[61]

Marcos's performance as Johnson's "right hand in Asia" indeed had its compensations. In exchange for promising a two-thousand-man army engineering battalion to assist U.S. troops in 1966, he acquired $45 million in economic assistance, $31 million in settlement of Philippine veterans' claims, and $3.5 million to assist the First Lady's cultural projects.[62] And yet, in subsequent negotiations for increased military aid, he repeatedly threatened to approach China should such assistance not be forthcoming. Simply put, Marcos was playing both sides. He used the Vietnam conflict to simultaneously curry favor with Washington and demonstrate to his critics at home that he was not a supplicant to U.S. interests. It was a foretaste of the opportunistic nature of the red-scare tactics that he would implement in the aftermath of the First Quarter Storm.

From January to April 1970, Marcos twice raised the possibility of martial law.[63] This was a politically risky move, given that just a year before, during his reelection campaign, he had downplayed reports of stepped-up insurgency in the countryside, confidently assuring Washington and the Philippine public that his administration could "handle the Communist threat." In May 1970 he predicted an "inevitable confrontation" with Maoist communists. His alarmist prognosis elicited bipartisan criticism in the Philippine Senate. A special committee headed by Senator Salvador Laurel, a Marcos opponent, asserted that there was "no clear and present danger of a Communist-inspired insurrection or rebellion," and that NPA activity in the countryside posed "no real military threat to the security of the country."[64]

The Department of National Defense and the communist media painted a drastically different picture. Based on secret intelligence gathered by the Armed Forces of the Philippines, Marcos announced in August 1971 that the NPA now had one thousand men on the frontline, with support troops of about fifty thousand. Reports from the CPP-NPA's periodicals, *Ang bayan* (The nation) and *Pulang bandila* (Red flag), indicated that the well-equipped and highly mobile NPA was widening its operations in Central and southeastern Luzon. Closely monitoring the NPA's progress were the Peking media, which had reported in December 1970 that the NPA had wiped out "more than 200 reactionary Philippine troops and police," and fifteen U.S. military personnel in over eighty operations that year.[65]

The oligarchy-controlled media, on the other hand, took an overwhelmingly skeptical position, accusing Marcos of sensationalizing the Maoist threat. They accused him of "swallowing all that military commanders were telling him" and asking the public to do the same.[66] The Lopez-controlled *Manila Chronicle,* the most outspoken of the anti-Marcos dailies, would write, "Since the government cannot seem to stop the rising price of bread, it is apparently trying to offer us circuses as a diversion. And these in the form of endless warnings about the rise of subversion."[67]

As his critics were quick to point out, Marcos's counterinsurgency campaign was a public extravagance. It created an "imaginary" crisis, which ironically deflected attention away from "real" crisis conditions voiced by demonstrators in the streets. The *spectral* nature of the underground Maoists was crucial in this regard. The CPP-NPA seemed to invite fabulous portrayals and mystifications on the part of the government. As Eduardo Lachica put it in 1970,

> If a Manilan does not read the newspapers, he would never suspect that a dissident struggle was going on in the countryside only 50 kilometers north of the capital. Most Manilans go through their daily rounds, completely unaffected by what is going on in Central Luzon. One sometimes wonders indeed whether the Huks are not just a convenient invention of the Armed Forces for purposes of raising their budget. . . . The Department of National Defense is the only legitimate source

of day-to-day information about the Huks and one of the few agencies officially quotable on the subject. . . . The Huks thus carry on a *strangely twilight existence* on the front pages based entirely on what the AFP claims they are doing.[68]

In a series of dazzling pseudo-events that call to mind the covert operations described by Rogin, Marcos would produce "visible evidence" of the communist threat. His anticommunist performance was used not to protect "free institutions," however, but to justify the imposition of martial law in the country.

Marcos's uptake of the covert spectacle began with a public bloodbath. On August 21, 1971, at least three fragmentation grenades were hurled at the speaker's stage at a Liberal Party rally in downtown Manila's Plaza Miranda. Over ten thousand people were present to witness the presentation of candidates for the November congressional and local elections. Nine people were killed in the explosion. All the Liberal Party's eight senatorial candidates were among the more than one hundred persons seriously injured. Broadcast before a live national audience, the attack was the most shocking political crime the country had ever seen, an event described by Gregg Jones as the "Philippine equivalent of the assassination of President John F. Kennedy."[69]

Marcos's opponents widely believed that the president had himself ordered the massacre—a suspicion that acquired the status of fact until the 1988 confessions of top-ranking CPP-NPA officials revealed that Sison was the true mastermind behind the attack.[70] Be that as it may, Marcos manipulated the trauma unleashed by the event for his own political purposes. Eerily reminiscent of Kennedy's alarmist performance during the Cuban Missile Crisis, Marcos yet again played the role of heroic leader for the national audience, and in a highly dramatic televised address, declared a state of national emergency. Marcos's televised message climaxed with his announcement that he had suspended the writ of habeas corpus.

As radical students and labor leaders were simultaneously being rounded up, Marcos dropped a second bombshell, announcing the discovery of the CPP-NPA's "July-August plan" to burn Manila to the ground and assassinate government officials and prominent citizens.[71] "Subversives have made this plan," Marcos told the national audience. "We are aware of the fact that they have certain signals for their members, and these signals are supposed to then mark the initiation of aggressive action."[72]

Six months later, an outbreak of terrorist bombings seemed to confirm Marcos's claim that the communists were communicating by deadly "signals." In March 1972 the target was the Arca Building; in April, it was the Filipinas Orient Airways office; in May, the porch of the South Vietnamese embassy; in June, the Philippine Trust Company; in July, the Philam Life Building. Later that month, after an American Express office was bombed, authorities discovered an unexploded bomb in the Senate's publications office. The bombings continued almost daily throughout August, hitting the Philippine Long Distance Telephone Company office, the Philippine Sugar Institute, and the Department of Social Welfare and Development, among others.[73]

The so-called terrorist attacks occurred late at night or early in the morning, when the bombing targets were virtually empty. In some cases, the explosives were discovered before they could be detonated. Except for the bombing of a department store, in which one woman was killed and forty-one persons injured, no serious injuries were reported.[74] The well-timed attacks were clearly intended to amplify the national trauma generated by the Plaza Miranda massacre. To borrow Rogin's terms, the attacks had become interchangeable parts in a string of crisis spectacles, each one producing a sensory overload that reduced to invisibility the corollary countersubversive measures taken by the state.

The Plaza Miranda massacre and the terrorist bombings were all conducive to spectacularization. Each event generated intense, short-lived, and repeatable images of apocalyptic violence that Marcos used to represent the invisible threat of "subversion" in the nation. Like the covert operations described by Rogin, these mass-mediated events were significant for their intended demonstration effect. Whether they were taken as evidence of the CPP-NPA's strength (confirming Marcos's warnings) or as signs of Marcos's red-scare tactics (confirming his cunning), they made it abundantly clear that Marcos was in control—that he had the power to intervene.

Preparing for the Coup: A Propaganda Film

During the final countdown to martial law, the Marcos administration released a propaganda film that was a retrospective summary of the First Quarter Storm as well as a chilling preview of Marcos's final coup.[75] Designed as an anticommunist primer, the film speaks in the language of U.S. political demonology. And yet, in transforming Marcos's covert operations into political spectacles, the film, titled *The Threat—Communism,* is also a self-reflexive commentary on the difficulties of representing what the president called subversion.

The film makes the case that the violent demonstrations of the First Quarter Storm were but surface manifestations of a deeper social evil that paradoxically defied visualization. The film opens with a disembodied voice intoning, "is the communist threat real or imaginary?" Standard pedagogical devices of the newsreel format—authoritative voice-over narration, expository titles, dramatic commentative music—are employed to weave horrific images of the demonstrations into an unequivocal argument for the affirmative. "The purpose of this documentary film," the unseen narrator states, "is to show that the danger is real." The narration traces a dramatic arc that begins with the capture in June 1969 of "communist documents" revealing a possible plot to overthrow the government,[76] followed by the violent demonstrations of 1970, and ends with the recent wave of terrorism initiated by the Plaza Miranda bombings.

Conceding that visible signs of the state's antisubversion military campaigns would seem too drastic to the average citizen, the film argues that anything less would open the floodgates to invisible subversive forces. Parroting the defensive nationalism of the Kennedy era, the film asks the citizen whose "apathy stems from a lack of knowledge of the gravity of the situation" to put his or her faith in "the president and the members of our military community who have access to classified information."

As the primary target of the film's message, the citizen is crucially invoked as an ethically incomplete subject whose fundamentally flawed knowledge of the political situation demands urgent attention. For in contrast to this cipher is a political savvy other, the subversive, which the film defines as one engaged in covert activities "calculated to undermine our national soil." Photographs of CPP leaders fraternizing with "Chinese Communists" are repeatedly presented as evidence of the otherness of this estranged element of the national community.[77]

In casting the CPP-NPA as secret agents of communist China, the film presents a version of political demonology to draw rigid boundaries between citizens and subversives. It would be helpful to recall Rogin's take on the countersubversive tradition in U.S. political culture. Pivoting on fears of secret penetration and social contamination, U.S. political demonology has historically relied on *visible* markers of otherness to perpetuate an image of a "self-making people, engaged in a national purifying mission." But the anticommunist moment in the history of U.S. countersubversion marks a critical shift. Because the subversives in question are no longer identified along clear racial and ethnic lines, it is now imperative to discover exactly who is under foreign control—hence the central importance of the surveillance state.[78] The film borrows the form, if not the content, of political demonology to legitimize the amassment of secret intelligence by the Department of National Defense to profile the CPP-NPA and decimate its ranks. In doing so, it implicitly presents state efforts to weed out the Maoist threat as a mirror image, if not an extension of, the anticommunist mission of the United States.

The binary opposition between citizens and subversives is secured by a series of stylistic moves. Handheld, high-contrast black-and-white footage of the First Quarter Storm captures the iconography of student dissidence. The students are shown engaging in now-legendary acts of defiance—provoking police with lascivious slogans, torching an effigy of the president, hurling rocks at military personnel, setting fire to buildings and cars. We cut to daytime shots of random citizens navigating a bustling city in the light of day. These normative shots of a disciplined citizenry clearly stand in stark contrast to the nighttime shots of students "chanting communist slogans" against the backdrop of a burning city. The film thus co-opts the students' affective performance of nonnormative conduct to present radical youths as a savage, anarchic force flouting the codes of emotional restraint that diacritically define the public sphere. The association of the dissidents with darkness and their identification with animalistic drives and regressive tendencies are the cinematic correlates of political demonology. The film uses these stock tropes to stigmatize and dehumanize the students.[79]

As the film proceeds to trace the mounting escalation of political violence in 1971, the "subversives" in question ironically become more and more invisible. The visual traces of their personhood become increasingly rare, in inverse proportion to the tally of their offenses. Thus, police procedural photographs of bombsites and captured weapons gradually replace the news footage of the First Quarter Storm with which the film begins. The viewer is asked to make a leap of faith, to connect the fully embodied representations of the demonstrations with these disembodied symbols of "terrorism" at the film's climax. One such photograph presents an array of carefully labeled explosives ("nitrogen liquid, pill boxes, Molotov bombs"), presumably the subversives' weapons of choice. The pithy caption reads: "Are these legitimate tools of dissent?" By fiat, objects like these are made to stand in for the absent subversives, who are ultimately knowable to the citizen only from the trail of destruction they are alleged to leave behind.

While self-consciously drawing attention to the authenticity of the images ("all the events depicted here are actual happenings"), the documentary grapples with an inescapable problem: how to represent subversion. All but sensationalizing the First Quarter

Storm, the film has a decidedly alarmist tone calculated to convince the incredulous citizen that a full-scale urban guerrilla war was not far from happening. And yet, the film insists that evidence of this war can come to light only if subversive forces are allowed to gain ground. The government is thus placed in the untenable position of making this invisible threat manifest to the citizen and, at the same time, of defusing it. In this zero-sum game, the subversives in question are either allowed too much power or none at all.

A clip of President Marcos's televised address after the Plaza Miranda bombings captures the film's overall solution to this dilemma. "I am the president," Marcos says, directly addressing the camera. "I am sworn under my oath of office to protect our people and execute the law. Rather than wait for this rebellion to be initiated, and to wait for our people to be massacred in the fighting between the military and the subversives, I would rather stop that rebellion now." Proffered as the authorial voice of the film, this address plays a performative function: it allows Marcos to present himself as a heroic leader with the requisite power to exert social control over all things seen and unseen. In that performance, Marcos himself enacts what Rogin describes as the "fiction of a center." The trope of a center is here employed to make Marcos's opportunistic red-scare tactics jibe with U.S. Cold War national security interests. To be more precise, Marcos's performance rests on blurring the distinction between the two. He thus presents himself as "freedom fighter" in a world of secret agents "at once connected to a directing power and also able to act heroically on their own."[80]

In "indigenizing" the covert spectacles of U.S. foreign policy, the film channels the racial violence underpinning the countersubversive tradition in U.S. political culture and applies it to the CPP-NPA—herewith depicted as agents of an alien power. But insofar as political demonology simultaneously reflects the countersubversive's fear of, and identification with, the subversive, the film cannot help but portray the symbiotic relationship between Marcos and his avowed nemesis. As Jones reminds us, Marcos needed the communist rebellion just as much as the CPP-NPA needed him:

without the communist rebellion, Marcos might have found the public less than acquiescent to the prospect of martial law; and without Marcos's repressive tactics, the CPP-NPA might not have acquired its romantic, revolutionary aura.[81]

Positioned at the end of the film, Marcos's address brings meaning and order to balance the spectacles of social breakdown with which the film begins. *The nation will have nothing to fear,* Marcos suggests, *if only citizens place their absolute trust in the government's covert operations.* Thus inviting citizens to participate vicariously in the government's invisible war, the film exhorts each citizen to identify with an increasingly powerful surveillance state.

Zero Hour: Martial Law

Marcos's propaganda film underscored the need for secret planning "accountable to no one and to no standard of truth outside itself."[82] This recourse to secrecy parroted the "national security" principles underpinning the crisis spectacles of the Kennedy era. Marcos's countersubversive performance had in fact earned the approval of Washington. U.S. diplomats and intelligence officers stationed in Manila at the time believed that strong governmental action was needed to restore order to the nation and that Marcos was the man to do it. As a U.S. embassy political officer put it, "The Philippines needs a strong man, a man on horseback to get the country organized and going again."[83]

In August 1972, Marcos frequently met with U.S. ambassador Henry A. Byroade to discuss the possibility of martial law. Byroade at first counseled Marcos of the undesirability of martial law, which was sure to trigger a backlash in the U.S. Congress. Marcos, the "freedom fighter," put pressure on the ambassador to check with President Nixon. After meeting with Nixon and Kissinger in the White House, Byroade delivered Washington's new policy: "If martial law were needed to put down the Communist insurgency, then Washington would back the Philippine president."[84]

At 9:00 p.m. on September 22, 1972, Marcos signed the order implementing martial law.[85] Marcos's military moved with alarming precision to arrest the president's political enemies, beginning with Senator Benigno Aquino, Jr., Marcos's political archrival within the oligarchy.[86] By 4:00 a.m., scores of prominent citizens—politicians, journalists, priests, and students—had been seized. Radio and television stations were padlocked, newspaper presses closed down.

In the months following martial law, the Department of National Defense perfected its surveillance techniques against suspected communists. Marcos, who in 1965 had placed all four of the military's services under presidential control, completely reorganized the nation's military and security forces. This new command structure gave him personal control over an emerging national security state. Substantial resources were funneled into the Presidential Security Command (PSC) and the National Intelligence Coordinating Agency (NICA). The PSC, originally a small security force, grew to about fifteen thousand men with responsibilities for both domestic and foreign intelligence. Marcos's secret police were given the responsibility of ferreting out information, not so much on the state's enemies as on Marcos's political foes.[87]

The atmosphere of heightened surveillance engendered by Marcos's martial-law declaration was a Third World reflection of the political culture of surveillance that peaked in the United States at the height of the Cold War. In Rogin's words, "Political repression went underground, intimidating by its invisibility. Surveillance worked by concealing the identity of its actors but letting the existence of its network be known. Like warders in Jeremy Bentham's model prison, the panopticon, the surveillants planted in subversive organizations could see without being seen. The political activist . . . was always to wonder whether he or she was being observed."[88]

In likening the surveillance state to Bentham's panopticon, Rogin provocatively gestures at the links between "national security" and cultural policy, understood as the process whereby a population's modes of thought, feeling, and behavior are targeted for transformation. The linchpin between the two is governmentality: modes of self-surveillance that function to mold a citizenry who, under the constant threat of being secretly observed, learns to comport itself accordingly. Marcos sought to recalibrate social conduct as a necessary first step toward building a new social order (see chapter 2). However, his so-called New Society belied deep tensions between the regime's espousal of U.S.-sponsored modernization theory and its co-optation of the discourse of national liberation from the young dissidents of the First Quarter Storm. Borrowing from both discourses, the New Society's cultural policies would do damage to both.

Chapter 2

SOCIAL CONDUCT AND
THE NEW SOCIETY

Sa ikauunlad ng bayan, disiplina ang kailangan (For national development, what we need is discipline). The founding motto of the New Society, which citizens were to learn by rote upon the declaration of martial law, encapsulated the Marcos regime's concerted efforts to place social conduct within the purview of state policy.[1] In his *Notes on the New Society of the Philippines,* Marcos explains the martial-law state's abiding interest in national discipline. Like its counterparts in the decolonizing world, the Philippines, Marcos averred, was a "transitional society" preoccupied with the intertwined problems of fostering a national identity and achieving rapid social and economic development. Contradictory values and institutions undermined these goals, thus underscoring the importance of regimenting social conduct.[2]

Marcos, whose countersubversive performance blurred the boundaries between U.S. foreign policy and his own personal political agendas, yet again subjected the Philippines to the discourse of U.S. political demonology. This time, however, he assumed the voice of U.S. social theorists whose Washington-funded research "analyzed a foreign world in ways that stressed their own nation's historical virtue, continuing superiority, and right of benevolent intervention."[3] Modernization, the grand narrative of the Cold War, posited the United States as the model society that Third World nations should seek to emulate. It was believed that the replication of the "consensual" framework of the United States—its capitalist economy, "liberal" media and modern values—could drive "traditional" societies through the difficult transitional process.

As a former U.S. colony, the Philippines was in fact one of the earliest laboratories of modernization. It was touted as the "showcase of democracy" in Asia. It had five television stations, 190 movie theaters, and twenty-six daily newspapers in Manila alone—placing it well ahead of most Southeast Asian countries in terms of mass media outlets. Unlike its Asian neighbors, which had responded to threats of political disunity and social chaos in the postindependence period by nationalizing or socializing their mass media, the Philippines had earned the reputation for having the "freest press in Asia."[4] But rather than bolster a genuinely participatory democracy, an oligarchy-controlled media fed en elite-dominated political culture characterized by political violence and electoral fraud. And while capitalism was firmly in place, it was overrun by the rent-seeking practices of the oligarchy. In every respect, the Philippines presented a distorted portrait of modernization.

With Marcos's declaration of martial law, the Philippines seemed poised to follow in the footsteps of late-industrializing countries where the modernization thesis was being radically rewritten. In these states, authoritarianism was increasingly recognized not as an aberration but as a prerequisite to modernization and development.[5] U.S. support for dictatorial regimes dramatically increased at this time, with a concomitant slackening of concern about the defense of democracy.[6] Constituting a new domino effect, the turn toward authoritarian rule may be traced back to a fundamental weakness in modernization theory: rather than bolster democracy, the extension of electoral politics to the decolonizing world produced volatile political situations conducive to military regimes, ethnic conflict, or civil war.[7]

Harvard University political scientist Samuel P. Huntington was among the earliest modernization theorists to point this out. In his influential treatise *Political Order in Changing Societies,* Huntington took the theory to task for paying insufficient attention to the problem of building political order in the so-called transitional states. Commenting on the social upheavals plaguing these states, Huntington argued that such manifestations of political instability were "the product of rapid social change and rapid mobilization of new groups into politics coupled with the slow development of political institutions."[8] Later known as the Huntington thesis, this refinement of modernization theory argued that in the Third World the building of political order must take precedence over the exercise of procedural democracy.

The Huntington thesis corroborated U.S. support for martial law in the Philippines, underscoring the need for national discipline. As Bonner points out,

> Americans demanded law and order, at home and abroad. They also expect the people of other countries to govern themselves as Americans do; when they don't measure up, the reaction is to assume that they are not capable of the responsibility that democracy requires and therefore not worthy of the freedom that it allows. . . . That is precisely what many American leaders and journalists thought. The Philippines just wasn't ready for democracy.[9]

The notion that the Philippines "just wasn't ready for democracy"—a striking instance of colonial infantilization—is indicative of the continuity between modernization and colonial thinking. In his political treatises concerning martial law, Marcos claimed that the Philippine experiment in modernization had failed because of the profound incompatibility between liberal democracy and the cultural values generated by the nation's colonial past. Marcos's uptake of the Huntington thesis was in fact based on an internalization of an imputed lack—a cultural and moral deficiency that rendered the nation unfit to govern itself as a democracy.

As Marcos would have it, colonial rule created a "Filipino personality" marked by "indolence, docility, passivity, a pervading consciousness of racial inferiority, shyness and resistance to being enlightened."[10] Having bred "habits of subservience," colonial rule was supplanted by a "western democratic system," which was adopted, Marcos argued, "unexamined" by the postindependence state. The cultural inertias of colonial rule, Marcos claimed, undermined the nation's uptake of democracy, such that, rather than revolutionize Philippine society, it had "bred corruption, subversion, and sectarianism."[11]

To legitimize authoritarian rule, and to co-opt the rhetorical suasion of the Huntington thesis, Marcos provocatively claimed that the Cold War created a false choice between democracy and socialism. Third World nations, he argued, should opt for a third alternative:

> The exigencies, the conditions, and the crises in the Third World are peculiar to the Third World and must, consequently, be met with tactics suitable to the temperament and character of its peoples. We can no longer inordinately and gratuitously adopt western political models. We have seen, at an enormous cost, their failure to advance our national goals. . . . [Third World] leadership must possess an authority that is both tough and flexible, realistic and visionary.[12]

For Marcos, the "third alternative" was strong leadership (i.e., authoritarianism) tempered by nationalism. Loosely referencing Peronism and Juan Perón's "third way," Marcos's statement also appropriated the anticolonialist perspective of Frantz Fanon's *The Wretched of the Earth*. Fanon had argued that the Cold War battle between capitalism and socialism obscured the true struggle faced by Third World nations: decolonization. Always a violent phenomenon, decolonization, Fanon argued, necessitated "the replacing of a certain 'species' of men by another 'species' of men." National liberation entailed the material eradication of colonialism; but more fundamentally, it required the psychoaffective transformation of the colonized subject. It is in light of this overriding imperative that Fanon exhorted Third World nations to reject the colonizers' definitions of their values and identities and to seek instead to "find their own particular values and methods and a style which shall be peculiar to them." Fanon is emphatic on this count: "Let us not pay tribute to Europe by creating states, institutions and societies which draw their inspiration from her. Humanity is waiting for something from us other than such an imitation, which would be almost an obscene caricature."[13]

In his *Notes on the New Society of the Philippines,* Marcos paraphrases Fanon: "It is important . . . that we extricate ourselves from the mental conditioning of ideologies foreign to our experience."[14] Clearly sharing Fanon's views on the psychic wounds inflicted on the colonized subject, Marcos likewise prescribes the eradication of colonial subalternity. He advances his notion of a third way as nothing less than the symbolic slaying of a colonial father figure: "By choosing to take up a third alternative as other Third World nations have, we are conducting not America's experiment but our own, free, independent and unfettered. Anti-American, one may say, because it involves the slaying of the great white father's image; but more Pro-Filipino, on closer look, for the slaying of the father image means liberation for the brown son, his coming of age, his passage into full manhood in the community of nations."[15]

Marcos's allusion to the brown son's coming of age is indeed consistent with Fanon's theorization of the new man born out of the struggle for national liberation. As Fanon put it, "the 'thing' which has been colonized becomes man during the same process by which it frees itself."[16] By invoking the slaying of the great white father, Marcos gestures toward the racial politics of modernization, which, in the Philippine context, could be traced back to the American colonial policy of benevolent assimilation. Indeed, a long historical thread linked modernization to this policy, which saw (white) U.S. citizens as the moral superiors, hence political exemplars, of America's "little brown brothers." Marcos's third way was anti-American to the extent that it outwardly rejected this racist bias masquerading as cultural paternalism. However, in valorizing his third way as a "pro-Filipino" experiment, Marcos nonetheless borrowed the great white father's rhetoric. His third way bore an ambivalent relation to what Vicente Rafael has described as *put-ing pagmamahal* (white love), the love of whiteness that has "come to inform if not inflict the varieties of Filipino nationalism that emerged under American patronage."[17]

White Love, Modernization, and Marcos's Third Way

To understand the operation of "white love" in Marcos's third-way discourse, it is perhaps necessary to take a short detour into the history of U.S. colonialism in the Philippines. After the Spanish-American War, some seventy-five thousand U.S. troops were dispatched to the Philippines in 1899 to crush an indigenous revolutionary struggle. It would in fact take the United States almost four years of brutal warfare to wrest its booty from Filipino nationalists, a conflict that has since been tagged by revisionist historians as the forgotten war.[18] Popularly regarded at the time as yet another "Indian war" in America's expansionist history, the brutal conflict saw political demonology in action: American observers arriving in the islands in 1899 claimed that the indigenous leaders of the Philippine revolution were illegitimate representatives of the Filipino people. In fact, they claimed that *there were no Filipinos* as such, only a mixed collection of polyglot savages lacking a common culture and prone to impulsive and irrational behavior.[19] Given the "absence" of a Filipino nation, the new colonizers rationalized U.S. presence in the islands, not as an act of imperialist aggression (since after all there was no nation to usurp), but as a benevolent act: they were in the islands to defuse the political instability unleashed by "deluded peasants and workers" led by a gang of mixed-race leaders.[20]

The fourteen-year conflict was thus paradoxically perceived as a humane war. Despite the thousands of Filipino deaths, it was characterized as a valuable learning experience for Filipinos and Americans alike. David Prescott Barrows, head of the Bureau of

Non-Christian Tribes, wrote in 1901 that the conflict was a blessing, "for without it the Filipinos would never have recognized their own weaknesses; without it we would never had done our work thoroughly."[21]

It is well worth reiterating the racial politics underpinning the U.S. policy of Benevolent Assimilation. President McKinley, who coined the term, argued that the "earnest and paramount aim" of colonization was to "win the confidence, respect and affection" of the people.[22] In William Howard Taft's view, Filipinos were orphaned children, "little brown brothers" abandoned by their Spanish fathers. It was therefore imperative to enfold them within the compassionate and protective embrace of the United States. It was, in short, an instance of white love. As Rafael puts it, "As a father is bound to guide his son, the United States was charged with the development of native others. Neither exploitative nor enslaving, colonization entailed the cultivation of the 'felicity and perfection of the Philippine people' through the 'uninterrupted devotion' to those 'noble ideals which constitute the higher civilization of mankind.'"[23]

Such has been the colonial thread of white love: the allegorical projection of a great white father whose love for his wayward children is served by creating a reciprocal relationship between a civilizing love and a love of civilization. Cultural paternalism clearly underpinned the policy of Benevolent Assimilation, which "required making native inhabitants desire what colonial authority desired for them."[24] It also involved the enforcement of constant surveillance, for the Filipino, it was believed, was incapable of self-government. This fundamental incapacity—something we have seen repeated in Marcos's time with the Huntington thesis and the view that Filipinos "just weren't ready for democracy"—was in fact the official reason why U.S. colonial rule lasted until 1946. Benevolent Assimilation projected U.S. colonial rule as merely a transitional stage; self-rule would be granted as soon as the natives, in Taft's words, "have been elevated and taught the dignity of labor . . . and self-restraint."[25] In other words, self-government can be achieved only when the subject has learned to colonize itself. In

Woodrow Wilson's words, "Self-government is a form of character. It follows upon the long discipline which gives a people self-possession, self-mastery, and the habit of order and peace . . . the steadiness of self-control and political mastery. And these things cannot be had without long discipline. . . . No people can be 'given' the self-control of maturity. Only a long apprenticeship of obedience can secure them the precious possession."[26]

As a precondition of Filipino self-rule, white love set standards of discipline and civility that required the tutelary subject to submit to strict regimens of training and the constant supervision of a sovereign master. By mid-century, white love evolved into the Cold War technology of modernization. Replacing direct colonial supervision with the application of the social sciences to the problems of decolonizing states, modernization worked to spread the culture and values of the United States throughout the Third World. Modernization, in expanding and reconstituting the colonial project of white love, had definite, if unstated, racial overtones. Its humanistic teleology, to borrow Fanon's terms, "invit[ed] the submen to become human and to take as their prototype Western humanity."[27]

Marcos strategically sidesteps modernization's emphasis on the social replication of Western culture and values to focus instead on the theory's normative construction of human emancipation. In his *Five Years of the New Society,* Marcos projects an outwardly radiating series of transformations centering on the recalibration of national "values": first, such values will foster a sense of pride in the individual; it follows that this pride will foster a sense of belonging to a larger national community; and finally, a sense of belonging to a national community will enjoin individuals to seek "oneness with mankind."[28]

To "Third Worldize" this model of human emancipation, Marcos sought the psychoaffective creation of a "decolonized" cultural subject. The New Society's cultural policy indeed hinged on eradicating colonial subalternity by restoring the dignity and self-respect of the New Filipino. But as we shall see, Marcos's program of cultural rehabilitation nonetheless called on the cultural sphere to effect an internal colonization along the lines of the cultural paternalism of white love. Its promise of a perfect social order presupposed the citizenry's submission to the dictator's "paternal" authority and the consolidation of a social hierarchy through the internalization of traditions invented by, and grounded in, the martial-law state.

The Internal Revolution and Governmentality

Despite its First World narcissism, the salience of modernization theory, as far as Marcos was concerned, lay in its emphasis on the power of cultural values to shape patterns of social conduct. The New Society was indeed the first deliberate attempt ever made in the Philippines to realign the cultural values of the populace with the development initiatives of the state.[29] For Marcos, this process involved "restructuring mental dispositions and evolving an authentic individual and social consciousness."[30]

Just months after the declaration of martial law, veteran psychological warfare specialist Jose Ma. Crisol, working through the auspices of the Armed Forces of the Philippines' Office of Civil Relations, convened an academic think tank to construct a master plan for moral reform. Their report, *Towards a Restructuring of Filipino Values,* gave the following recommendation: "We should treat the country as our very own family, where the President of the Republic is the father and all the citizens as our brothers. From this new value we develop a strong sense of oneness, loyalty to the country, and a feeling of nationalism."[31]

Thus elevating the *family* as the principal institution for formulating national values, the report anticipated Foucault's description of the intimate connection between the family and the science of policing, Jacques Donzelot's term for the "methods for developing the quality of the population and the strength of the nation."[32] For Foucault, the task of policing led to the rise of governmentality via a modern state that "exerci[zed] towards its inhabitants, and the wealth and behavior of each and all, a form of surveillance and control as attentive as that of the head of the family over his household and goods."[33] In Marcos's own writings on the New Society, metaphors of the father's role in a well-run household abound. Like the head of the household (in Tagalog, *ama ng tahanan*), the president's primary role is to ensure that his house is in order, for this "does not only ensure the regularity of one's daily bread; it provides the vitality that fills both the thirst for productive labor and creative contemplation."[34]

In matters of culture, Marcos's ama ng tahanan blended the cultural paternalism of the great white father of Benevolent Assimilation with the anticolonial stance of Fanon's *Wretched of the Earth*. Though he actively promoted modernization to bring about the humanist project of national development, he also prescribed a cultural liberation program that would correct the colonial mentality of the populace.

Marcos's notion of cultural liberation closely follows Fanon's conception of cultural rehabilitation. Because colonialism distorted, disfigured, and destroyed the native's past, it devolves on the postcolonial state to seek a national culture in the past. Thus enmeshed in the psychoaffective operations of cultural rehabilitation, the creation of a national culture is a necessary feature of decolonization, for without it, liberated peoples would be "colorless, stateless, rootless—a race of angels."[35]

The search for a national culture was a priority for Marcos, who saw it—in clearly Fanonian terms—as the "anchor" of a proud and noble race:

> One of the most crucial tasks we faced after the declaration of martial law was to mend the tattered fabric of our society, to resuscitate the dying spirit of the nation. Clearly, the strategy for decolonization lay in a cultural liberation program directed toward an understanding, appreciation and internalization of our rich cultural heritage as a foundation for

developing pride in ourselves as a people . . . meaningful and lasting change entails the reshaping not only of the existing social order but also of the consciousness of the individuals that together make up that order.[36]

For Marcos, national discipline rested on a concept of culture as both object and instrument of social and moral reform. Such faith in culture's capacity to effect inner transformation as a necessary step toward securing external social transformation points to what Tony Bennett describes as a different mode of government, one "aimed at producing a citizenry, which, rather than needing to be externally and coercively directed, would increasingly monitor and regulate its own conduct."[37] For indeed, as Marcos put it, "We cannot permanently depend on the coercive powers of the state. We must give to the new political bond the force of our own individual discipline."[38] Marcos's cultural liberation program was a bid to "governmentalize" culture—to "use culture as a resource through which those exposed to its influence would be led to ongoingly and progressively modify their thoughts, feelings and behaviour."[39]

Marcos's projection of a self-monitoring and self-regulating cultural subject bears a striking affinity with Foucault's theory of governmentality. For Foucault, governmentality marked a radical shift in conceptions of the instruments and ends of government. Based on Machiavellian principles, earlier theories of governance gave to the state a single purpose: to secure the political obedience of the populace. This imperative was seen as the very precondition to the exercise of sovereignty, which in turn was pursued as an end in itself.[40] Obedience to the law, in other words, made the *end* of sovereignty the exercise of sovereignty. With the rise of the modern state, Machiavellian notions of sovereignty gave way to a new conception of governance premised on the population as objects of care of the state. Eschewing the "self-referring circularity" of sovereignty, this mode of governance was characterized by a plurality of specific aims—for example, ensuring that the greatest possible quantity of wealth is produced, that the people are provided with the sufficient means of subsistence, and that the population is enabled to multiply. And so, while sovereignty looked to the law as the principal instrument for achieving obedience to the law, governmentality looked to how things were disposed to meet specific social ends.

In his *Notes on the New Society of the Philippines*, Marcos echoes Foucault's observations on the circular logic of sovereignty (what Foucault calls juridico-discursive power). He concedes that the New Society readily calls to mind a Machiavellian "command society." But such a society, he argues, has a weak social basis—a fear of authority—and can only engender a "crude discipline . . . the kind we have been subjected to as children." It is therefore imperative to transcend the command society's basis in notions of punishment: "We should be afraid of wrongdoing not because of the personal consequences to ourselves but because it might destroy the 'balance' of our community . . . Only in this way can our covenant with one another be made into a 'lasting institution.'"[41] Marcos introduces the notion of an "internal revolution" as the key to fostering a deeper social covenant:

> We should not fall into the trap of a 'surveilled' society: this will defeat our purpose. Happily, our recourse was prescribed by Apolinario Mabini in another revolution, when he said that an 'internal' revolution was necessary for the success of an 'external' one. What this ultimately means is that we should be able to internalize the democratic revolution, make its objectives, principles and ideals a part of our being, if we expect to succeed—and make our success an enduring one.[42]

That other revolution, of course, was the 1898 revolution. Marcos is here channeling the hero Mabini, the nationalist leader widely regarded as one of the brains of the revolutionary movement. He argues, after Mabini, that the attainment of the revolutionary social agendas of the New Society necessarily hinges on each and every

Filipino internalizing the "objectives, principles and ideals" of the martial-law state. This implies an "inner discipline that is not a response to coercion" but rather a critical engagement with, and active participation in, the developmental projects of the state.[43]

Significantly, the internal revolution was premised on making the cultural subject aware of his deficiencies. The self-monitoring cultural subject, in short, had to be trained to recognize his ethical incompleteness as a first step to developing a drive for self-improvement. This critical fixture of cultural policy was promoted and disseminated by the Marcos regime in and through melodrama. And it was First Lady Imelda Romualdez Marcos and the Cultural Center of the Philippines that embodied the nexus between the cultural paternalism of Marcos's modernizing stance and the anticolonial populism of his cultural liberation program.

The Marcos Romance

In a 2003 *Philippine Daily Inquirer* interview, a nostalgic Imelda Marcos gave the following rationale for the Cultural Center of the Philippines: "When Ferdinand Marcos became President, he told me, 'I'll make a strong house for the Filipino people. You make it a home.' That kept me thinking. What makes a home? Values, art. . . . So I built the Cultural Center of the Philippines."[44] The statement points to the thematic importance of domesticity and familial relationships in the discursive construction of the Cultural Center of the Philippines, the bastion of the Marcos regime's cultural policy. Opened in 1969, the center is the most prominent symbol of the Marcos romance—the national allegory that codifies the central tenets of the regime's cultural policy.[45]

The Marcos romance allegorizes the center's two competing rationales: the normalization of the popular classes into discriminating citizens and the creation of a dramatic space in which disenfranchised classes may vicariously realize their demands for social recognition. The former encapsulated the center's bid to effect an internal colonization of the cultural subject in ways eerily reminiscent of white love. The latter represented Marcos's avowed interest in the psychoaffective transformation of the cultural subject, based on Fanonian notions of cultural rehabilitation. To begin to understand these two contradictory impulses underpinning the national allegory of the Marcos romance, we must first examine the relationship between melodrama and cultural policy.

Cultural policy embraces the institutional webs that enable and facilitate aesthetic activity as well as the uptake of cultural forms in the day-to-day renewal of public subjectivity.[46] Significantly, cultural policy, which implies the management of populations through the standardization of conduct and tastes, imagines individuals as cultural subjects endowed with a drive toward self-improvement. What generates this drive is the notion of ethical incompleteness, which Toby Miller describes as a determinate indeterminacy, a lack that subjects are encouraged to find within themselves and to remedy. This lack is ethical in as much as it is premised on each individual's capacity to draw upon moral codes as a means of managing one's conduct.[47]

To the extent that it offers a moral framework for the world, melodrama can serve as a potential resource for inscribing ethical incompleteness in individuals. As a literary genre, it is particularly interested in the private lives of individuals and proffers for public discussion "exemplary individual lives to be emulated (or abjured)."[48] Christine Gledhill flags the confluence of the personal and the social in melodrama, where the "webs of economic, political and social power in which melodrama's characters get caught up are represented not as abstract forces but in terms of desires which express conflicting ethical and political identities."[49] The genre's focus on personal desire can illuminate the subjective aspects of the discourse of ethical incompleteness whereby "the irrational aspects of subjects would be made known to them as a preliminary to their mastery of life and its drives." Furthermore, the genre provides a template of the challenges that the socially excluded must face in "devising forms of ethical legitimacy."[50]

Significantly, the Marcos romance locates the impetus for the cultural center in the social exclusion of the popular classes. Alongside claims to educate the citizenry to fit into a set of tastes, the center was also conceived as a means to revalue the identities and cultural products of disempowered Filipinos. These two processes were to be simultaneously pursued with a view toward enhancing the dignity and self-confidence—in short, the emotional and psychological makeup—of the cultural citizen.

The melodramatic imaginary of the Marcos romance lent itself well to the "authoring process" necessary for making emotional needs the proper object of the cultural center's therapeutic cultural policy. As Yúdice points out, whenever actors in the cultural sphere demand recognition of their identities as a means of claiming entitlements, they do so by drawing on the genre conventions through which "they are variously imaged, valued and devalued."[51] In what follows, we shall explore how the Marcos romance drew on melodramatic codes and conventions to articulate the ethical incompleteness of Imelda Marcos and the popular classes. It is a drama of disenfranchisement and transcendence that underwrote a populist cultural policy based on therapeutic notions of social exclusion and emotional empowerment.

Strong and Beautiful

Imelda's mission to build a cultural center first entered public consciousness during Ferdinand's 1965 presidential campaign. In the midst of a campaign rally in Cebu City, the future first lady publicly declared her desire to build a cultural institution that would become a "showcase of Filipino artistic expression," and a "mansion of the Filipino Soul."[52] In a subsequent campaign interview, she swore to personally undertake two programs to complement her husband's nation-building platform: social action aimed at improving the welfare of the population and a program to foster pride in Filipino cultural heritage.[53] It is significant that Imelda's chosen fields of intervention conformed to the maternal duties of women—as the primary caregivers and formative educators—in the domestic sphere. Laying claim to social policy and cultural policy as "women's work," she went on to posit cultural development to be not merely an appendage to social development but its necessary counterpart.

Imelda presented her role of social-cultural worker as the "natural" outgrowth of a social order conceived in familial and domestic terms. In her own words, "What the Filipino people needed was a mother."[54] Imelda's desire to be mother to the Filipino people dovetailed with the familial tropes with which the future First Couple conceived their relationship to the nation at large. Notions of family and domesticity in fact dominated their political rhetoric on the 1965 campaign trail. This rhetoric drew its force from Ferdinand Marcos's astute manipulation of the myth of Malakas (strong) and Maganda (beautiful), the first Filipino man and woman, who as legend has it, emerged from a single bamboo stalk.[55] The popular meanings attached to these heteronormative symbols of (masculine) strength and (feminine) beauty allowed the future First Couple to present themselves as ideal helpmates destined to govern the nation as though it were a household—a national family.

Imelda is an ideal melodramatic heroine because of her colorful past. Ferdinand's 1965 inauguration program claims for her a noble birth: "She considers herself to be of the South, being a Romualdez of Leyte, where her forebears founded the town of Tolosa and established a family that has since become one of the mightiest political clans in the country."[56] Her 1969 campaign biography goes so far as to portray her as having been bred to be a first lady.[57] The official texts of the Marcos romance thus take pains to individuate Imelda as an "aristocratic woman," whose function is to serve as an "ornamental body representing the family's place in an intricately precise set of kinship relations determined by the metaphysics of blood."[58]

But, following the conventions of the family melodrama, this persona acquires a negative identity—negative, because of the suffering with which the melodramatic heroine comes into being.

Imelda's negative identity surfaced with the controversial publication, also in 1969, of her unofficial biography, *The Untold Story of Imelda Marcos,* which revealed that Imelda was a child of tragedy.[59] Though a gentleman in temperament and upbringing, her father, Vicente Romualdez, was a widower with a struggling law practice and five children when he married Imelda's mother, Remedios Trinidad. Because of unbearable family conflicts between Remedios and her stepchildren, Imelda, at age two, was consigned to live in the family garage with her mother. When Imelda was eight, the long-suffering Remedios succumbed to pneumonia. Vicente, now a broken man, moved the entire family to Tacloban, Leyte, where they were forced to live in a "poor man's Quonset hut."[60]

The Marcos romance presents Imelda's ambivalent class position using standard tropes of the family melodrama: the sudden reversal of fortune, the shameful family secret, and the long-suffering mother. Imelda, whose "noble birth" had been effectively erased by the moral infractions of others, is the victimized heroine in whose name the melodramatic imaginary of the Marcos romance must put all things to right. If, in melodrama, human desires shape human actions, then Imelda's trajectory is governed by one all-consuming desire: social recognition. Poetic justice is her due. Fast-forward to 1953. Imelda, now a stunning beauty, returns to the big city as a country cousin seeking accommodation with rich relatives. The stage is set for her fateful meeting with the ambitious parvenu and presidential hopeful Ferdinand Marcos.

The story of Imelda and Ferdinand's first meeting is immortalized on film in Marcos's 1965 campaign biopic, *Iginuhit ng tadhana* (Drawn by destiny). Coming half way into the film, the scene that introduces Imelda (Gloria Romero) into the diegesis creates a critical break in the narrative that until then had been Ferdinand's bildungsroman.[61] In inhabiting the medium of narrative cinema, the Marcos romance here obeys the gendered economy of spectacle and gaze that Laura Mulvey identifies in her seminal essay "Visual Pleasure and Narrative Cinema."[62] Coded for strong visual impact, Imelda's cinematic double is offered up as a passive object for an active male gaze. Her entry into the diegesis freezes the flow of the action. But what is particularly noteworthy about this spectacle is its blending of Imelda's two melodramatic personas—the aristocratic woman of the official Marcos biographies and the victim-heroine of the *Untold Story*.

The scene opens in the cafeteria of the Congress Building, where Imelda, dressed in a checked shirt and trousers, is eating dried watermelon seeds. Her shabby work clothes and poor man's snack appear incongruous in the stately setting. To punctuate the point, a close shot of Imelda's dainty feet reveals that she is wearing mismatched house slippers. These visual cues clearly align her with the unformed tastes of the popular classes. But the film is also careful to establish her political pedigree. Brief expository dialogue between Imelda and a lady companion reveals that she is waiting to collect her cousin, House Speaker Pro-Tempore Daniel Romualdez.

The film abruptly cuts to Ferdinand (Luis Gonzales), standing transfixed at the entrance to the cafeteria. The scene reenacts the couple's first encounter, made legendary by Marcos's official biography, *For Every Tear a Victory*. Marcos, we are told in another official biography, "stood motionless for a moment, an action which did not go unnoticed by canny politicians present, whose eyes miss nothing unusual."[63] The difference here is the scene's cinematic enlistment of point-of-view devices. Seen through Ferdinand's gaze, Imelda, now glamorized in close-up, assumes the regal aura of the heroine of the official Marcos biographies. Crucially, it is Ferdinand's gaze that transforms Imelda from a cipher embodying the cultural perfectibility of the popular classes to a spectacle of feminine perfection and civility.

The scene may be read as an allegory of ethical incompleteness and cultural uplift. The spectacle of Imelda interpellates the discriminating citizen, the imagined subject of cultural policy who, as Miller and Yúdice put it, "can locate and luxuriate in the radiance of an object of beauty." Ferdinand is a template of this "feeling, sensate romantic" figure, whose encounter with perfection must be transferred onto his "lesser co-nationals." Such a paternalistic model of cultural dissemination rests on shoring up the value of a chosen aesthetic object and making it "available for redisposal as a method for pedagogic formation."[64] The melodramatic imaginary of the Marcos romance advances Imelda as the very instrument for civilizing the popular classes; and indeed, so much of the cultural center's programs hinged on literally disseminating her spectacle. But Imelda's spectacle derives its aesthetic power from the story of her own pedagogical formation under Ferdinand's tutelage. As we shall see, this bittersweet family melodrama marks Imelda's apotheosis from victim-heroine to the perfect civilizing agent of the national family.

The Sentimental Education of Imelda

According to the official Marcos biographies, Ferdinand was so taken by Imelda's natural charms—her simplicity, gentleness, and unspoiled character—that he famously wooed and married her in eleven days. One unofficial biography argues otherwise: "To Marcos, who fell in love with Imelda's impressive name, the Rose of Tacloban had a long way to go. He was the superior being, the master who would mold Imelda to his likeness and make her the patrician wife he wanted." Following their storybook church wedding, an event carefully stage-managed to mark Ferdinand's debut as a presidential contender, Imelda came to live in the Marcos household—a sprawling bungalow with magnificent gardens in a fashionable Manila suburb. Bundles of cash—acquired through mysterious means—were always at hand. Ferdinand, we are told, pushed Imelda to "adopt a new, assertive, and self-confident persona," and pressured her to buy only the best clothing and jewelry. She was initially unprepared for this decadent lifestyle: "Her beliefs and attitudes had been shaped by her simple life in Tacloban. . . . If she was ambitious and coveted the good things in life, she had nevertheless been brought up to pursue these goals within a moral framework. Moreover, years at the bottom of the heap had taught her the virtues of meekness, humility and resignation—virtues that were ill-suited to Marcos' ambitions."[65]

A clash of moral codes disturbed the harmony of the Marcos household. The victim-heroine of the Marcos romance had been conditioned to perceive "meekness, humility and resignation" as virtues that would be divinely rewarded. In a society governed by favor and patronage, such values were in fact used to keep the popular classes in their place. Though he had enriched himself spectacularly in public office, Marcos routinely condemned the culture of patronage and espoused the liberal values of modernization. He propagated an ideal type: the self-maximizing individual guided by the rational, utilitarian, and scientific precepts of the Enlightenment. This modern subject was the reverse image of a colonized "Filipino personality" that he vowed to correct via strict regimens of training. Imelda was his first test subject.

Imelda's new domestic life was ruled by one philosophy: good taste. Kerima Polotan's official biography states that Imelda saw it as her wifely duty to cultivate her intellectual and aesthetic sensibilities, and that she saw it as her public duty to enable others to do the same. In her own words, "Culture and art and the taste for the beautiful must lead to goodness."[66] Imelda's dictum synthesizes Kant's notion of taste as a "public sense" and Matthew Arnold's notion of culture as the "study of perfection." For these philosophers of taste, being "cultured" entails the deliberate and systematic acquisition of aesthetic sensibilities, which crucially serve to buttress social harmony. For Kant, aesthetic training produces a critical faculty in the subject who must weigh his judgment with the collective reason of mankind. For Arnold, the study of culture derives "not merely or primarily of the scientific passion for pure knowledge, but also of the moral and social passion for doing good." Aesthetic activity, in short, is a conduit to public subjectivity, making good taste "both a sign of and means towards better citizenship."[67]

Imelda's pronouncements on the intrinsic value of good taste posit the aesthetic as an autonomous sphere of activity. But as Terry

Eagleton argues, aesthetic activity necessarily involves balancing two competing forces: the rule of reason and the pull of sensual inclination.[68] Cultural programs, which must negotiate the provision of pleasure and the provocation of thought, have historically been linked to hegemonic contests over the definition of those aesthetic values that would curb the irrational aspects of pleasure and desire. Consequently, the aesthetic channeling of social harmony, Miller and Yúdice remind us, has been "bought at the expense of those whose tastes are not only aesthetically unacceptable, but more importantly, potentially contestatory."[69]

In insisting that human desire is inextricably linked to political conflict, melodrama gestures toward the hegemonic forces that shape the aesthetic. Standards of taste are not autonomous concepts deriving, according to Kant, from "universally valid 'morally practical precepts.'"[70] Rather, they are another means of keeping the popular classes in their place. In her pursuit of perfection, Imelda wrestled with standards of taste that had previously excluded her and those like her. In melodramatic terms, being "cultured" meant renouncing her identity as a subaltern subject and assuming a "modernized" identity that was both whitened and bourgeois.

Imelda's biographies curiously employ the language of mental health to describe her conflicting identities as manifestations of a torn psyche. Carmen Navarro Pedrosa's unofficial biography (1987) states that Imelda's pedagogical formation caused her to become socially withdrawn. She "escaped into excruciating and interminable migraine headaches."[71] No longer able to claim a clear psychic and moral identity, she suffered a nervous breakdown. She was admitted to a psychiatric hospital in New York for treatment.[72] Ferdinand's publicists state that her treatment involved daily sessions of autosuggestion, thanks to which, we are told, Imelda came to realize that the "cure lay within her own will." A critical moment in the Marcos romance, Imelda's epiphany is clearly figured as a moment of "voluntary transformation," bringing into being a new person: "She began to cast away her inhibitions and uncertainties and expressed a willingness to try new things, to become more extroverted, resourceful, and adaptable."[73] Thus would she fit the specifications of the New Filipino espoused by Marcos.

The People's Star, the People's Culture

In the race for the presidency, the Marcos camp got incredible political mileage out of the "improved" Imelda. Popular press reports of the couple's public appearances on the campaign trail underscore her role as Marcos's "secret weapon."[74] She was in fact the star of the show, and Marcos was party to this arrangement.

The mise-en-scène of Marcos's political rallies revolved around Imelda, whose entrance, much like that of the female star in narrative film, would come after a dramatic buildup that played on audience expectations. Ferdinand would use his bombastic oratory to work up the crowd; but it is only at the sight of Imelda that the crowd found emotional release. "Isolated, glamorous, on display, sexualized,"[75] her stage presence had a cinematic aura of to-be-looked-at-ness. But rather than disrupt Ferdinand's power, "Imelda's striking presence . . . allowed power to circulate between Ferdinand and the crowd. While she reduced the people to spectators, he overwhelmed them with slogans. . . . They *looked at her* while he spoke to them."[76]

Imelda's spectacle was directed at a specific audience, the *probinsiyano* (barrio folk), for whom she was just then fashioning a new persona for herself as the People's Star. This new identity was based on her philosophy that the "poor needed dreams and she fulfilled their wishes by being a star."[77] In her public appearances, Imelda was careful to tailor her star persona to suit the tastes and preferences of the common folk. She wore *ternos*—the traditional formal costume consisting of floor-length skirt, tight bodice and stiff butterfly sleeves. Trained in classical voice, she serenaded the crowd—not with operatic arias but with sentimental love songs in the vernacular. These choices allowed her to forge a powerful bond with the folk:

Led to the microphone, she touches it, and prepares to sing her winning repertoire: *Dahil sa Iyo, Waray, Dungduguen can to la unay.* She has lost weight considerably, her bones show through her terno—it is a slight and vulnerable back that rises above the scoop of her neckline. . . . From the convention floor at the Manila Hotel nine months ago, to this stage tonight stretch innumerable miles, and countless lessons and she has learned each one very well. . . . She knows the excitement of power—the crowd waits, like a trapped and unresisting prey, for Imelda to begin using that power: this is the secret they share, the crowd and Imelda, Imelda and the crowd. She will smile and flick those wrists and sing her little songs. . . . She bends and barely sways, beating time, glancing at the guitar and then lifts her face to point with her chin at the night bright with neon lights and the moon—the old charisma, with its look of suffering, potent tonight as never before, the brilliance of beauty commingling with the brilliance of pain, the haunted, agonized, tragic look encircling the plaza and holding her audience in thrall.[78]

Imelda's charisma seems to hinge on her ability to create a homology between her own melodramatic persona as the victim-heroine of the Marcos romance and the collective imaginary of the folk as victims of history. An intimate knowledge of ethical incompleteness and social victimization is the secret they share.

As the People's Star, Imelda does not just aestheticize the victimhood of the popular classes, she performs the people's "best self"—to use Matthew Arnold's terms. She does this by embodying a cultural state-in-the-making. She exteriorizes the painful process of self-improvement necessary for overcoming ethical incompleteness. It is a melodramatic performance of cultural paternalism that sees Imelda inspiring the folk on behalf of Ferdinand, her mentor and senior partner. Enervated by the psychic costs of her pedagogical formation, yet profoundly beautiful by virtue of the "countless lessons she has learned," the spectacle of Imelda serves as an invitation to transcendence.

But in appropriating the vernacular, Imelda's performance also gives voice to the people's feelings of social exclusion. The sentimental love songs in her repertoire are wrenched free from a long history of aesthetic marginalization: what elite society had long repressed as markers of the folk's backwardness becomes a powerful talisman for engendering group identity. These songs support a drama of public recognition in which the People's Star arrogates unto herself the power to speak for the folk. She must do for them what they cannot do for themselves: voice their demands that their devalued identities and cultural practices be officially recognized and revalued.

Imelda's performance is a foretaste of the cultural center's therapeutic ethos; one that interprets the ethical incompleteness of the folk in terms of psychological needs and approaches their disenfranchisement in subjective terms. As we shall see, the melodramatic imaginary of the Marcos romance has Imelda administering a cultural "cure" for the folk. It is a course of cultural therapy that will pay close attention to their psychic pathologies. Just as her own pedagogical training had culminated in the treatment of a malformed personality, so too would the folk's road to aesthetic enlightenment end in their psychological rehabilitation as New Filipinos.

The Cultural Center of the Philippines

At her first press conference as first lady of the land, Imelda Marcos declared: "My dream is to have a theatre—a completely equipped auditorium where artists can find full expression of their talent. Something like Carnegie Hall, perhaps."[79] It comes as no surprise that Imelda should decide on a performance space as her first cultural project. Pubic gatherings were intermittent, and therefore inefficient for displaying herself as the People's Star; a cultural technology had to be built to monumentalize this persona.

Designed by National Artist for Architecture Leandro Locsin, the cultural center cuts a striking silhouette against the backdrop of Manila Bay. At eye level, the main theater appears as a massive rectangular slab of stone floating above the ground. The twelve-story block is actually cantilevered on thin supports that recede into the shadows created by the structure's enormous eaves.[80] Visitors navigate a "complex of pavilions . . . interspersed by plazas, lush gardens, serene reflecting pools and shaded areas."[81] The main theater, which seats 2,598, is done up in red and gold opera colors. Cantilevered side boxes offer a privileged vantage point to both the stage and the orchestra seats.

Clearly governed by elite standards of taste, the center operationalizes ethico-aesthetic exercises in three important ways: as a space of emulation, in which the folk might learn civilized forms of behavior from their social betters; as a space of representation, staging cultural performances in such ways as to educate the folk into a set of tastes; and as a space of observation, which constantly reminds the visitor to monitor his or her conduct because one never knows when one is being watched.[82] The center's spatial arrangements compel the visitor to demonstrate the skills, taste, and values necessary to "belong" there. To borrow Laurajane Smith's terms, the site has an affective power that is dictated by the way the Marcos romance values the trappings of high culture as "items of desire, as possessing innate values and properties."[83]

But the center's grand design is equally invested in vernacular culture. The center's "floating" structure was famously inspired by the *bahay kubo,* the modest dwelling of the popular classes, consisting primarily of a rectangular living space embellished only with functional ornaments and elevated from the ground by wooden stilts. The center was in fact at the forefront of a state-supported architectural movement that valorized folk culture in both anthropological and aesthetic terms. Imelda and her stable of architects understood such culture to be "timeless, locally rooted, and expressive of the authentic indigenous identity, character, and soul of the people."[84]

Marrying monumental and vernacular forms, the center gave physical shape to the paternalist and populist cultural policy agendas of the Marcos romance. These agendas came under public attack in 1969 as the center's construction costs ballooned to a spectacular Php 50 million. Ferdinand Marcos was up for reelection that year. With the public coffers all but depleted on campaign spending, Imelda secured a $7 million foreign loan to ensure the completion of the building. Senator Benigno Aquino, Jr., demanded a Senate investigation. In a legendary speech delivered on the Senate floor, he assailed the center as an elitist institution and likened its benefactor to Eva Perón, the wife of the Argentine dictator. "To spend 50 million pesos on a national theater that will cater mainly to the elite, the members of the Establishment, at a time when the country's poor cry out for immediate solutions, is not only the height of callousness but borders on the criminal," he railed.[85]

We find a reverse image of Aquino's antielitism in Imelda's populist defense of the center. She claimed that the center would in fact democratize culture. The poor would have access to the center's offerings for as low as one peso, less than the cost of a movie ticket. The idea was to "have the affluent sectors pay heavily on opening nights" and thereby subsidize subsequent showings. Her supporters vaunted the center's programs as much-needed cultural entitlements that would "giv[e] the Filipino what his political and economic worlds have failed to provide."[86]

If Aquino's attack focused on the material needs of the popular classes, Imelda's defense focused on psychological ones. The center would heal a national psyche suffering from cultural amnesia. In Imelda's words, "When history and circumstances cause a blurring of the past, the result is confusion of traditions and values. A people with national amnesia suffer a lack of balance and sense of direction. Rootless and purposeless, they must find firm traditions . . . or they will wither and die."[87] The statement strikingly paraphrases Fanon's notion that without "tradition," postcolonial subjects are cast adrift, becoming "colorless, stateless, rootless—a race of angels."

Imelda's condemnation of the "confusion of traditions and values" plaguing the nation follows Marcos's description of the Philippines as a "transitional society" whose path to "national development" has been stymied by contradictory values and institutions. Both notions mesh well with the melodramatic imaginary. In melodrama, a conflict of identities drives desire. Redemption is achieved with the confirmation of a clear psychic and moral identity—a "true" self. If the nation's colonial history had repressed the nation's true self, then the key to unlocking the national unconscious lay in folk culture. To this end, the center invented traditions and reinvented vernacular practices as evidences of a "great Malayan culture." For the center's grand opening, in September 1969, Imelda commissioned an original work, *Dularawan,* an epic opera set in a pre-colonial village. The performance called for a musical ensemble made up entirely of indigenous instruments so that "not even a violin would figure on the stage."[88]

Dularawan looked to the past to recover the nation's "true" identity in a "noble" race, which the exigencies of history had buried underneath a false colonial identity. This was in keeping with Ferdinand Marcos's prognostications on the "sterility, mediocrity and timidity" of the "Filipino personality" scarred by the colonial experience. Of the psychic suffering of the colonized cultural subject, Ferdinand would write, "No one can truly measure the intensity of his hurt and shame. A moving shadow, he . . . feel[s] unworthy of his own true self." As an instrument of national glorification, the center's great Malayan culture supported Ferdinand's modernization platform. It was hoped that such culture would lead to the creation of a more "assertive and self-confident" subject, the New Filipino, on whom the state's nation-building programs depended. Just as the victim-heroine of the Marcos romance had to overcome her affliction by realizing that the "cure lay within her own will," the psychically scarred Filipino must look deep into himself for self-affirmation. Only by rediscovering his "true" heritage would he be sufficiently primed to be a "dynamic instrument of nation-building and social reconstruction."[89] I turn now to the martial-law state's formalization of the nation's heritage culture to explore how the regime's rhetoric bent and stretched cultural-policy realities.

Heritage Culture and the New Society

On December 11, 1972, a symposium on cultural policy sponsored by the Philippine commission to the United Nations Educational, Scientific and Cultural Organization (UNESCO) was held at the controversial Cultural Center of the Philippines. The unprecedented conference saw representatives of the cultural sector debating the meanings to be attached to *culture* and *cultural development* in the New Society.[90]

The Philippine commission drew on the basic principles of modernization to arrive at a definition of *culture* as "an awareness possessed by a human community of its own historical evolution"; *cultural promotion* as "the measures taken to improve the quality of social life by the communication of men's ideas, thought and works"; and *cultural development* as involving "the organization, stimulation and promotion of a living culture but also the accession of the greatest possible number of people to the activities and works of the arts and the intellect."[91]

The symposium revisited the question of state subvention of the arts, the controversial issue in Imelda's and Aquino's war of words in 1969. Leonidas V. Benesa, then president of the Art Association of the Philippines (AAP), a private organization of artists, delivered a position statement arguing that legal precedent made such support a matter of citizenship rights.[92] The 1935 constitution decreed that "Filipino culture shall be preserved and developed for national identity," and that "the arts and letters shall be under the patronage of the state."[93] Benesa's position statement imagines a vertical structure for the administration of culture. Emanating from state bureaucracies, high culture would produce a trickle-down effect that is predicated on the transfer of taste. Crucially for Benesa, only a centralized cultural state could provide the adequate infrastructure that would allow the arts and letters to do their ethico-aesthetic work: mold the critical faculties of the cultural citizen.

Expanding the discussion of cultural policy beyond the immediate ambit of state patronage of the arts, Jose D. Ingles, undersecretary of the Department of Foreign Affairs, offered a different vision. He argued that the martial-law state's abiding interest in the preservation of heritage culture must be matched by the development of a *living* culture as a corrective to the elitist tendencies of the former: "The national culture must not remain a commodity for museums or other types of intellectual contemplation."[94] Significantly, Ingles questions the notion of a static heritage culture. Characterizing such culture as "dead," he strikes at a critical issue in postcolonial theorizations of national "traditions." As Fanon rightly argues, such traditions are often misunderstood as the mummified "proofs" of a national culture; when in fact, in the postcolonial context, national "traditions" are profoundly unstable, reflecting "the fluctuating movement which the people are just giving shape to." For Fanon, the postcolonial subject must transcend his initial instinct to recover and monumentalize a lost heritage in favor of forging a new cultural praxis geared toward the struggling nation's political, economic and social realities.[95]

Ingles's position statement grafts the political and economic imperatives of modernization onto a clearly Fanonian understanding of heritage traditions, arguing that such culture is of little use to the martial-law state unless it is purposively integrated into the state's development initiatives. What is needed is a *living* national culture—a useful culture that would empower popular classes "in an age of competitive economies and super-power relations." A living culture is such not because of any transcendent property of the cultural object, but because of its pragmatic applications as a marketable heritage culture. Crucially, the ideal cultural citizen imagined by Ingles is a cultural entrepreneur, one who enters into a development-oriented partnership with the state.[96]

The two position statements encapsulate the ambivalent priorities enmeshed in the New Society's creation of a heritage culture:

the imperative to facilitate the cultural liberation of the populace on the one hand and the implicit demand that this domestic cultural-policy agenda, directed at the internal revolution of the New Filipino, be geared as well toward the state's external economic relations. The avowed therapeutic ethos of the Cultural Center of the Philippines—the imperative to restore the dignity and self-confidence of the cultural citizen—was indeed to play a subservient role to the creation of a "viable" heritage culture that could be marketed abroad.

Throughout the 1970s and into the 1980s, Imelda Marcos oversaw the construction of a mushrooming number of cultural institutions, which all fell under the purview of the cultural center. Collectively designated as the Cultural Center of the Philippines Complex (CCP Complex), the center and its progeny institutions constituted a cultural city-within-a-city. It consisted of the Folk Arts Theater, the Philippine International Convention Center, the Philippine Center for International Trade and Expositions, the Philippine Trade Pavilions, the Coconut Palace, and the Manila Film Center. The "lives" of these cultural monuments were tied to ephemeral international events: the Miss Universe Pageant in 1974, the IMF-World Bank conference in 1976, the United Nations Conference on Trade and Development in 1979, the papal visit in 1981, and the Manila International Film Festival in 1982 and 1983. All these events saw the repurposing and commercialization of heritage culture.

The 1974 Miss Universe Pageant set the tone for all the international events that followed. Built in just seventy-seven days, the Folk Arts Theater was especially erected for the pageant. A mass ceremony dubbed Kasaysayan ng Lahi, or History of the Race, was staged to inaugurate the unveiling of the new theater.[97] For this event, Imelda enlisted 20,400 citizens representing fifty tribal groups to reenact the history of the Philippines. Witnessed by over a hundred thousand Filipino spectators, the ceremony also targeted a shadow audience—the international community. The regime hoped that the lavish production would enhance the nation's image as an attractive tourist destination.

Kasaysayang ng Lahi and the Miss Universe Pageant were in fact part of a massive effort to package Manila as a "global" city. This involved major investments in cultural infrastructure that would attract tourists and bring together the service, information, and culture industries. Between 1972 and 1977, the Philippine government invested over Php 19 billion in building projects, the jewels of which were concentrated in the CCP Complex.[98] To maintain the aesthetic integrity of her "cultural city," Imelda Marcos ordered sixty thousand squatter's shacks bulldozed from view. She conscripted ten thousand slum dwellers to sweep the streets. She had concrete walls erected to shield visitors' eyes from urban blight. Meanwhile, numerous luxury hotels were quickly built, fourteen of which were funded by foreign loans. By 1976 the government had spent at least $500 million on hotel construction—compared with $13.3 million that same year for public housing.[99]

The economic pressures bearing on the CCP Complex shifted the center's cultural priorities away from the social empowerment of the folk to the rerouting of public resources into cosmetic improvements and amenities that would primarily serve transnational end users. Consequently, the folk were regarded less as clients of a therapeutic cultural state than as providers of muchneeded cultural services—as low-level service workers and performers of marketable touristic experiences. In short, the turn to an instrumental conception of heritage culture in the New Society generated unexpected social outcomes that were incommensurable with Marcos's cultural rehabilitation program.

Marcos invoked culture as the handmaiden of an internal revolution. But as a consequence of the centralized structure of Marcos's cultural state, the "people's culture" fell prey to accounts of ethical incompleteness predicated on the circular and self-referential power of the national family. Nowhere was this dynamic more pronounced than in the New Society's efforts to build a national cinema. As we shall see in the next chapter, the emergence of the New Cinema was never far removed from the state's efforts to secure the political obedience of the wayward children of the national family.

Chapter 3

NATIONAL DISCIPLINE
AND THE CINEMA

On September 29, 1972, just one week after the declaration of
martial law (Proclamation 1081), Ferdinand Marcos issued Letter
of Instruction no. 13, ordering the Board of Censors for Motion
Pictures (BCMP) to ban

(1) Films which tend to incite subversion, insurrection or
rebellion against the State;

(2) Films which tend to undermine the faith and confidence of
the people in their government and/or their duly constituted
authorities;

(3) Films which glorify criminals or condone crimes;

(4) Films which serve no other purpose but to satisfy the market
for violence and pornography;

(5) Films which offend any race or religion;

(6) Films which tend to abet the traffic in and use of prohibited
drugs;

(7) Films contrary to law, public order, morals, good customs,
established policies, lawful orders, decrees or edicts; any and
all films which in the judgment of the Board are similarly
objectionable and contrary to the letter and spirit of
Proclamation No. 1081.[1]

It would seem that Marcos was worried about the cinema's promotion of unethical values (notably through pornographic and violent films) and, more fundamentally, its capacity to "incite subversion." As it turns out, these concerns were well placed. A special relationship existed between the cinema and the dissidents of the First Quarter Storm. Often romanticized in most historical accounts of the cinema, the love affair between the cinema and radical youth in fact began with sex and violence.

From Bakya *to* Bomba

In the 1970s the film industry was highly prolific, producing an average of 182 feature films per year, while charging one of the lowest admission prices in the world (Php 5.00, or roughly $0.40, for an orchestra ticket in first-run theaters in Metro Manila).[2] But up until the early 1960s, the vast majority of movie theaters in the Manila area catered to the Americanized tastes of urban audiences, and therefore exhibited mostly Hollywood imports. Local films were "dumped" in the provinces. Indeed, as a cultural institution, the cinema was historically associated with the unformed tastes and irrational behavior of the peasantry. It was a structurally marginalized institution.

One must revisit the colonial period to understand how the indigenous film industry had become structurally marginalized. The introduction of cinema technology to the Philippines overlapped with the country's annexation to the United States, in 1898. Since that time, Filipino producers had to labor at a disadvantage against the unrestricted entry of film imports, the majority of which came from the colonial metropolis. The introduction of sound technology, in the 1930s, ushered in the standardization of Tagalog as the local cinema's lingua franca. Since Hollywood products thoroughly dominated urban areas, local film companies redirected their linguistically differentiated products at provincial audiences. So strong was the local cinema's identification with country folk that it became synonymous with the so-called *bakya* crowd. *Bakya* is Tagalog for clog, the functional, albeit déclassé, footwear favored by the peasantry. It was a metonym of the ethical incompleteness of the cinema and its abject audience. As a 1968 *Manila Times* editorial put it: "The *bakya* crowd is not so much a matter of class distinctions as a certain mentality. . . . They watch *bakbakan* (violent) movies where the hero shoots down seven men with six bullets, seated in bedbug-ridden, knife-slashed [Php] 1.20 seat, their feet on the backrest in front of them, cracking peanuts and repeating loudly every line said on the screen."[3]

The statement projected a good fit between the degenerate content of local films and the squalid atmosphere of provincial theaters. Both encouraged unruly behavior among a purportedly boorish audience. The stigma attached to the local cinema was exacerbated in the 1960s by the proliferation of sex and violence movies, popularly known as *bombas*.

In the local cinema, *bomba* (lit., bomb) referred to female nudity or scenes simulating sexual acts (or both). Such content was strictly prohibited until 1961, when the BCMP adopted a system of classification that distinguished between "for general patronage" and "for adults only." By the end of the decade, the hitherto repressed sexuality of Philippine films "exploded" in such "for adults only" films as *Uhaw* (Thirsty), *Dayukdok* (Starved), *Laman sa laman* (Flesh on flesh), *Luray* (Crushed), and *Sabik* (Excited). In these films, the sexual repression of the female protagonist motivates the display of nudity; the eventual release of repressed desires propels narratives climaxing with graphic depictions of the sex act.

The bomba film's textual protocols were reinforced by institutional practices that rendered it especially unruly. In February 1970 the BCMP revealed some of the most rampant violations then being committed at the point of exhibition: the insertion of pornographic content into otherwise "legitimate" films passed by the board; the admission of underage audiences into movies classified for adults only; and the splicing of sexual content onto film posters and billboards.[4] The bomba's institutional protocols thus created a potentially subversive filmic experience. Not only did such films *represent* deviant behavior, they also occasioned the violation of laws safeguarding the gregarious communitas of cinema spectatorship.[5]

It is profoundly ironic, then, that the bomba film sparked a rediscovery of local films by urban elites. In 1961 only three Manila theaters showed local films regularly.[6] By 1970, however, all the nation's nine hundred theaters were exhibiting local films. As the bomba film drew an ever-widening circle of devotees to the cinema, the gregarious nature of cinema spectatorship became increasingly sexualized, even promiscuous:

> Some of the *bomba* fans were carryovers from the [bakya] folk, the ones who regularly went to local movies rain or shine. Another portion of the *bomba* audience was made up of teenagers and young people for whom this kind of movie . . . was a visual introduction to the facts of life. Normally, young people would have been indifferent to the Tagalog film, but the sex bit drew them in. Still another portion of the new audience was made up of college-educated professionals and middle-class employees who constituted the great bulk of the English-language movie crowd in the Greater Manila area, but who discovered the local film industry for themselves with the appearance of its adult movies.[7]

Perplexingly, the addition of youth and middle-class professionals to the ranks of the bomba audience, far from sparking a moral panic, inspired then chief censor Jose L. Guevara to proclaim in 1970 that the "Filipino film industry was finally growing up." This backhanded compliment took as a given that the local cinema had been languishing in a state of "arrested development." And the litmus test of the cinema's purported coming of age was not so much the films as the audience drawn to them. As if by osmosis, the cultural capital of these urbane groups was projected onto the screen, adding value, as it were, to the filmic texts. In this exchange between text and audience, the bomba film suddenly became praiseworthy for its "adult themes, realistic plots and acceptable characterizations."[8]

Historians of Philippine cinema hold a less sanguine view of the bomba film. By most accounts, the bomba phenomenon was an indication that the cinema had reached its nadir in the 1960s.[9] The literature on the subject tends to explain the pathology of the bomba film through the lens of industrial economics. It is said that the bomba trend was symptomatic of the breakdown of a previously stable studio system, which had peaked a decade earlier when a cartel consisting of four studios controlled the domestic market for Philippine films. Labor troubles forced one of the studios to shut down in the mid-1960s. This created an opening that independent producers would fill. On a macro level, however, the new competitive environment made the local industry more vulnerable to foreign imports. The Philippines placed no restrictions on the entry of foreign films even after formal independence, in 1946. Meanwhile, the film industry paid the highest amusement taxes in the country while being the cheapest form of entertainment. Taxed as luxury entertainment—like cockfighting and horse racing—the cinema surrendered up to 30 percent of each film's gross earnings to the government.[10] Indeed, the local cinema represented an inverted picture of most film industries in the Asian region, where the importation of foreign films was generally restricted and where taxes levied on foreign films were considerably higher than those imposed on local productions.

Despite these complications, 1970 and 1971 were highly prolific years for the industry. In 1970 the BCMP reviewed 245 local films, and in 1971 this figure climbed to 268.[11] Some twenty-one local films were produced every month during this period, and approximately five new movies were introduced into the nation's theater circuit every week. However, the majority of the films were hastily produced "quickies," with running times averaging seventy-five minutes. Retrospectively assessing the quality of these films in the wake of Letter of Instruction no. 13, Guillermo C. de

Vega, Marcos's newly appointed chief censor, gave the following prognosis: the films "were sex-and-violence oriented and did not require any complex dramatic structure, sophisticated character delineation, or complicated technical values in cinematography, editing and musical scoring." The films, in other words, were just "vehicles for inserting bombas."[12]

At this juncture, film imports tended to be sexploitation films. To hold on to its market, the industry endeavored to surpass the graphic content of these imports. As Bienvenido Lumbera puts it, "The result was a plethora of films that tried to outdo foreign films in the depiction of sex and violence, giving rise to such curiosities as Filipino samurai and kung fu masters, Filipino James Bonds, and most notorious of them all, the bomba queen."[13]

The derivative quality of the films, combined with their commercial logic, made the local cinema of the 1960s anathema to historians of Philippine cinema. And yet, it has become a truism in Philippine film historiography that the cinema's vapid productions were irrevocably transformed in the early 1970s, when the cinema became nationalistic. Replicating the board of censors' sleight of hand, the literature isolates the entry of a nationalist intelligentsia to the ranks of the audience as the historical signpost of the cinema's turn to nationalism.

Of the disparate groups now regularly attending bomba screenings, it was the youth—and in particular, radical college students—who were closely associated with the cinema's so-called coming of age. Invoked as mirror images of each other, this new, youthful audience for Philippine films and the film industry were on the cusp of something new and dangerous. The radical youth politics associated with this audience group bled into the potentially subversive qualities of the bomba film, making it doubly threatening. And indeed, the specter of the First Quarter Storm loomed large over the cinema's new horizon of possibility: "Nationalist students were drawn to local films, hoping to gain understanding of the masses as represented by the audience for Filipino films and cultural forces that intensify oppression of the masses."[14]

The bomba's transformation into a nationalist filmic experience, however elliptical its account in the established literature, nonetheless bears an uncanny resemblance to Marcos's own assessment of the cinema. For Marcos as well, the apparent revitalization of the cinema during the 1970s was symptomatic of "the upsurge of nationalist sentiment during the decade of intense ferment."[15] To begin to understand the relationship between the new subversive film culture unleashed by the bomba film and the social ferment of the 1970s, it is necessary to revisit the violent political climate of the nation on the eve of the First Quarter Storm. As we shall see, the cinema's bomba culture was a mirror image of the excesses associated with "Philippine-style" democracy. Its libidinous energy, in particular, overlapped with the sex scandal that marred Marcos's presidency.

The Bomba in Politics and Film

At the close of 1969 a nationwide poll conducted by Senator Helena Benitez found that 20 percent of the respondents "favored violence as the only means of bringing about change." In March 1970 another poll revealed that 30 percent expressed "readiness to take the law into their own hands."[16] Coming on the heels of the November 1969 election, these responses were almost certainly conditioned by the record-setting upsurge of political violence that year. The Commission on Elections (COMELEC) recorded at least seventy-two political assassinations in an election further marred by massive vote buying and fraud.[17]

The 1969 election was the culmination of a decade-long escalation of political violence: each biennial campaign throughout the 1960s had been characterized by the formulaic mobilization of "gold, goons, and guns," which had led to a "few hundred political deaths."[18] In 1965, the year Marcos was first elected, the homicide rate was at thirty-five per hundred thousand persons (compared to twenty-five for Colombia that same year—a time of upheaval known there as La Violencia.). The violence, as Alfred McCoy points out, "was neither random nor widespread," but was "integral to the electoral process." In one provincial town, for instance, the murder rate jumped from two in the months before elections to thirty during the 1965 presidential campaign. Two years later, during the 1967 congressional elections, one provincial municipality achieved a record annual homicide rate of 134 per hundred thousand.[19]

As electoral violence escalated and gained increasing visibility, campaign politics reflected a more acute and systematic use of political bombas. It was common practice for politicians to "explode" political exposés onto the nation's scandal sheets as a means of smearing opponents with allegations of graft or corruption. The political bombas of the 1960s, however, set unprecedented standards of sensationalism. The U.S. embassy described the Liberal Party's campaign against Marcos in 1965 as a "year-long propaganda orgy."[20] Charging Marcos with land grabbing, taking bribes from U.S. business groups, and filing fraudulent war damage claims, the party's smear campaign was so extensive that, in the words of a foreign correspondent for the *Far Eastern Economic Review,* "few are willing to believe that anyone can possibly be so bad."[21]

The Liberal Party's smear tactics did not spare Imelda Marcos from a character assassination of commensurate proportions. In addition to tales of her extravagant lifestyle, party backers floated rumors that the celebrated beauty had starred in a pornographic film. While the film in question never materialized beyond hearsay accounts, a nude photograph of Imelda did in fact surface.

> Copies of a photograph of [Imelda] in the nude began to circulate around universities and nightclubs. She called a 3 A.M. meeting to discuss strategy. Although hurt by the smear tactic, Imelda appeared quite unruffled. She viewed the whole matter with detachment, took the picture—a collage of another woman's body with her face—and asked the

dozen political aides she had assembled, "And what shall we do about this?" The embarrassed men fumbled for a suitable reply, but Imelda spared them from further embarrassment, shrugging her shoulders and saying, "Well, at least I hope that the body they supplied for my face is nice."[22]

The above vignette from Imelda's unofficial biography points to the increasingly porous boundaries between the political bomba and its cinematic counterpart. Ferdinand's opponents clearly seized on the gendered voyeurism underpinning Imelda's self-performance as the People's Star and pushed its libidinal connotations to an extreme. Eliciting the leering gaze of the bomba film's urbane audiences, Imelda's "doctored" photograph was not just a parody of Maganda; it was meant to humiliate Maganda's master.

The scandal did not hurt Marcos's political career, however. In 1969 he won reelection—the first president in the history of the republic to do so—by a margin of 2 million votes (of 11 million votes cast), a landslide his critics attributed to payoffs and intimidation.[23] The candidates spent the equivalent of nearly one-fourth of the national budget, but Marcos led the pack, spending no less than $50 million during the campaign. As his opponent, Senator Sergio Osmeña, Jr., famously grumbled, "[We were] out-gooned, out-gunned, out-gold."[24]

The COMELEC duly noted: "During all these election years, the dice have been loaded in favor of the affluent, the rich and powerful. . . . Indeed, this is one of the primary causes of the youth unrest and the student demonstrations that we witness today."[25] The statement came in the heels of a spate of student demonstrations protesting the fraud and violence of the 1969 elections. In a matter of weeks, the First Quarter Storm erupted, and Marcos found "himself the object of personal and political attack, hanged in effigy, scorned in placards and editorials, jeered and taunted."[26] The uproar over the elections would soon be amplified by a bomba spectacular never before seen in the country: a sex scandal starring the president himself.

The Dovie Beams Scandal

The scandal began with a campaign film, *Ang maharlika* (The noble). Maharlika was Marcos's nom de guerre.[27] If the Marcos romance were to be believed, Ang mga Maharlika (the nobles) was the name of the anti-Japanese guerrilla unit organized by Marcos during World War II.[28] The film, which starred Hollywood actors Paul Burke (as Marcos) and Farley Granger, was a big-budget action-adventure billed as "the story of Ferdinand Marcos, war hero."[29] Shooting began in May 1969. Principal photography was completed in September. However, the film, which was intended for release in advance of the 1969 presidential elections, stalled when Marcos's campaign funds dried up. The project was eventually completed in 1970, and though a rough cut of the film was concurrently released in Guam, the film was banned in the Philippines. The controversy over the film hinged on Marcos's affair with Dovie Beams, the American starlet playing the female lead in *Ang maharlika*.[30]

Dovie Beams arrived in Manila in December 1968. The thirty-eight-year-old starlet soon after became the president's kept woman. A retinue of armed guards, intelligence agents and Colonel Fabian Ver, Marcos's future chief of staff, coordinated the top-secret affair.[31]

Before Beams returned to the United States, in September 1969, to do postproduction work on the film, the lovers exchanged a few souvenirs that would later gain untold notoriety. Beams's souvenir was an audiotape of Marcos singing "Pamulinawen," his favorite folk song, supposedly recorded in their bedroom—and in flagrante delicto. Marcos's souvenir was a cache of Polaroid snapshots of Beams in the nude. The lovers also exchanged highly unusual mementos: locks of each other's pubic hair.[32]

Beams was back in Manila when the First Quarter Storm broke out. Unbeknownst to Marcos, Beams had been recording other "souvenir" audiotapes of her bedroom relations with the president. Published transcripts of one tape revealed Colonel Fabian Ver interrupting a tryst with urgent news about a student demonstration. "They're attacking and bombing. Here I am fucking around," Marcos said on the tape.[33]

By August 1970, Marcos had cut all ties with Beams. When he reportedly refused to give her a "separation allowance," she pressed *Ang maharlika*'s producers to pay her $100,000. She said she was "prepared to embarrass the President," if the money was not forthcoming.[34] She was paid only $10,000 by the film's investors, partners in a production company called USV Arts. Beams persisted in her quest, even appealing to the U.S. embassy for protection.[35]

The scandal eventually exploded—in classic bomba fashion—in October 1970 when the *Philippines Free Press* put a picture of the bikini-clad starlet on the cover, under the headline "Dovie Beams— A Lovely Argument for Special Relations." The very morning that the Beams issue hit the stands, a distraught Imelda Marcos telephoned the wife of *Free Press* publisher Teodoro Locsin, Sr., demanding to know why the magazine dared to "put [Marcos's] mistress on the cover."[36]

The story of the confrontation between Imelda and Locsin was sensational news and triggered a chain reaction. Reporters hounded Beams, who was gradually "persuaded" to supply every minute detail of her affair with the president. On November 11, 1970, Beams held a press conference. As it turned out, the real star of the occasion was an audiotape. As Carmen Navarro Pedrosa recounts, "There were sighs, breathless half-minute pauses, and, most titillating of all, singing while it happened. The voice, Marcos watchers avowed, sounded uncomfortably reminiscent of the president's baritone vowing to lead the country to greatness."[37]

Beams left the Philippines for good immediately following the press conference, but the scandal persisted well into 1971, for there were other "souvenirs" yet to be exploded. The Marcos camp started the offensive by publicizing Ferdinand's Polaroid shots of the starlet, along with a deposition, from Beams's former psychiatrist, testifying that she had "schizoid traits." The Marcos offensive appeared in a ten-week series of articles in the Marcos-controlled

Republic Weekly. From Beverly Hills, Beams retaliated with more audiotapes and sent Manila publications some bonus evidence—strands of presidential pubic hair. Her sensational rebuttal package appeared in a series of articles—the "Dovie Beams Claws Back" series—in the *Graphic.*[38]

The Dovie Beams scandal exacerbated the dramatic drop in Marcos's popularity immediately following the outbreak of the First Quarter Storm. These two "pseudo-events" would indeed become mutually reinforcing features of the president's bid to recuperate his public image as Malakas. Not without irony, he would do so by clamping down on the bomba film.

National Sexuality

When Congress reconvened on the Monday after the January 30 "revolt," Marcos was confronted with an actual bomba, this one hurled from the Senate floor by Aquino, who assailed the president for the deaths of four students in the much-publicized Battle of Mendiola Bridge:

> Four Filipino students are dead, Mr. President. They were shot, not by strangers, but by their own countrymen; not by invaders, but by the soldiers of their own government, by the guards of their own president. These were young students, not grizzled rebels—innocent, unarmed, defenseless. ... The greatest sin we in this chamber can commit today, Mr. President, is not to tolerate disorder by the youth but to allow them to be cowed and coerced. To allow our youth to be frightened will be a sin against our people, a sin against history, a sin against our future.[39]

As the national allegory played out, the political rivals assumed unequivocal roles: Marcos was the target of the student demonstrators; Aquino, their champion. Aquino went on to compare the violence and vandalism committed by the student dissidents with the graft and corruption underpinning the 1969 elections: "The students destroyed 250,000 pesos worth of property Friday night," Aquino shouted, "but these leaders have pillaged and ravaged the Republic down to its last dollar!" In a final declaration that "roused cheering from the packed gallery," he concluded: "I stand with the students, Mr. President—not with Malacañang's tools of violence, not with Mr. Marcos' bloodthirsty troops. They are the fomenters of violence, the harbingers of unrest. Yes, Mr. President, we are gripped by crisis, a crisis fraught with danger to us all. But not the crisis born of the imagined conspiracies and conspirators of Mr. Marcos. Our crisis, sir, is a crisis of aspiration among our young and a crisis of conscience among their elders. How shall we respond?"[40]

Marcos's response to Aquino's bomba was to staunchly uphold the threat of communist subversion. Privately, however, he blamed his political enemies—and the oligarchy-controlled press—for the First Quarter Storm. The next day, in his own private diary, Marcos would write, "We must unmask these would be anarchists hiding behind children."[41]

The First Quarter Storm and Aquino's political bomba placed the radical youth movement at the center of the mounting power struggle between Marcos and the media. But if there was one sector in the media landscape with which the youth were now readily associated, it was the local cinema. It did not take long for Marcos to blame the cinema and the bomba film for the "crisis of aspiration" allegedly suffered by this vulnerable segment of the population. In his search for an elusive force directing the subversive actions of the students, Marcos would have recourse to the sex and violence flooding the nation's movie screens.

On February 22, 1970, civic and religious groups picketed the Palace and Mayfair theaters in downtown Manila. The theaters were known for specializing in sex-and-violence movies. A congressional investigation followed, prompted by the "rampant production and exhibition of movies commercializing sex, promiscuity and vices."[42] Eight months later the Dovie Beams scandal exploded. The press's sensational treatment of the scandal created an inevitable backlash that sharply called to mind Aquino's allegation that the "crisis of aspiration" suffered by the nation's youth was mirrored by a "crisis of conscience" suffered by their elders. Following these developments, Marcos issued a memorandum to the board of censors prescribing new standards of film censorship. The presidential memo conceded to the BCMP the difficulty of maintaining a "balanced and enlightened censorship policy," particularly in the face of "strong competition posed by the more heavily-budgeted foreign films." Marcos nevertheless urged the board to protect the populace from the "exploitation of their anxieties."[43] The First Quarter Storm could not have been far removed from Marcos's meaning.

Before the memo, the BCMP considered objectionable scenes depicting "bloody fights with one protagonist more or less unable to defend himself, brutal kicks in the face and the abdomen, strangulation, flogging, torture and shooting further a man who is already down on the ground."[44] It is ironic that the spectacles of the First Quarter Storm depicted the police and the military performing various versions of these scenarios on the bodies of unarmed students. As if in acknowledgment of these ignominious scenes of police brutality, the presidential memo urged the board to proscribe "scenes of gruesome and gory killing, showing for more than two seconds bloodied faces or hacked and disjointed parts of the human body." And, as if in recognition of the hero worship inspired by the so-called Four Martyrs of the January 30 "revolt," the presidential memo urged the board to ban films "glorifying criminals or condoning crimes," and films "having at their end no redeeming social message or retribution."[45]

The remainder of the memo was devoted to the elucidation of objectionable sexual content. Extant censorship standards proscribed scenes depicting "acts of self-gratification," "full shots of naked bodies," "the pumping motions associated with intercourse," "the female breast being caressed, either by hand or by mouth, whether by a man or by a woman," and "any tongue-licking of the anatomy, at least for reasons of sanitation alone."[46] To these restrictions, Marcos added "scenes exposing pubic hair."[47]

One could do worse than interpret Marcos's personal crusade against the bomba film as a feeble attempt to restore the heteronormative framework of the national family. Ferdinand and Imelda secured two presidential terms on the strength of a rhetorical promise to govern the nation as a loving household. The Dovie Beams scandal brought to light how notions of intimacy so deeply woven into the ideology of the national family could be profoundly destabilized by the public exposure of sex acts hitherto protected behind a wall of privacy. At stake were the institutions of economic privilege and social reproduction cherished and protected by the organization of a hegemonic national public around sex.

Lauren Berlant and Michael Warner have identified the salient features of the U.S. version of what I have been calling the national family: the "structural differentiation of 'personal life' from work, politics, and the public sphere"; the linkage of intimacy "only to the institutions of social reproduction, the accumulation and transfer of capital, and self-development"; and the blocking of "nonnormative or explicit public sexual cultures." In making sex seem merely personal, U.S.-style intimacy, Berlant and Warner argue, works to make the intimate relations of private personhood appear to be the realm of sexuality itself. Or to put it another way, it makes sexuality appear to be a property of subjectivity, a fundamental aspect of one's inner personal essence. And so, the above conventions of intimacy produce the mirage of "a home base of prepolitical humanity from which citizens are thought to come into political discourse and to which they are expected to return in the (always imaginary) future after political conflict." Intimate life thus becomes the *"elsewhere* of political discourse." It serves an important compensatory function, distracting citizens from the structural inequalities and social injustices subtending their economic and political lives. And it keeps them in line by shaming them "for any divergence between their lives and the intimate sphere that is alleged to be simple personhood."[48]

From the 1969 elections (which demonstrated the porosity of cinematic and political bombas), to the First Quarter Storm (which placed the country's youth at the center of a moral-cum-political panic), to the Dovie Beams scandal (which exposed the father of the national family as a philanderer), the intimacy governing Marcos's national family was exposed as a mirage. The ideal of a privatized sexual culture, so dear to the U.S. notion of intimacy, was just impossible to sustain, given the blatant violations of intimacy norms in those pseudo-events. To hold on to his role as Malakas, Marcos would have to reestablish the sense of rightness and normalcy—in short, the heteronormativity—conceptually embodied in the national family. And here, heteronormativity is more than ideology or prejudice; it is the very index of a disciplined social order.[49]

Marcos's campaign to clean up the cinema asserts a "national heterosexuality," which Berlant and Warner describe as "the mechanism by which a core national culture can be imagined as a sanitized space of sentimental feeling and immaculate behavior, a space for pure citizenship."[50] Such a space of pure citizenship is secured by the spectacular demonization of any represented sex. When martial law was declared, Marcos's version of "national sexuality" was more strongly enforced. With the heavy hand of the law, the dictator made the privatization of sex (and the sexualization of private life) an important feature of his regime's national symbolic, whereby the body and subjectivity of the citizen was to be strictly disciplined as a precondition to entry into the political sphere.

A New Cinema for a New Society

In 1972 the BCMP withdrew from public exhibition 148 film imports and fifty locally produced films in accordance with the New Society's new censorship guidelines.[51] The onset of martial law in fact drove the bomba film close to extinction. In the twelve months following Marcos's martial-law declaration, only ten films out of the 173 local films reviewed by the board were classified "for adults only."[52]

The board's move to expunge the bomba film was part of a larger project to reinvent the cinema. As dictated by the BCMP, the film industry's new role in the New Society was to "produce quality films that do not merely entertain or inform, but prod the moviegoer to rethink his values and inspire him to constitutive action."[53] Clearly referencing Marcos's internal revolution, the BCMP's conception of "quality films" drew on the ethico-aesthetic functions of the heritage culture that was just then being formalized by the Philippine Commission to UNESCO. In the words of BCMP chairman De Vega,

> With the commitment of the New Society to the enrichment of Philippine culture, the reawakening of the people to traditional values and historical heritage, and the clarification of the Filipino image, through the revival and refurbishment of native arts such as painting, sculpture, dance, architecture, music and plays, it is imperative that the Filipino cinema must reorganize itself, examine its techniques, improve its attitudes, in short, rediscover itself by upholding its inherent artistic and social responsibility.[54]

De Vega's statement clearly anthropomorphizes the cinema, invoking it as an ethically incomplete subject that must discover its true worth—much like the New Filipino, whose psychoaffective rehabilitation hinges on internalizing the heritage culture invented by the state. Significantly, the statement insists that the cinema has an "inherent" artistic responsibility. This is a provocative claim, for at no other time in the history of the republic has the government valorized the local cinema as a cultural institution comparable to the seven so-called native arts (architecture, painting, sculpture, dance, music, drama, literature). A popular institution historically stigmatized by its association with the bakya crowd is now being invoked as an instrument of cultural uplift.

True to her self-appointed role as cultural custodian of the New Society, it was Imelda Marcos who would define the cinema's new artistic calling, in a 1974 speech delivered before the Filipino Academy of Movie Arts and Sciences:

> I can no longer accept the idea that the Filipino is frivolous, for example, or that the audience for films—the much-derided mass audience—is too ignorant and indifferent to appreciate productions which follow the timeless dictum of all art: the exaltation of the human spirit. We would like to see films of our native epics, portrayals of our native soul. Dramatizations of our authentic lives as individuals and as a people. . . . At a time when the eyes of the world are upon us, at a time when we are embarked on the task of regeneration through discipline, the challenge begins with our artists. Let us not, therefore, betray this vision. Let us be worthy of it.[55]

The last line of Imelda's speech powerfully encapsulates the principle of ethical incompleteness, which as we saw in the previous chapter, was the linchpin of the paternalist cultural policy of the martial-law state. The film industry, like the cultural subject, must prove its worth by acquiring artistic competencies consistent with universal standards of good taste. But in enjoining the cinema to provide an "authentic" mirror of the "native soul," Imelda's speech simultaneously gestures at the therapeutic ethos governing the regime's populist stance toward culture: the imperative to facilitate the psychoaffective rehabilitation of the New Filipino through the internalization of a rich cultural heritage.

These simultaneous pursuits made conflicting demands on, and set impossible expectations for, the film industry: while strict censorship guidelines were to be enforced to facilitate the creation of authentic "national" texts, the real measure of success for these texts lay in pragmatic outcomes that had noting to do with the therapeutic rehabilitation of the New Filipino. Success meant capturing an international standard of excellence, which was in turn to be measured by a film's ability to gain international recognition for the New Cinema.

As Imelda put it, the local cinema should aspire to "present Philippine life and culture not only to Filipinos but also to people abroad." Producers should therefore "aim for higher artistry and technical excellence so that they would merit international exhibition."[56] The local cinema, in other words, was being enjoined to create a heritage film industry that could compete in international film festivals and earn much-needed cultural revenue for the New Society. Such a mandate for a New Cinema clearly followed the instrumental logic of the New Society's heritage culture: the imperative to create a marketable heritage that would service the state's tourism and heritage-industry projects.

In July 1975 the BCMP issued a set of guidelines that would codify the textual frameworks of the regime's simultaneously paternalist, populist, and instrumentalist heritage film culture. Giving formal substance to Imelda's demand that local films authentically mirror the culture of the people while also serving the developmental initiatives of the martial law cultural state, the BCMP prescribed the following themes and topics as the appropriate textual parameters of the cinema:

1. *Materials that are of national interest and significance:* Film subjects that complement the developmental goals of the government, such as land reform, tourism, national integration, food production, infrastructure development, etc.

2. *Patently Filipino themes and characters:* Moviemakers are urged to project on film the Filipino image in its varied aspects. Rich sources of materials readily available to filmmakers are the following:

   A. Folk literature
   B. Metrical tales
   C. Zarzuelas (popular stage spectacles)
   D. Fiction
   E. Drama
   F. Historical events and personalities.[57]

The BCMP would thus define "local content" according to "folk" traditions actively promoted by the Cultural Center of the Philippines and its great Malayan culture. The remainder of the BCMP's guidelines on local content drew on the language of mental health to ban, among other things: *"Perverted or abnormal personalities* (homosexuals, prostitutes and the like as central figures in films); *Drug addiction and traffic in drugs* (If these subjects must be used, the film must positively emphasize that their use is undesirable, anti-social and criminal; *Incest and adultery* (portrayal of abnormal and illegal sex relations); *Violence and Brutality* (brutal killings, excessive cruelty and prolonged torture perpetrated on human beings and even animals."[58]

Thus proscribing "abnormal" affects, appetites, and intimacies, the BCMP's content guidelines must be seen as an extension of Marcos's national sexuality campaign against the bomba film. It was as though a New Cinema was being invented to finish the job of expunging the sex and violence that disgraced the nation's cinematic and political landscapes around the time of the First Quarter Storm. But as we shall see, the rebellious performance of nonnormative conduct by the youth during the First Quarter Storm would deeply inform the antiauthoritarian cultural politics of an emergent New Cinema.

Memories of the First Quarter Storm

Perhaps the most striking feature of the youth politics on display during the First Quarter Storm was the fighting language of the dissidents. Indeed, their much remarked upon shibboleths carried clearly libidinous connotations: *"Pulis, pulis, titi mong matulis!"* [Pigs, pigs, uncircumcised dicks!] . . . *Baka magreyp pa kayo, lima-lima na ang asawa ninyo!"* [You might be thinking of raping someone, you already have so many wives!]." Rafael notes the logic behind the students' impolitic language: "Cusswords and obscenities were at once infuriating to the cops that they were directed to as much as they were a source of pleasure and solidarity among the youth."[59] What needs emphasizing here is that the students were performing their own version of the bomba. One could indeed substitute the word *bomba* for the "cusswords and obscenities" in Rafael's statement to arrive at the similarities between the bomba's subversive pleasures and the rebellious conduct of the young dissidents during the First Quarter Storm. The bomba film thrived because of the complicit subversion of censorship rules by producers and consumers. The prospect of agitating the authorities was a very real part of the bomba experience, as were the consequences—real or imagined—of getting caught. And the bomba's status as first and foremost a native-language cinema in no small part influenced its recent patronage by radical youth. For these new audiences of the local cinema, familiarity with the linguistic codes of the bomba guaranteed one's membership in a community of fellow nationalists.

Radical students regarded the bomba as a touchstone for the "masses"— the abject audience long belittled by Westernized elites as bakya. But by virtue of their social categorization as youth, the students were, like the bakya audience, symbols of ethical incompleteness themselves. As Rafael reminds us, "youth" can exist on the social map only as "a highly unstable and transitory location: an embodiment of a history that is always yet to arrive from the future."[60]

The young dissidents opted out of the discourse of ethical incompleteness associated not only with their social categorization as youth but also with their ethico-aesthetic training as students. They performed instead scenes of liberatory violence, as idealized by Fanon. "Decolonization," Fanon writes, "transforms spectators crushed by their own inessentiality into privileged actors, with the grandiose glare of history's floodlights upon them."[61] In their self-conscious performance of national allegories, they channeled the impulsive behavior and boorish appetites associated with the bakya crowd. To borrow Fanon's terms, the "accumulated libido, the hampered aggressivity" of their allegorical performances instantiated the "therapeutic violence" that must accompany decolonization. Such a mode of "therapy" rests, not on asserting the essential "nobility" of the native, but on its opposite: the psychoaffective release of the repressed rage of subaltern subjects long conditioned to imagine themselves as ethically deficient—and indeed, as less than human.

Incessantly invoking the sex act in their national allegories, the students reflexively violated the traditional split between the private and public spheres. Their mode of protest made a mockery of the twin ideals of privatized sex and sexualized privacy so dear to the ideology of heteronormativity embodied by the national family. And their performative invocation of nonnormal intimacies effected the dangerous contamination of the political realm by the irrational impulses of the psyche. They performed just the kind of bad behavior first pathologized in Gustav Le Bon's 1895 study of crowd psychology and later taken up by sociologists in the "collective behavior" school.[62] This classic paradigm viewed mass actions as the "emotionally-driven working out of participants' psychological distress." The students' nonnormative conduct would most certainly be read by proponents of the paradigm as proof of being "self-evidently alienated from society, unfulfilled from their personal desires; narcissistic and arrested in their development; perhaps even latently homosexual."[63]

The dissidents' unruly passions were indeed of urgent concern to Marcos, who demonized the national allegories of the First Quarter Storm. He absolutely refused to recognize the protests as legitimate expressions of political grievances (see chapter 1). Indeed, he refused to acknowledge the students as legitimate political actors, even going so far as to effect their *public erasure* from the First Quarter Storm. Marcos's demonization of the protests bore the stamp of a broad cultural prejudice against political emotion: the belief that political action must preclude the exercise of emotion, and that political contestation must suppress the event of the body.

The students, on the other hand, saw no contradiction between affect and cognition in political action. They clearly understood the power of affect and emotions to mobilize people, and chose a protest style that showcased the messiness of political emotion. They made a point of showing that such emotion is necessarily "ambiguous, ambivalent, contradictory, noncoherent, undisciplined and surprising."[64] And bearing an affinity with the subversive libidinousness of the bomba film, their spectacularization of political emotion hinged on assuming a hypercorporeality.

In their obscene language and in their bodily performances of abjection, hypercorporeality was not just a source of pleasure for the students. It was more than just a means of establishing a group identity; it was a mode of political action that worked by *negation:* it negated the dominant, hegemonic formation of the public sphere and its myth of abstract personhood; and it negated the mirage of intimacy and its compartmentalization of the sexual (or the deeply personal) from the political. It projected the body as a site of countermemory and national allegorical truth telling.

The students' performative style was powered by the bodily, visceral qualities of feelings (i.e., affect), and the coded and conventional expression of those feelings (i.e., emotion). It translated the subversive pleasures of the bomba film into a hyperembodied mode of political contestation that was staged as *jouissance.* In this mode of contestation, political grievances took the form of "inchoate, emergent, not yet articulate ways of feeling"—producing an affective sense that something was not right and must, therefore, be changed.[65] This was the legacy left by the young dissidents of the First Quarter Storm to the would-be auteurs of the New Cinema.

The auteurs of the New Cinema were a highly ambivalent vanguard, however. Widely regarded as the cinema's answer to the student-dissidents of the First Quarter Storm, the group also became the poster children for Imelda's much-vaunted "artistic cinema." Consequently, their antiauthoritarian cultural politics very often fell prey to the discourse of ethical incompleteness articulated by the martial-law state.

A Cinema Vanguard Comes of Age

A discursive overlap exists between standard accounts of the New Cinema's coming of age and the paternalism of the New Society's cultural policy. Consider, for a moment, Nicanor Tiongson's description of the birth of the vanguard movement:

> The New Cinema, which refers to feature films characterized by innovativeness and artistic integrity, was born in the 1970s and grew through the 1980s because of the confluence of social and cultural conditions prevailing during those decades. First, the 1970s saw the rise and development of film directors, scriptwriters, actors, and designers who were familiar with Italian neorealists (Rosselini, de Sica) and surrealists (Fellini), the Swedish art film (Bergman), the French "Nouvelle Vague" (Truffaut, Godard, Resnais) and the Japanese (Kurosawa) and Indian (Ray) art films, many of whom had studied films abroad or in local universities. Second, the decade witnessed the birth of a new social consciousness, which was the product of the activist movement of the early 1970s. As the consciousness of economic oppression grew, as the Marcos regime grew more and more repressive . . . film artists could no longer remain indifferent or uninvolved and decided to create films that would at least reflect the far-from-ideal conditions of that period.[66]

Tiongson's account of the emergence of the New Cinema tellingly begins with the cinematic competencies of the young filmmakers at the forefront of this group. Clearly valorizing the aesthetic training of these filmmakers and their specialized knowledge of international film styles, the passage conforms to, and even perpetuates, Imelda Marcos's injunction that the New Cinema prove its "worth." Not coincidentally, the established literature on the New Cinema defines the political agency of the group in terms of the "artistic integrity" of their films. Indeed, Philippine film historiography tends to use the Great Man approach, outlining how the would-be auteurs of the New Cinema managed to transform "political and industrial liabilities into aesthetic assets."[67]

The established literature identifies filmmaker Lino Brocka as a leading figure of the New Cinema. In a 1986 interview, he recalled the perceptible "changing of the guard" at the time of the First Quarter Storm: "The movie industry was a closed system then—like a big family, and those with a college background were anathema because the old directors thought they would make boring art films."[68] But with the bourgeoisification of the cinema following the bomba trend, the industry had to adapt to the "tastes and preferences of college-age youths in terms of subject matter and themes."[69] The upshot of these developments, Brocka recalls, was "a fad," in which "college-educated people" like himself and his contemporary, the now equally renowned filmmaker Ishmael Bernal (formerly a *Manila Chronicle* film critic) were allowed into the inner circle. By the end of the 1970s, this group would include other young, college-educated and politically conscious filmmakers: Mike de Leon, Marilou Diaz-Abaya, Celso Ad Castillo, Joey Gosengfiao, Elwood Perez, and Peque Gallaga.[70]

Brocka, who began his career in the theater, made his directorial debut with the film *Wanted: Perfect Mother* (1970). The film was based on a long-running *komiks* serial. Komiks are cheaply made graphic magazines written in the vernacular. At the time, 30 to 40 percent of local films were adaptations of komiks material.[71] Brocka adhered to the industry's established practices by creating a komiks film; and yet, given the popularity of the bomba film, his choice of komiks material was somewhat anachronistic—a serial loosely based on the popular Hollywood film *The Sound of Music*.

Eschewing the sexploitation themes favored by bourgeois audiences, Brocka's debut film worked within the established codes and conventions of the family melodrama—a genre long associated with the bakya audience. Mirroring the affective performance of subalternity by the dissidents of the First Quarter Storm, Brocka assumed the burden of representing and speaking for this marginalized group. His choice of genre—melodrama—would very quickly become a constitutive feature of his sentimental mode of address, earning him fame as the expositor and moral champion of the bakya folk.

Brocka's *Wanted: Perfect Mother* garnered several awards— including Most Wholesome Picture—at the 1970 Manila Film

Festival. Soon after, the youth-oriented *Sixteen* magazine praised the film and its young filmmaker in clearly auteurist terms: "The fortunate thing about Lino Brocka . . . is the tempered combination of his burning desire to create an artistic piece of work while realizing the external and material limitations of others concerned in the production." Drawing attention to the profound tensions between the director's creative personality, *Wanted*'s popular source text and the economic constraints of filmmaking, *Sixteen*'s auteurist evaluation of the film jibed with Imelda's simultaneously ethico-aesthetic, populist and instrumentalist conceptions of the cinema. But allusions to the First Quarter Storm nonetheless peppered the review, which drew on a romantic image of youth politics to establish auteurism as an aesthetic force that would revolutionize Philippine cinema.

Emphasizing Brocka's youth (he was thirty-one) and college background (he majored in speech and drama at the University of the Philippines), *Sixteen* cast Brocka and his peer group as the film industry's answer to the youthful heroes of the First Quarter Storm. These filmmakers were poised to "revolutionize" the movies. The modest Brocka demurred: "I am not here to revolutionize the Filipino movies. That is something which we cannot achieve with one picture. I am only hoping to pave the way for 'revolutionizing.'"[72]

Brocka nonetheless prized filmmaking as a means of social analysis. His explorations of the social worlds of the bakya folk very often ran afoul of Imelda's ongoing efforts to sanitize folk culture. Indeed, Brocka's melodramas characteristically pivot on the exploitation of subaltern subjects in the slum areas of Imelda's vaunted cultural city—for example, *Maynila sa kuko ng liwanag* (Manila in the claws of light, 1975), *Insiang* (1976), *Jaguar* (1979), *Bona* (1980). In these films, victimized heroes turn against their exploiters with shocking fury. The victim's violent revenge coupled with a "camera verité approach to poverty . . . rendered Brocka's films subversive in the eyes of Marcos and his watchdogs."[73] Working principally by political indirection, Brocka's film praxis, like the youth politics of the First Quarter Storm, hinged on the production of highly emotional national allegories.

Brocka's *Tinimbang ka ngunit kulang* (Weighed and found wanting, 1974) strikingly captures this allegorical mode of antiauthoritarian cultural politics. Ostensibly adhering to the populist ethos
of Imelda's heritage cinema, the film focuses on the cultural mores
of the folk. Turning on the theme of social conformity, however,
the film allegorizes small-town life as a microcosm of the repressive normalization of social conduct in the New Society. Crucially,
two of the film's principal characters are "abnormal" personalities—an insane woman and a leper—who are both demonized by
the townsfolk as diseased, and therefore contaminating, presences
threatening to disturb the town's social harmony.

The film opens with a botched abortion. In a visually striking
sequence filmed in monochromatic sepia tones, we watch the illegal procedure that traumatizes Kuala (Lolita Rodriguez).[74] Mr.
Cesar Blanco (Eddie Garcia), a mayoral candidate, presides over
the bloody affair, which takes place in a secluded hut away from
the prying eyes of his electorate. Prominently displayed in the
background, however, is a presidential photo of Ferdinand Marcos, whose commanding gaze envelops Mr. Blanco, Kuala, and the
abortionist. The prologue ends with Kuala silently going insane.

The mise-en-scène invites the viewer to decipher the film as a
national allegory. Marcos photograph, in particular, acquires an
allegorical density that absorbs the perverse familial dynamics
between Kuala, Mr. Blanco, and her unborn child. Kuala, it is revealed, is Mr. Blanco's mistress. He had ordered her abortion to
protect his political career. In juxtaposing the philandering politician with the father of the national family, the film not only alludes
to Marcos's sexual indiscretions, it flags the social hypocrisy linking
Kuala's botched abortion and Marcos's national sexuality campaign
against the bomba film following the Dovie Beams scandal. The
sequence is punctuated with shock cuts of Kuala's dead fetus.
These shock cuts powerfully establish what will become critical
features of the film's oppositional aesthetic: the mobilization of the
splice-and-shock methods of the bomba film and the resuscitation
of the bomba's "illegal" tropes.

The plot obeys the emotive conventions of melodrama: We flash forward several years to observe Kuala, now a vagrant physically disfigured by years of neglect, being molested by the townsfolk. In need of female companionship, the leper Bertong Ketong (Mario O'Hara), takes her in. She becomes pregnant. The "abnormal" union polarizes the town. Junior (Christopher de Leon), Mr. Blanco's son, takes an interest in the couple. He "adopts" the ostracized couple and vows to protect them. When Kuala goes into labor, Berto tries to get the town doctor, but is refused help. In desperation, Berto takes the doctor hostage. He is chased by an angry mob and is gunned down by the police. The film ends with Junior ministering to Kuala and her newborn as the townsfolk look on.

Tinimbang ka is a coming-of-age film, depicting Junior's acquisition of manhood—literally, through an illicit sexual encounter with Milagros (Laurice Guillen), an enigmatic woman from the Big City; and symbolically, by assuming protective custody of Berto and Kuala. Initially depicted as childlike and somewhat effeminate, Junior focalizes the film's persistent thematization of masculinity. His narrative arc follows an Oedipal trajectory that sees him profoundly transformed by his contact with Berto and Kuala. In "delivering" Kuala's child, he disinters the long-repressed "sins" of his father. Indeed, he symbolically slays his father, whose hypersexuality allegorizes the continuity of the political excesses of the Old Society in the New Society. The sentimental message of the film's final sequence is clear: Junior will model for the townsfolk a compassionate policy of social tolerance, and thereby bring about more egalitarian social relations in the town.

The film is clearly critical of Imelda's "heritage" film culture. Satirizing "small-town penchant for gossip, social and religious hypocrisy and ostracism of social outcasts,"[75] *Tinimbang ka* provocatively subverts the regime's national symbolic. Its depiction of the folk is indeed profoundly unflattering: they are shown to be simpleminded and merciless, compensating for their own subaltern status by victimizing the weakest among their ranks. More to the point, they exercise a mode of moral policing that calls to mind the draconian censorship standards of the martial-law cultural state. Ironically figured as the New Society's exemplary cultural subjects, the folk enact the *voluntary* self-policing advocated by Marcos.

Brocka's contemporaries similarly operated within the confines of the popular cinema to create national allegories that were highly critical of the New Society. As a group, however, the New Cinema filmmakers did not cohere around a formally articulated aesthetic, nor did they issue militant manifesto essays, as had been the case in other "new" cinema movements in the Third World. If there was one thematic that unified their work as a group, it was the affective dynamics of national allegory discussed above. Bernal's *Manila by Night* (1980), which explores prostitution and drug addiction in Imelda's cultural city, highlights the shibboleths of the bomba film to critique the heteronormativity of the national family. A central character is a "failed" mother, a former prostitute, who cannot save her son from the city's drug culture. Indeed, in many of these films, familial dynamics or patriarchal power structures (or both) are used to allegorize cultural repression in the New Society: De Leon's antifascist film *Batch '81* (1981), a film ostensibly about fraternity hazing, is clearly an allegory of Marcos's police state; and in Diaz-Abaya's *Karnal* (1984), parricide ends the tyrannical rule of an oppressive patriarch.

How these films managed to evade Imelda's censors is a puzzle that historians of Philippine cinema are hard pressed to explain. The received notion is that a great deal of arbitrariness characterized the regime's censorship record. However, the puzzle has as much to do with our discussion of ethical incompleteness as it does the mercurial whims of the censors.

Imelda, it must be pointed out, actively nurtured an image of the New Cinema filmmakers as a modernist vanguard. But it was ultimately the interest that the New Cinema films generated in international film festivals that would be the yardstick by which she measured their worth. For as long as their films generated international accolades, Imelda tolerated their veiled political allusions. Ironically, international critics regarded these filmmakers as first and foremost anti-Marcos activists. Indeed, the accolades heaped on their films focused more on their political themes than on their cinematic competencies.

Imelda Marcos and the New Cinema auteurs were locked in a symbiotic relationship that uncannily reprised the reciprocal relations between Marcos and the underground communist insurgency explored in chapter 1. Without the communist "threat," Marcos could not have legitimized martial law; and without Marcos's repressive police state, the communists could not have acquired their romantic aura as a revolutionary force. In a similar fashion, Imelda needed the New Cinema vanguard just as much as these anti-Marcos activists needed her. The New Cinema auteurs clearly benefited from Imelda's valorization of the ethico-aesthetic functions of the cinema; and indeed, it was Imelda's promotion of the cinema as a "national art" that made possible their very identities as "film artists." Imelda, on the other hand, needed the New Cinema auteurs—despite their unflattering allegories of the martial-law cultural state—for without them, her "national art" could not have garnered the international attention that she desired for the New Cinema. Significantly, without the political repression of "socially aware" filmmakers in the New Society, the New Cinema vanguard might not have acquired their national and international reputations as radical political artists.

Did the New Cinema in fact promote the "discourse of excellence" symbolized by the Cultural Center of the Philippines? Fanon's description of the dilemma of the postcolonial cultural subject captures the pitfalls of this discourse: "The Negro, never so much a Negro as since he has been dominated by the whites," must inevitably "prove that he has a culture and . . . behave like a cultured person."[76] The New Cinema auteurs, in constantly asserting their worth as "cultured persons," subscribed to the same ethico-aesthetic discourse promoted by Imelda. And yet, like the youthful heroes of the First Quarter Storm, they saw themselves as the champions of the folk. It may be argued, however, that their social distance from the folk—and their insistent assertions of their cultural leadership over these subaltern groups—blunted the force of their sentimental cultural politics and, by extension, their social critique of the martial law state.

Nevertheless, the New Cinema auteurs proved that the bomba's subversive film culture and the memory of the First Quarter Storm could be harnessed to produce affective national allegories critical of the New Society. They proved as well that such a mode of cultural politics could be commercially viable. However, focusing exclusively on the aesthetic and commercial successes of the New Cinema auteurs produces a distorted picture of the film industry in the 1970s. The gains made by the New Cinema auteurs were in fact atypical of the broader film industry; indeed, a profound gap existed between the regime's avowed patronage of the cinema and the industry's actual economic realities.

Throughout the 1970s the local cinema was still largely a commercial cinema enjoying minimal protection from the government and almost no public subvention to speak of. Though it had become the most prominent symbol of cultural patronage in the New Society, public subvention was in fact limited to a few token gestures. The regime gave its support to an annual Metro Manila Film Festival, requiring all first-run theaters in the capital city to show only Filipino films in the lucrative period between Christmas and the New Year.[77] The state required 30 percent of the gross receipts from the annual event to be shared by the Cultural Center of the Philippines and the Movie Workers Welfare Foundation (MOWELFUND), a private organization providing social and medical benefits to two thousand film workers.[78] The regime also made Philippine National Bank loans available to filmmakers for the production of "quality" pictures geared for export.[79]

But foreign films continued to enjoy unrestricted access to the local market. Indeed, from 1970 through 1979 of all local films, the proportion previewed by the BCMP decreased, from a high of 33.1 percent in 1970 to 23.9 percent in 1979, with a record-setting low of 19.1 percent in 1974. In the decade following the onset of martial law, the proportion of foreign films previewed by the BCMP increased by 7.3 percent.[80] Meanwhile, onerous taxes continued to be levied on local films—taxes that were disproportionately higher than those imposed on film imports.

The institutional supports promised by the regime would only materialize—and in highly contradictory and invidious ways—in the 1980s with the creation of the Experimental Cinema of the Philippines (ECP), a comprehensive film body ostensibly geared toward the artistic development of local films. Working alongside, and in some cases within, the protective embrace of the ECP, politically conscious filmmakers like Brocka created highly ambivalent films at once beholden to and highly critical of the Marcos regime and its new film culture.

Chapter 4

POPULAR STRUGGLES
AND ELITE POLITICS

In 1969 the oligarchy so dominated the economic and political spheres that some foreign commentators could only describe their hegemony as a form of internal colonization. Consider the following sketch, made by an American observer, of the power structure of the country on the eve of the First Quarter Storm:

> The Philippines is a colony still, but not an American one. It is colonized by 50 families who flaunt their wealth more, and exploit their factory workers and farm hands more than any foreigner or foreign company would dare do. . . . The Filipinos hold frequent elections and vastly enjoy them, though quite a few people get killed in shooting affrays during the campaigns. Most Filipinos, rich and poor, plantation owner and sharecropper, are cousins to some degree, and blood generally proves to be stronger than class consciousness.[1]

Here again is another reminder that the Philippines just "wasn't ready for democracy." But it is worth retracing how the nation's elite families came to exercise such unbridled power in the republic. As the above sketch demonstrates, the oligarchy's hegemonic rule was protected by collective habits of thought enshrining the primacy of the family in Philippine life. Article 216 of the Civil Code of the Philippines states, "The family is a basic social institution which public policy cherishes and protects." The Civil Code further states: "Mutual aid, both moral and material, shall be rendered among members of the same family. Judicial and administrative officials shall foster this mutual assistance."[2] These legal provisions must be seen in relation to a key feature of the Philippine political system: a weak and incoherent state bureaucracy. And the Philippines has the United States to thank for that.

"Huge, autocratic, white-run bureaucracies" were typical of the colonial regimes of Southeast Asia. The Philippines, as Benedict Anderson points out, was the exception: "American authorities in Manila created only a minimal civil service, and quickly turned over most of its component positions to the natives." The introduction of representative institutions allowed some local patrimonial lords to gain purchase over the state, which "remained weak and divided."[3] Known as *caciques,* these native elites possessed vast economic power (they were landowners whose agricultural exports were the backbone of the nation's economy) and assumed quasi-military and quasi-judicial functions (they were political warlords in their home provinces).

In the twentieth century the Philippine state collapsed no less than four times in the midst of war and revolution. And in the continuing absence of a strong state apparatus in the postwar years, it devolved on the family unit to provide employment and capital to its members, educate and socialize its young, shelter the handicapped and the aged, and above all else, "transmit its name, honor, lands, capital and values to the next generation."[4]

The dictates of social reproduction drove elite families to engage in—monopolize, in fact—one particular activity: electoral politics.

Though party politics in the Philippines cleaved to the two-party system introduced by the United States, the nation's political parties were not defined by their political ideologies so much as by the loose coalitions of powerful political families that made up their ranks. Competitive elections ensured the alternation of power between the Liberal and Nacionalista Parties and the family factions they represented. For their part, political families regarded political candidacies as intangible legacies, to be apportioned among heirs in much the same way as the distribution of land and heirlooms. Intense intrafamilial conflicts resulted from such arrangements, and internal family battles actively shaped electoral politics at both the local and national levels.[5]

When formal independence was granted, in 1946, a bundle of postwar economic and military treaties ensured the Philippines' "special relations" with the United States: (1) the Bell Trade Act, which established a "free-trade" system to run with the gradual application of duties until 1974; (2) a "parity" agreement, which guaranteed equal rights for U.S. citizens in all economic ventures; (3) the Military Bases Treaty, which gave the United States twenty-three military bases for a period of ninety-nine years; and (4) the Military Assistance Agreement, which placed the Armed Forces of the Philippines under the direct supervision of the so-called Joint United States Military Advisory Group (JUSMAG).[6] These arrangements further bolstered the power of the landed oligarchy.

The free-trade agreement gave the oligarchy's agricultural products preferential access to a protected U.S. market. Added to this were various U.S. economic-assistance packages that they plundered from the state. After World War II, the Philippines received $620 million in U.S. rehabilitation assistance. Rather than use this windfall for capital investments, the oligarchy used it to purchase imported luxury goods. The oligarchy's appetite for such goods was so insatiable in fact that the economy nearly collapsed when the government could not stanch the hemorrhage of foreign exchange for these items.[7] Against this dire economic backdrop, the Huk rebellion erupted. Washington stepped in with military and economic rescue missions, establishing a basic pattern that would remain in effect throughout the postwar era: "while the state was plundered internally, it was repeatedly rescued externally."[8]

Marcos often trumpeted his hostility toward the oligarchy. But in practice, his attacks were limited to a fraction of their number, notably, his two most threatening rivals, Senator Benigno Aquino, Jr., and sugar baron and *Manila Chronicle* publisher Eugenio Lopez. Indeed, despite Marcos's claims to use martial law to correct the political irrationalities of the Old Society, the New

Society crucially adhered to the familial foundation of the nation's patrimonial political economy. Rather than disband a national network of patron-client relations, Marcos, as David Wurfel puts it, used his martial-law powers to become "supreme godfather."[9] He divided the whole economy into "different fiefs managed by relatives and cronies who regularly shared their earnings with the dictator."[10] Marcos's national family may thus be understood on a material level as a new coalition of elite families that was considerably smaller and more cohesive than the large and fragmented oligarchy of the Old Society. Crucially, this new national elite was loyal not to Marcos's vision of a democratic revolution but to the system of plunder over which he presided.[11]

Marcos against the Sugar Elite

A cornerstone of the New Society—and a crucial component of the dictator's populist image—was a land reform program that Marcos signed into law in October 1972. The success of the New Society, he declared, hinged on the transfer of ownership of agricultural land from landlord to tenant, resulting in the emancipation of the latter from the "bondage of the soil."[12] Operation Land Transfer aimed to redistribute 3.75 million hectares of rice and corn land among 915,000 peasants. The project bogged down toward the late 1970s, however, due to mismanagement. Only a little over 2 percent of the targeted beneficiaries had become actual landowners. Tenancy had in fact increased from 865,000 farms covering 2 million hectares in 1960 to 872,000 farms covering 2.4 million hectares in 1980.[13]

The landed oligarchy emerged unscathed from Marcos's largely symbolic moves to eliminate land tenancy. But when Marcos moved to organize export monopolies on behalf of his cronies, landlord resistance escalated. This was especially true in the sugar lands, which were exempted from Operation Land Transfer.

Up through the 1970s the Philippines ranked tenth among the world's top sugar producers. Sugar was the leading earner of foreign exchange—providing one-third to as much as one-half of the nation's export earnings. And it was on the island of Negros, the richest sugar-producing area in the country, where the nation's wealthiest families—a good number of senators and ex-presidents among them—maintained their power bases. Indeed, the sugar elite was the most powerful elite faction in the country before martial law.[14]

In November 1974 the *New York Times* exposed the extreme disparities of wealth and poverty on Negros, where ownership of sugar lands was in the hands of less than 2 percent of the population of 1.9 million.[15] Visible signs of the landowners' almost unimaginable wealth—mansions, servants, luxury cars—coexisted with just as visible signs of extreme poverty. One needed only to look at the bloated stomachs and open sores of the severely malnourished children of the farmworkers, numbering about half a million, employed in large haciendas and sugar mills.

The extreme poverty of the Negros sugar workers was a controversial issue. A 1975 study by the Association of Major Religious Superiors of the Philippines (AMRSP) found that these workers were employed for an average of only 9 months per year; 58 percent did not receive the legal minimum wage, and 80 percent did not receive social security benefits.[16] A 1977 study by the national wage commission found that at Php 6.00 a day, even minimum wage recipients could not afford the Php 19.28 required daily to purchase the minimum nutritional requirements of a family of six, the average sugar worker's household size.[17] Conditions steadily worsened throughout the decade, and a 1979 *Time* magazine feature story likened the dire situation on Negros to the famines in Bangladesh and sub-Saharan Africa.[18] Indeed, at least two-thirds of the children on Negros were suffering from second- and third-degree malnutrition.[19]

The Negros crisis must be seen in relation to the government's takeover of sugar trading. In 1974, Marcos gave the Philippine Exchange Company (PHILEX), a subsidiary of the Philippine National Bank, complete authority as the nation's sole exporter of sugar. That same year, a world shortage saw sugar prices soar to $0.67 per pound. Buying sugar from millers at below-market prices, PHILEX sold the nation's sugar at a profit of about 30 cents per pound.

Speculating that the world price would peak at $1.00 per pound, PHILEX hoarded the nation's sugar. When the world price crashed to $0.11 per pound, in 1976, PHILEX was stuck with 2 million tons of sugar—almost the total crop for the year. Meanwhile, mills continued to produce sugar without buyers, forcing PHILEX to store sugar in schools, swimming pools, and even roadways. The sugar-hoarding disaster required immediate rectification. The government sold the nation's sugar at prices at or below the cost of production, raised the domestic price of sugar, refused loans to small producers, and exempted land transferred from sugar to rice and corn production from land reform policies. The losses of the sugar barons were thereby "buffered, while wage laborers, small farmers, and consumers suffered."[20]

In 1976, PHILEX's Roberto Benedicto, who had been Marcos's fraternity brother at the University of the Philippines, announced the signing of a five-year contract with U.S. refineries for 75 percent of the nation's sugar crop. PHILEX, in effect, was the gatekeeper for this U.S. market. The sugar barons now found themselves in the ambivalent position of supporting the regime for the export quotas they needed, while also condemning the Benedicto group's monopoly on the sugar trade.

In 1977, Marcos consolidated his position over the sugar elite by transferring the control of sugar trading to a new agency, the Philippine Sugar Commission (PHILSUCOM), with Benedicto as chairman. The marketing of sugar was given to a PHILSUCOM subsidiary, the National Sugar Trading Corporation (NASUTRA). Under Benedicto, these two agencies not only had sole authority to buy and sell sugar (both domestically and internationally), but also the power to set the price paid to planters and millers. PHILSUCOM was furthermore empowered to assume control of any mill deemed not to be operating efficiently.

As the world price of sugar continued to plummet in 1977 and 1978, the sugar elite found that it could "no longer risk new investments, or even maximize production." Land formerly dedicated to sugar cane were left idle, and many sugar workers went without work because "planters had lost confidence in the government's marketing system."[21]

The regime's sugar monopoly brought the once mighty sugar elite to its knees; only those sugar barons who managed to ingratiate themselves with the Benedicto group survived the industry recession. But capturing control of the industry proved to be costly for Marcos in the long run. With planters buried in debt, with mills on the verge of closing down, and, most important, with desperate workers appealing to church activists and communist groups, Marcos faced an opposition that would turn out to be even more threatening than the oligarchy.

The Plight of Sugar Workers and the Film Sakada

With Marcos's enemies among the oligarchy effectively demobilized by martial law, church activists and communist groups took the lead in the anti-Marcos struggle. They earned the loyalty of disempowered communities, who regarded the church and the CPP-NPA as better alternatives to the elite-controlled political system.

Following the sugar recession, church activism on behalf of the sugar workers veered more sharply to the left. Meanwhile, the NPA was actively recruiting rural unemployed youths who had no access to land—not even as tenants. At the same time, a small number of priests and nuns joined the NPA as active combatants, while many more indirectly supported the communist insurgency through their membership in the National Democratic Front (NDF), which the CPP created in 1973 to "take the lead in developing a broad alliance of all forces opposing the dictatorship."[22]

At this time, Marcos and his cronies fully controlled the media.[23] Philsucom's Benedicto also happened to own one of the largest newspaper combines, the Philippine Daily Express Company (*Daily Express, Filipino Express,* and *Expressweek*). Hans Menzi, a former military aid to the president, owned the national dailies *Bulletin Today* and *Balita mula Maynila.* Imelda's brother and governor of Leyte, Benjamin Romualdez, was the publisher of the *Times Journal.* Presidential assistant Juan Tuvera and his wife, Kerima Polotan, the First Lady's official biographer, owned the *Evening Post, Focus Philippines,* and the *Orient Express.* Marcos's cronies also dominated the radio and television sectors. The Benedicto group owned Radio Philippines Network (RPN), which had been the beneficiary of Marcos's expropriation of the ABS-CBN network from Eugenio Lopez, in 1972.[24]

No surprise, then, that the crony media kept silent on the sugar crisis. The regime even went so far as to pull from local newsstands the September 24, 1979, issue of *Time* magazine in which the controversial article "Powder Keg of the Pacific" appeared, exposing the explosive situation on Negros.[25] But the radicalization of the church and the leadership role assumed by the CPP-NPA in the struggle of the sugar workers were nonetheless documented in the 1976 film *Sakada* by New Cinema filmmaker Behn Cervantes.

The film opens with an epigraph highlighting the general public's lack of knowledge of the political economy of the sugar industry: "The problem described in this film is a problem long endured by some of our people. For those not yet aware of their plight, this is an exposition." The "problem" at the center of the docudrama's social analysis is the sugar industry's systematic exploitation of migrant workers, the *sakadas* of the film's title.

The film's expositor is an activist youth who happens to be the scion of a wealthy landowning family, the Montemayors. In a key sequence, Juan Miguel (Joseph Sytangco) explains the sakada system to Father Vic, a Jesuit priest who has come to the hacienda to study the social situation. The sakadas, he learns, are a special category of laborers. Already the most poorly paid, they do not qualify for most benefits because of their status as seasonal workers. Contractors lure them from the neighboring provinces of

Antique, Capiz and Cebu with generous "advances." But since the work cycle typically lasts only five months, the advances are paid for dearly. Basic provisions at the hacienda's dispensary are costly, medicines costlier still. By the end of the migrants' work cycle, they are buried in debt.[26]

Juan Miguel takes Father Vic on a tour of the workers' quarters, where fifty persons—including whole families—share a living space meant for ten to fifteen. "This is where they sleep . . . where they eat . . . where they give birth . . . and where they die," Juan Miguel's voice-over proclaims over a montage of the emaciated bodies of workers and children in makeshift bunks. We cut to a long shot of Father Vic saying mass to a congregation of sugar workers. His tour of the hacienda has clearly opened his eyes, as his sermon quickly attests.

"A father set aside a plentiful meal for his beloved children, but most of them remained hungry because one or two children took all they could, not leaving anything for the rest." Father Vic's parable encapsulates the social-justice concerns of liberation theology, a current of religious thought that was radicalizing young priests and nuns in the Philippines.[27] At the center of liberation theology is the concept of structural violence, which sees poverty "less as [a] result of individual sinfulness (and sloth) than the consequence of 'structural injustices' inherent in liberal capitalism."[28] Father Vic's sermon uses Christian symbolism to attack the four major structural sins—debt, hunger, sickness, lack of education— keeping the sakadas from attaining their basic dignity as persons. It is an act of consciousness raising that is clearly influenced by a major statement, issued by the AMRSP in 1971, affirming the need not just to raise consciousness but to arouse social action among the oppressed.[29] The goal of such social action, the film's diegesis asserts, is to break the dependency syndrome of the sakadas and to encourage them to find social solutions to their plight.

Crucially, the film presents Father Vic's activities among the sugar workers as just one version of consciousness raising. Another version is presented in a key sequence juxtaposing two youth activists—Juan Miguel and David (Bembol Roco)—at a CPP student meeting. As the clear leaders of the group, the two youths allegorize the alliance between peasant groups and the CPP-NPA.

David, the son of a slain labor leader at the Montemayor hacienda, opens the discussion with an eloquent speech derived from *Philippine Society and Revolution,* penned by CPP founder Jose Maria Sison. Identifying imperialism as the historical cause of the nation's structural inequities, David proclaims (in Tagalog), "Unity among all oppressed classes is the only solution." The camera pans around the room to reveal visual "signatures" of the CPP—placards bearing the rally cry *Makibaka!* (Fight!), and more explicitly, the Maoist slogan Serve the People. The camera settles on Juan Miguel, who, in impeccable English, attacks another social evil, cultural imperialism, which he describes as an "insidious form of corruption, that of taste and culture." Its function is to "perpetuate the American system and to protect American investments." We cut back to David, who states (again, in Tagalog), "Our liberation cannot be achieved in peaceful ways." Thus rehearsing central tenets of CPP ideology, the sequence concludes with David condemning the Western democratic system (in Tagalog): "This system only serves the interests of the wealthy and the powerful."

The strategic use of English in the sequence draws attention to Juan Miguel's class background—and indeed, the urban and middle-class outlook of the student activists at the meeting. The CPP, it must be remembered, had a Manila-educated middle-class core. Since the party's inception, in 1968, CPP cadres devoted much of their energies to indoctrinating peasants, thereby building up a nationwide grassroots organization with surprising speed.[30] But the CPP's middle-class origins gave the party invaluable connections with the Philippine elite—connections that would later prove to be decisive for the party. *Sakada* foregrounds this tactical asset through the character of Juan Miguel, who has allies in both sides of the landowner-sakada divide.

Unlike the other activists at the student meeting, David can claim to have an organic understanding of the sugar workers' plight.

Significantly, however, David's own involvement in the organization was made possible by his special status as a seminarian at the Loyola House of Studies, at Ateneo de Manila University. Father Vic had brought him to Manila to train at the Jesuit institution, known for its commitment to liberation theology. David's presence at the meeting in layman's clothes, and more directly, his speech condemning the democratic process, mark his break with the essentially reformist politics of the moderate Catholic opposition.

Later, David and Juan Miguel are shown participating in an industrial strike. Prominently displayed in the background are red banners with KM and CPP insignias. The mise-en-scène's focal point is a centrally placed placard that reads, The Strike Weapon Is a Just One.

It must be noted that a massive strike in October 1975 at the La Tondeña distillery led Marcos to issue Presidential Decree 823, prohibiting strikes, picketing, and lockouts.[31] *Sakada,* which was released within a year of the La Tondeña strike, makes a clear statement in support of Catholic clergy and civil-rights activists currently opposing the regime's strike ban.

The scene depicting David and Juan Miguel's involvement in an illegal strike climaxes with a violent confrontation with hired goons sent in to break the strike. In a clearly allegorical gesture, the ex-seminarian strikes down his aggressor and rallies his comrades with the KM chant: *Makibaka! Huwag Matakot!* David is later arrested and it is Father Vic who bails him out of prison. In the sanctuary of a deserted church, the two men have a quiet confrontation.

Father Vic gently rebukes David for betraying his Christian calling. David responds, "It is perhaps in my blood to revolt because I was born poor." David thus understands his class identity in organic terms (as dictated by blood and lineage), and has come to regard his "authenticity" as a double-edged sword that sets him apart from his allies—Father Vic and Juan Miguel. Asked by Father Vic about his immediate plans, David responds, "Not plans, Father. Action." He has chosen the Left's route of mass action, which, he explains, must necessarily be violent. The camera lingers on a wooden crucifix at the altar. What for the priest is a symbol of the redemptive power of Christ's love is now for David a symbol of the need for liberatory violence in the present. "I am a priest," Father Vic says (in English). And as a priest, his primary duty is to his church, he tells David. "And that's where your contribution to the struggle ends," David responds pointedly in Tagalog. "What a pity, priests can still play an important role in our alliance," he says.

The scene rehearses the longstanding rift between the Catholic Church and the radical Left. To explain: Filipino Marxists and Catholics became mortal enemies in the 1950s. Huk rebels harassed priests, who in turn assisted the government's counterinsurgency operations. During the First Quarter Storm, the CPP continued the Left's anticlerical posture, calling Christian reformers "clerico-fascists."[32] When martial law was declared, the Church hierarchy, notably the conservative Catholic Bishops' Conference of the Philippines (CBCP), adopted a strategy of "critical collaboration" with the regime.[33] But some priests and nuns influenced by liberation theology joined ranks with the CPP through the NDF. Called Nat-Dems, or National Democrats, radical clerics and Marxists were challenged by progressive Catholics who continued to regard communists with profound antipathy. These Soc-Dems, or Social Democrats, formed their own underground network. They represented a "revolutionary, but non-Communist" alternative to the CPP-NPA.[34] David, in rebuking his former mentor for his indecisiveness, was in effect provoking him to choose sides.

Later, at a CPP safe house, Juan Miguel chastises David for his actions. "What you did was wrong," he says (in English), "You owe Father Vic an apology." David responds, "*Idinaramdam ko. Hindi ko na maunawaan ang salitang Ingles. Salitang pamburgis*" (I regret to say that I can no longer understand English, the language of the bourgeoisie). The statement makes a fine point of the bilingual structure of the key scenes discussed above. David's refusal to communicate in English marks his alienation, not just from the "elitist" Church, but also from the middle-class core of the CPP.

Juan Miguel takes up David's challenge. In a long speech that highlights his ability to switch linguistic codes, he says,

> I can accept that I am bourgeois [Tagalog]. But it's not my fault that I was born rich, or that you were born poor [English]. In your case, you have no choice [Tagalog]. But me, I have a choice [English]. I am here because I choose to be here. Doesn't that weigh more? You will say that you are poor, and that only you can understand the problems of the poor [Tagalog]. . . . But you won't make me feel guilty. Not the way you made Father Vic feel guilty [English].

The confrontation between the two allies flags the ambivalent class politics of the radical Left. As tellingly revealed by Juan Miguel's speech, some CPP cadres regarded subaltern groups with profound paternalism. For these cadres, an informed commitment to Maoist principles "weighed more" than the grievances of the oppressed groups in whose name the CPP was fighting the regime. Indeed, for CPP cadres, the moral outrage of the oppressed classes was still only a raw force that needed to be tamed and properly channeled by enlightened leadership.

Juan Miguel informs David that his former mentor is now considering leaving the priesthood. "I didn't know," David responds with clear remorse. Once again expressing his paternalistic stance toward David, Juan Miguel says, "There are still a lot of things you don't understand." "The little that I do know, I hold in conviction," David replies. David informs Juan Miguel that the sugar workers at his family hacienda are about to revolt. "I know I am needed there. And you? Whose side are you on?"

As a sentimental text, *Sakada* is remarkably self-reflexive in that it gives powerful voice to the often-conflicting views of the privileged and the socially abject protagonists of the anti-Marcos struggle. These sentimental heroes are allegorized by three characters: Fr. Vic (the Catholic Left), Juan Miguel (the CPP-NPA), and David (who represents all the oppressed groups in whose name the anti-Marcos struggle was being waged). Highlighting issues of class "authenticity" and cultural leadership, the film tellingly ends with Juan Miguel killed in the worker's uprising that explodes at the Montemayor hacienda. In an ironic twist, he is gunned down by his father's henchman. Also killed in the shooting affray is David's brother Badong (Robert Arevalo), the clear successor to the peasant family's legacy of labor organizing. The film's final shot shows David, in work clothes, fraternizing with migrant workers. His "organic" connections to the sakadas, and his political education under the Jesuits and the CPP, have prepared him to take up the fight. By implication, he will avoid the political mistakes of his slain father and brother, as well as those of his former ally, Juan Miguel. Thus presented as the synthesis of the various oppositional outlooks dividing the elite and popular forces in the anti-Marcos struggle, David is a symbol of hope for the opposition.

Director Behn Cervantes, like the youthful activists in the film's diegesis, had participated in numerous "illegal" strikes and demonstrations during martial law. Indeed, he was twice imprisoned for his activism.[35] Cervantes's extratextual activism would later lead to his participation, along with fellow New Cinema filmmaker Lino Brocka, in the Free the Artist Movement—a historic anticensorship movement organized by the film industry in 1983. But that was seven years away. With the regime's hold on the media still tight in 1976, *Sakada*'s critique of the exploitation of the sugar workers is understandably silent about the government's mismanagement of the sugar crisis. Offering David as the ideal type of the popular forces in the anti-Marcos struggle, *Sakada* must by necessity rely on allegory to invoke other oppressed groups whose struggles against the regime were being suppressed in the crony media. The extratextual activism of these groups must be seen as a distorted mirror image of *Sakada*'s sentimental plot. While the latter focalizes its narrative of compassionate politics from the perspective of its socially privileged heroes, the real-world activism of subaltern groups consisted of self-driven expressions of their demands for social justice. The scenes and stories of their political rage constituted striking instances of democracy from below. As we shall see in a moment, however, tribal Filipinos and the urban poor, like the embattled peasantry and urban laborers in *Sakada*'s diegesis, also found the necessity to build alliances with the Catholic Left and the CPP-NPA.

Democracy from Below

Just five hundred kilometers north of Manila, a massive hydroelectric infrastructure program threatened the very existence of some hundred thousand indigenous Bontocs and Kalingas.[36] The Chico River Basin Development Project involved the construction of four dams that were promoted as a means of cutting down on the nation's dependence on oil imports. But the project required the flooding of Bontoc and Kalinga lands—including the spectacular terraced rice paddies climbing the steep mountain slopes along the Chico River. Built by hand several hundred years ago, the rice terraces constituted a complex and well-balanced ecosystem that singularly dominated the communal organization—indeed, the whole way of life of the Bontocs and Kalingas.[37]

Not without irony, the Presidential Assistant on National Minorities (PANAMIN), an agency created in 1968 to protect tribal Filipinos, became the primary instrument for "pacifying" resistant tribes and herding whole communities into American Indian–style reservations. By 1977, PANAMIN had forcibly relocated 2.6 million tribal Filipinos—or more than half the total population of tribal Filipinos—into four hundred such reservations.[38] The reservations were virtual armed camps, policed by PANAMIN's militias.

Priests and nuns worked with tribal Filipinos to expose the abuses of the military and the PANAMIN in the Catholic media. With few notable exceptions, the Marcos-controlled media took PANAMIN's official line. As far as PANAMIN was concerned, Church workers were a major obstacle to the state's development initiatives, and were thus "subversives" subject to "special treatment." As PANAMIN *News* rationalized it, "For the Church to work outside of the province of State concerns and preach ideas hostile to the state is to place itself within the punitive domain of the state."[39] The agency undertook various campaigns to harass and intimidate Catholic and Protestant social-action workers.

Throughout 1974 the Kalingas and Bontocs had tried without success to meet with Marcos to protest the Chico Dam project. As a last resort, they appealed to Bishop Francisco Claver for assistance. In April 1975 the bishop, himself a native Bontoc, wrote an open letter to Marcos expressing the concerns of the tribes and warning of an escalation of violence.[40] Less than a month later, 150 Bontoc and Kalinga leaders attended an ecumenical conference organized by an apostolate of the Catholic Church to discuss the dams. The leaders made a historic *pagta ti bodong* (peace pact) outlining the conditions under which the two tribes would oppose the project.[41] Indeed, Bontoc-Kalinga resistance to the dams was so strong that by July 1978, Marcos pulled PANAMIN out of the region. This was a bitter victory for the tribes. The 60th Philippine Constabulary (PC) battalion took over from PANAMIN, unleashing a reign of terror in the Chico River region.

During this time, NPA cadres began the long process of indoctrination required to win tribal Filipinos to the CPP's cause. A foreign correspondent described the process in 1979:

> Since the NPA must sell its ideology to a diverse nation, strategies differ greatly from region to region. Everywhere, however, the local people's confidence is the first prize, setting the stage for the communists to begin education, a process that an apolitical observer might describe as telling the poor why they are poor and the exploited, why they are exploited, and convincing them that there is something that they can and should do about it. As political awareness develops, the message gradually is refined down to the tenets of Marx, Lenin and Mao Zedong.[42]

The teachings of Marx, Lenin, and Mao may have helped the Kalingas see their struggle against the dams in more sophisticated terms, but it was the NPA's careful efforts to integrate into the closely knit Bontoc-Kalinga tribal system that made all the difference. Coming armed with knowledge of local customs and languages, NPA guerrillas had very quickly become advisers, friends, and even family to the Kalingas.[43]

The battle of the Kalingas and Bontocs against the Chico dams reverberated in the squalid areas of Metro Manila, where thousands of urban poor had been displaced by the regime's beautification and industrialization projects. From 1975 to 1976, about ten thousand of the city's approximately 1 million slum dwellers were evicted and sent back to their home provinces or to relocation sites outside Manila.[44] In the particularly depressed area of Tondo, squatters' shanties were demolished to make way for a container facility and a fish port in the foreshore area.[45] The government proposed to move the displaced residents into a nearby housing project, Dagat Dagatan. But charging rents of Php 70 a month, Dagat Dagatan was too expensive for the affected residents. Even if residents could eke out the full cost of Dagat Dagatan's rent, there was not enough room in the housing project to accommodate the twenty-eight thousand families living in Tondo.[46]

The militant squatter organization Zone One Tondo Organization (ZOTO) protested the demolitions and the government's inadequate housing alternative. ZOTO found an ally in the Catholic Church. The organization's activist stance meshed with the Church's promotion of grassroots community programs, called Basic Christian Communities (BCCs). Tondo squatters were indeed putting into practice the BCC model of social action, which encouraged oppressed communities to participate in decisions that affected them directly. In the words of Bishop Claver, the BCC model hinged on "discernment, involvement and shared responsibility."[47] To this end, the Church provided ZOTO with numerous venues—prayer vigils, masses, and social action projects—for airing squatters' grievances and facilitating community organization.[48]

The regime was especially harsh in its treatment of ZOTO workers. In April 1977, ZOTO president Trinidad Herrera was arrested and tortured. She was given electric shock to her fingertips and breasts as an inducement to "cooperate" with the military in identifying other "subversives."[49] Herrera's case was not an isolated one. Reports of the military's human-rights abuses against ZOTO and other activist groups would in fact force Marcos to make showy gestures of political normalization, culminating in the return of the ballot in 1978.

Human-Rights Abuses

The regime made sixty thousand political arrests between September 1972 and February 1977. The detainees constituted a veritable cross-section of the opposition, including traditional politicians, journalists, prominent businessmen, CPP-NPA cadres and Church activists who were deemed obstacles to the regime's development initiatives. But the popular classes—members of urban poor and peasant organizations and tribal minorities—constituted a disproportionate share of the arrests.

In 1972, Marcos denied that there were any political prisoners in the New Society. He eventually admitted to the arrests, but in December 1974 he flatly stated, "no one, but not one was tortured."[50] In 1977, however, a scathing report delivered by Amnesty International established that at least six thousand political prisoners were languishing in the New Society's various detentions centers and that torture was "part of the general approach to the treatment of suspects."[51]

The AMRSP took the lead in protesting the regime's human-rights violations. The organization's 4,500 priests, 7,000 nuns, and 450 monks had been strongly influenced by liberation theology and its leadership was in close contact with the NDF. In 1974 the AMRSP created the Task Force Detainees of the Philippines (TFDP). Among the new organization's immediate objectives were "protesting instances of torture to the authorities" and "publicizing the political detainee situation at home and abroad."[52] The TFDP would go on to document 1,093 cases of torture in the Philippines in 1983 and 1984.[53]

Among the cases that gained international attention were those of journalist Jose Lacaba and NDF leader Horacio Morales, Jr. Lacaba, whose reportage of the First Quarter Storm I analyzed in chapter 1, was arrested for publishing an underground newspaper that opposed martial law. He received the San Juanico Bridge treatment: for hours on end he was forced to lie with his feet on one bed, his head on another. Whenever his body sagged, he was beaten and kicked.[54] Morales received the "water cure" and electric-shock treatment "to force him, among other things, to sign a waiver of his rights to legal counsel."[55]

Traditional politicians—some of whom had been detained by the military at the onset of martial law—joined the TFDP's cause. Former senator Jose Diokno, who had been imprisoned from 1972 to 1974, founded the Free Legal Assistance Group. The organization worked with the TFDP to provide legal counsel to prisoners and their families.

To whitewash the bad publicity stirred up by the Amnesty International report, Marcos hosted a World Peace through Law Conference in August 1977. On the eve of Marcos's conference, ex-senator Jovito Salonga hosted the Filipino People's Convention on Human Rights. About one thousand people attended the opposition's conference, including some of the most prominent anti-Marcos politicians of the pre-martial-law era. The conference, which focused largely on civil-rights issues, called for the "immediate lifting of martial law, the removal of one-man rule, and the holding of elections."[56] The dictator was "determined not to let his image-building effort on human rights be undermined by the opposition."[57] Before delegates to the World Peace through Law Conference, he announced plans to hold legislative elections by 1978.[58]

A Stolen Election

Many Old Society politicians seized the legislative elections scheduled for April 7, 1978, as an opportunity to recover their leadership role in the anti-Marcos struggle. Catholic social-action workers, students, laborers, and slum organizers also seized the moment to extend their united-front activities. Both opposing groups chose to concentrate their organizing in Metro Manila, where they assumed they had a fighting chance against the regime.

Marcos created the Kilusang Bagong Lipunan (KBL; New Society Movement), a new political party that would balance his reliance on the powerful military. Its candidates included nearly half the existing cabinet, provincial and town officials, and not a few elite politicians (nine ex-senators and twenty-three ex-congressmen). In short, the KBL was a "party of officials and the locally prominent."[59] The democratic opposition formed Lakas ng Bayan (People Power) or LABAN (Fight) to run against the KBL. In the intensely contested region of Metro Manila, Imelda Marcos headed the KBL slate, while ex-senator Benigno Aquino, Jr., headed the LABAN ticket.

Aquino was among the Old Society politicians incarcerated at the onset of martial law. While most politicians were detained only briefly, he was enough of a threat to Marcos to warrant seven years in solitary confinement at Fort Bonifacio. He was charged with "murder, subversion, rebellion and illegal possession of firearms," and following a military court trial in 1977, he was sentenced to death by firing squad in November.[60] Aquino was appealing the verdict when he agreed to head LABAN's Manila slate. However, at this juncture, Aquino was "just a name and a fading memory to most Filipinos."[61]

Marcos relaxed restrictions on speech, press, and assembly during the campaign period, giving Aquino just enough room to reinvent his political image and reconnect with the Filipino people. Denied a temporary release from detention in order to campaign, Aquino was allowed only a single television appearance. The ninety-minute interview was the result of several days of negotiations between his sister, filmmaker Lupita Concio, and the government's National Media Production Center. The latter stood by its promise that none of Aquino's remarks would be edited, and in a dramatic interview recorded at Fort Bonifacio on March 10, the charismatic forty-five-year old politician presented himself as a "responsible, reasonable and constructive leader of the opposition."[62]

For the LABAN campaign, Aquino and his supporters carefully selected and arranged popular symbols of resistance: "the widely used acronym LABAN (fight) made clear that this was to be a struggle of people power against the Marcos dictatorship," and a thumb-and-index-finger salute forming the letter *L* powerfully captured the party's call for bravery.[63] Such symbolic cues proved to be effective in channeling cross-class solidarity among Manilans, in contrast to the more patronage-dependent campaign efforts of the KBL.[64]

The Manila campaign saw the two parties debating a single issue: the rightness of Marcos's rule. With Marcos's latest book and election tract, *Five Years of the New Society,* released in advance of the campaign, the KBL emphasized the regime's economic and administrative achievements. LABAN criticized Marcos's dictatorial powers and the rampant corruption of the regime. On April 6, the night before the balloting, Manilans made a clear statement against Marcos's rule: "what was to have been five minutes of horn-honking and pan-beating in support of LABAN turned into a large three-hour noise-making demonstration."[65]

The KBL swept Manila (21–0 seats, with Governor Marcos garnering 60 percent of the vote). In a performance that was striking for its sheer bravura, the regime had resurrected all the tried-and-true forms of electoral fraud in the Old Society. The U.S. embassy reported that at least two thousand "flying voters" were brought in from Ferdinand and Imelda's home provinces (Ilocos Norte and Leyte) to vote in Manila. The KBL also printed and marked 1 million fake ballots, engaged in massive ballot stuffing, and paid teachers recruited to supervise the polls Php 200 "under the table."[66] Electoral violence was so rampant that even the international press was not spared: upon witnessing a ballot-rigging episode, *New York Times* correspondent Fox Butterfield was thrown down a flight of stairs by government guards.[67]

Two days after the ballot, Manila residents staged a "death of democracy" demonstration. Marcos's troops broke up the march, arresting six hundred protestors, including ex-senator Lorenzo Tañada, who, at seventy-nine, was the "grand old man of the opposition."

It was Tañada who convinced Aquino to participate in the election. In this, he was backed by the Manila-Rizal branch of the CPP, which saw the elections as a "chance to further polarize the pro- and anti-Marcos elite, disseminate extensive anti-government propaganda, and build alliances with anti-Marcos reactionaries."[68] The Manila communists offered to provide LABAN with the staff it needed for poll watching, in exchange for four seats in the LABAN ticket and a chance to help write the party's platform. The alliance was far from sound, however. The CPP's National Central Committee had decided to boycott the elections. Consequently, much of the poll-watching responsibilities promised by the Manila communists devolved on the anti-Marcos—but equally anticommunist—Partido Demokratiko-Sosyalista ng Pilipinas (PDSP). And now, in the aftermath of the stolen election, the PDSP seized the moment to shore up the political clout of the Social Democrats in the anti-Marcos struggle.

As Tañada was hauled into a police van, he raised a clenched fist, prompting demonstrators to return the gesture with the LABAN salute. To keep the crowd's morale up, PDSP leaders defiantly sang an old Philippine protest song:[69]

Ibon mang may layang lumipad	Even birds that freely roam the Sky
Kulongin mo at umiiyak.	Loudly weep when not allowed to fly
Bayan pa kayang sakdal dilag	What more for a nation ensnared?
Ang di magnasang makaalpas	Would it not cry out for freedom?
Pilipinas kong minumutya	My beloved Philippines,
Pugad ng luha ko't dalita	nest of my tears and suffering,
Aking adhika	my one wish—
Makita kang sakdal laya.	to see you finally free.

Though this emotional moment added fuel to the opposition's moral fire, it triggered a devastating crackdown on the PDSP in the days that followed. The PDSP was the underground network of the Social Democrats. Though the organization was considerably weaker than the CPP during the early days of martial law, by 1978 it had earned the backing of progressive bishops and religious superiors. Among those arrested was Fr. Roman Intengan, a PDSP organizer and ideologue who had helped train poll watchers for LABAN. The day after Fr. Integnan's arrest, the Philippine Constabulary raided his office in the Loyola House of Studies. Among the "subversive materials" seized by the military were a few thousand copies of *Malayang Pilipinas* (Free Philippines), an ephemeral newspaper published by the opposition.[70] The PC arrested two young seminarians, one of whom would die from brutal beatings while in detention. Teotimo Taniado, seventeen years old, had worked with the opposition during the elections. His body displayed clear signs of torture: his intestines were ripped out, though a military press release stated that the cause of death was "acute pancreatis (sic)."[71]

With the PDSP's leaders arrested or forced underground, a new constellation of oppositional groups emerged. Both anti-Marcos and anticommunist, this so-called Third Force sought to use urban terrorism to bring down the regime.

Urban Terrorism and Militarization

Led by a handful of urban elites with close ties to Aquino, the Light-a-Fire Movement (LFM) advanced a strategy of insurrection. The organization hoped that *symbolic* acts of terror would obviate a protracted "people's war"—the strategy being pursued by the CPP-NPA. The organization was not interested in waging a violent revolution—the elites and moderates behind it were hardly inclined to bring about a drastic restructuring of society, but rather to "compel Marcos to negotiate a formula for the sharing of power."[72]

The LFM's inner circle included Eugenio Lopez's son-in-law, Steve Psinakis, and PDSP activist Eduardo Olaguer. The latter was deeply influenced by the Catholic Left—a brother was a Jesuit priest—and in his student days, led a Catholic organization at the University of the Philippines. In 1978, Olaguer traveled to the United States to meet with political exiles and raise money for the movement. He gained the support of the Movement for a Free Philippines (MFP), an organization founded by ex-senator Raul Manglapus in 1973 and headquartered in Washington, DC.

The MFP's role in the opposition was substantial; it had engaged in a propaganda drive to discredit Marcos, even offering testimony to expose the corruption of the regime to U.S. lawmakers.[73] Olaguer's meeting with Manglapus resulted in an insurrectionary plan, Project Public Justice, which would use urban terrorism to foster civil disobedience.[74] The group hoped that acts of sabotage would urge Washington to distance itself from Marcos or, at the very least, put pressure on the dictator to hold clean elections. Aquino endorsed the plan and from his prison cell plotted the targets to be attacked. A number of Aquino supporters—a good number of prominent businessmen among them—financed the campaign.

In 1979, the LFM attacked the COMELEC building—the hated symbol of the 1978 stolen election. Subsequent targets included several crony hotels and the regime's floating casino in Manila Bay. But these symbolic acts of violence, which were largely ignored by the Marcos-controlled media, accomplished little in the way of destabilizing the regime. An LFM member revealed the group's plans to a CIA official in Hong Kong, who shared the information with Marcos. The military quickly broke up the LFM, and by December 1979 most of its members, including Olaguer, were apprehended. Soon after, the crony media were exploding bombas about the group and its links to political exiles in the United States.[75]

At this critical juncture, Aquino was released from prison for health reasons. While doing daily exercises in his cell, the ex-senator had collapsed and was soon after diagnosed with a severe heart condition. The intervention of the Carter administration prompted Marcos to allow his nemesis to undergo triple-bypass surgery in the United States. Aquino arrived in this country in May 1980. Three months later, in a speech before the Asia Society in New York, he warned Marcos of a "gathering storm." He was referring to the April Sixth Liberation Movement (A6LM), a new insurrectionary movement organized by yet another group of Social Democrats, the Kapulungan ng mga Sandigang Pilipino (KASAPI, Sectoral Association of the Philippines). The organization was made up of former moderate student activists, who had an estimated two thousand followers among the poor in Manila. Named after the April 6, 1978, noise barrage, the A6LM sought to revive the spirit of protest harnessed during the 1978 LABAN campaign and to use symbolic acts of terror to spark a popular uprising.[76]

Aquino used the A6LM to pressure Marcos into holding clean elections. But the January 1980 election for provincial, city, and municipal officials did not bode well for the opposition's hopes of clean elections in the near future: massive fraud and violence at the polls resulted in yet another KBL sweep, with 69 of 73 governorships and 1,550 of 1,560 mayoral posts going to Marcos's candidates.[77]

In his speech warning Marcos of a gathering storm, Aquino stated that the A6LM's guerrillas were "well-educated, articulate young men and women who have patiently studied the latest tactics in urban warfare."[78] Within three weeks of Aquino's warning, the A6LM bombed nine buildings in Manila. As if to confirm Aquino's assessment of the A6LM's guerrillas, Defense Minister Juan Ponce Enrile noted some of the group's tactical advantages over the CPP-NPA: they had access to "money, talent and leadership, and . . . they were more acceptable to Filipinos because of their religious orientation." These advantages, Enrile said, made A6LM "more dangerous" than the communists.[79]

On October 19, 1980, the A6LM bombed the convention of the American Society of Travel Agents in Manila. While previous bombings of banks, hotels, shopping centers, and government buildings seemed to be intended for local consumption, the ASTA attack, which largely affected foreign travel agents, was done to undermine one of the cornerstones of the regime's economic strategy—tourism.

Marcos had assigned three thousand security personnel to protect the convention center and, in a speech before five thousand ASTA delegates, assured the international community that the recent wave of political terrorism was under control. Marcos's speech quickly took on a profoundly ironic cast when, minutes after concluding his remarks, a bomb exploded only fifteen meters from where the president stood. The terrorists had managed to circumvent Marcos's tight security precautions by smuggling the bomb in the briefcase of an ASTA delegate.[80] Eighteen persons, including eleven delegates and a popular Filipino singer, were injured.[81] The bombing triggered a slew of bombas in the crony media, and unlike A6LM's previous attacks, was extensively reported in the international press.[82]

When Marcos lifted martial law, in January 1981, and set presidential elections for June of that year, many in the elite opposition believed that the A6LM had done its job.[83] But the elite opposition's hopes were dashed when Marcos made several moves to ensure another KBL victory: he raised the minimum age of candidates to fifty (Aquino was forty-eight); refused the opposition equal access to the media; refused to reorganize the COMELEC to guarantee impartiality in supervising the election; refused to purge voters' list of unqualified voters; issued land titles in Tondo and disbursed Php 6,000 in pork barrel funds to *barangay* (village) chairmen. Marcos had so rigged the election terms in his favor that all major oppositionists opted to boycott.[84] And though twelve candidates eventually ran against the president, none was a serious threat. Marcos, of course, was reelected.

Not only did the A6LM fail to achieve its political goals, it also exacerbated militarization in Marcos's Philippines. The day before lifting martial law, Marcos issued Presidential Decree 1834, increasing penalties for rebellion, insurrection, and sedition. In the New Society, the maximum penalty for such crimes was seventeen years and four months in prison; in Marcos's so-called New Republic, the maximum penalties for all crimes involving rebellion, insurrection, and sedition was death.

By May 1981, Marcos was routinely ordering "preventive detentions" through the so-called Presidential Commitment Order (PCO): any person accused of national-security violations could be arrested and detained indefinitely prior to a court hearing. PD 1834 and the PCO allowed Marcos to detain hundreds of "subversives" allegedly connected with the Third Force. Middle-class students and Church activists—not its elite leadership—had indeed received the brunt of the military's wrath when the regime cracked down on the A6LM.[85] However, arrests documented by Amnesty International during this period revealed an important geographic shift. The organization found that arrests in the Metro Manila area had been steadily declining since 1976, but were rising in provincial areas after 1979.[86] Indeed, a pronounced trend of disappearances and "salvagings" affected many more Filipinos in the countryside.

In 1981, Amnesty International reported that 233 political detainees were "disappeared" between 1975 and 1980. Of 783 cases investigated by the organization, 181 were classified as "salvage" victims,[87] the military euphemism for summary execution. Salvagings differed from disappearances in one crucial way: while the authorities could deny knowledge of many disappearances, the "existence of corpses from 'salvagings' required an official explanation."[88] And the most common explanations given for the hundreds of corpses found on roadsides and other public places during this period were that they were NPA insurgents killed in military engagements or were the innocent victims of NPA "liquidations."[89]

Often caught in the crossfire between the NPA and the military, innocent civilians represented the bulk of the 145 disappearances and 368 salvagings documented by the TFD in 1983.[90] Many of the salvagings were attributed to paramilitary units and fanatical anticommunist groups like the Sagrado Corazon Señor (Sacred Heart of the Lord) and Tadtad (Chop Chop) gangs, who were notorious for their cannibalistic rituals.[91] Still more were attributed to "lost commands." Composed largely of court-martialed soldiers and other lumpen elements "whose records were expunged in return for killing 'rebels' or 'subversives,'" these lost commands committed the most unspeakable crimes in the name of national security.[92]

This climate of fear had largely paralyzed the media. The Catholic media, which had played a major role in exposing the struggles of the peasantry, tribal peoples, and urban squatters, had been the target of militarization throughout the martial law regime.[93] *Signs of the Times,* a weekly news bulletin of the AMRSP, was padlocked in December 1974 on charges of "inciting to sedition." *The Communicator,* a monthly publication of the Church's National Office of Mass Media, was similarly shuttered in December 1976 for printing articles critical of the regime. *Ang bandilyo,* a newsletter of the prelature of Bukidnon was shut down in November 1976 for criticizing "political normalization" in the New Society. Two missionaries, Fr. Eduard Gerlock and Fr. Albert Booms, were arrested and subsequently deported in connection with these shutdowns. The Catholic radio stations DXBB (Malaybalay, Bukidnon) and DXCO (Tagum, Davao) were shut down in November 1976 for allegedly broadcasting coded messages to NPA rebels.

The popular and elite forces of the anti-Marcos struggle were divided on issues of strategy and tactics. Working within a "democracy from below" model, marginalized communities, the Catholic Left and the CPP-NPA used grassroots activism to integrate the various "micro" causes of the oppressed into a nationwide popular struggle against the regime. Meanwhile, traditional politicians and the moderate Catholic opposition used human-rights activism—and failing that, urban terrorism—to press for the restoration of competitive elections, the linchpin of "elite democracy." Crucial alliances had nonetheless formed. All that was lacking was a media event that would galvanize the opposition's melodramatic imaginary.

Chapter 5

THE MEDIA AND THE SECOND COMING OF THE FIRST QUARTER STORM

Marcos's June 30, 1981, inaugural celebration was a made-for-TV spectacular dubbed "Ako ay Pilipino" [I am the new Filipino]: Rites of the New Republic." If the Marcos regime were to be believed, 30 million television viewers, or nearly three-fourths of the population, saw the live telecast of Marcos's swearing in at the Luneta grandstand.[1] Twenty-eight state visitors, including U.S. vice president George H. W. Bush, were present to watch an event that climaxed with a thousand-voice male chorus singing the "Hallelujah Chorus" from Handel's *Messiah.* "And he shall reign forever and ever."[2]

Panorama, the Sunday supplement to Manila's *Bulletin Today,* duly featured the inaugural. On the cover of the July 12, 1981, issue were three black-and-white photographs of the president, one in each of his inaugurations—1965, 1969, and 1981. Compared to the high production values of "Ako ay Pilipino," the *Panorama* cover seemed almost insipid. And, given the intense coverage that the inaugural had already received in the establishment press, nobody expected anything out of the ordinary from the magazine. But when editor Letty Jimenez-Magsanoc's story "There Goes the New Society, Welcome the New Republic" prompted the Ministry of Justice, the chairman of COMELEC, and the secretary-general of the KBL to threaten *Bulletin/Panorama* publisher Hans Menzi with "seditious libel" (and thereby force Magsanoc to resign), the offending *Panorama* issue became an instant collector's item. But "it was more than that," veteran journalist Marcelino B. Soriano points out. Magsanoc's swan song "marked an awakening of the journalism profession."[3]

Magsanoc's controversial article briefly mentions Presidential Decree 1737, issued in September 1980. The act authorized Marcos to direct the "closure of subversive publications or other media of mass communications." Magsanoc's reflexive dig at the legal measure intended to muzzle the media in the New Republic is followed by the ironic statement: "Yet with all the awesome powers at his disposal, [Marcos] needed, he said, to go before the people 'to be judged' on his performance in office for 16 consecutive years." Hinting at the fraudulence of the election, Magsanoc would draw the full ire of the regime with the following concluding lines: "The problem is a Marcos who with all his powers is powerless before corruption and the corruptors. It is a Marcos astride the same tired tiger (the discarded and discredited New Society) carrying on under a different name, the New Republic. If that continues, the Filipino, docile as he has been as the carabao [water buffalo] these 16 years cannot but give way and tear at the Republic."[4]

Magsanoc's acerbic piece was a bomba. Largely dormant since the imposition of martial law, the bomba occasionally appeared in the crony media; but it was largely used to "expose" the nefarious activities of the elite opposition. Magsanoc's impudent digs at "corruption and corruptors" within the regime was much more than a simple shift in bomba targets. The suggestion that the all-powerful Marcos was in fact "powerless" called into question the very linchpin of Marcos's national family.

The entire power structure of the regime rested on the personalistic rule of one man; but contrary to Marcos's musical selection for the inaugural, the head of the household couldn't possibly rule "forever and ever." In 1978 there were rumors that the president's health was failing. Visitors to Malacañang reported that the president could not rise from his chair unassisted. A year later, telltale signs of ill health became obvious even to television viewers: a rash covered his bloated face.[5] Marcos was suffering from lupus erythematosus, a chronic autoimmune disorder that had attacked his kidneys. Marcos campaigned vigorously for the presidential elections, thereby dispelling the worst rumors about his health. But the issue of political succession plagued the administration; and in the absence of a clear resolution, Magsanoc's insinuation that Marcos was ceding power to his cronies was high blasphemy in the New Republic.

What made Magsanoc's bomba particularly striking was its placement in a magazine owned by a powerful Marcos crony. To recall, publisher Hans Menzi was a former military aide of the president and one of his closest cronies. But Menzi's loyalties were divided between rival factions that had been growing since 1978 within the president's national family.

A Divided Household, a Divided Press

By the late 1970s, Imelda Marcos had become a formidable power broker within the national family. Ferdinand appointed her minister of human settlements in 1978, a position she held in addition to serving as governor of Manila. The Ministry of Human Settlements was a new government body charged with building roads, schools, housing, and public parks in the recently consolidated megalopolis of Metro Manila (4,338 square kilometers, population 7 million), which Imelda christened the City of Man.[6] With a budget of $1 billion, Imelda's ministry was a notorious patronage machine. Its seventy-three subsidiaries were never audited and served as a "source of income for cabinet members, military officers and cronies."[7] Imelda had cultivated a sizeable faction of loyalists—in the military, the business sector, and the bureaucracy—to rival her husband's own patronage network. By the end of 1978 her "ministerial portfolio" extended her "direct influence throughout the national administration."[8] The symbolic household of Malakas and

Maganda was in reality a house divided, in which key groups were "designated as 'his' as distinct from 'hers.'"[9]

As the publisher of *Bulletin Today,* the nation's largest newspaper chain, Menzi indeed wielded considerable power, but the Marcos loyalist was hardly predisposed to use that power against his patrons—Ferdinand and Imelda Marcos. And with the national family divided between "his and her" factions, Menzi had to take all precautions so as not to offend one or the other. Menzi's predicament underscored crucial differences—as well as surprising similarities—between the crony media in the New Republic and the pre-martial-law oligarchic media.

Before martial law, four oligarchic families controlled the mass media. The Elizalde family owned the *Evening News* and the *Philippines Sun* and the Metropolitan and Republic networks; the Roces family owned the *Manila Times,* the *Daily Mirror,* and *Taliba* and the Associated network; the Soriano family owned the *Philippines Herald* and the Inter-island network; and the Lopez family owned the *Manila Chronicle* and the ABS-CBN network.[10]

The diversified business holdings of these families ensured the diversity of views in the media. The Lopez family, for example, had interests in both traditional exports (sugar) and import-substitution industrialization (heavy machinery). It was to the family's best interest, then, to give rival factions—in this case, pro-U.S. groups and economic nationalists—fair play in the family's media outlets. After martial law, the cacophony of voices and viewpoints that diacritically defined the "freest press in Asia" gave way to a more subdued mood among the establishment media. This was because the cronies who had replaced the four oligarchic families were not only subservient to Marcos, they had "more pervasive and interlocking business interests."[11]

But the mere transfer of media ownership from the oligarchy to the cronies was not enough to kill the journalistic ideal of an independent press. To enforce the media's primary function as mobilizer of popular support for the regime's policies, the crony media were subject to several layers of control. Editors routinely screened journalists' copy for stories they deemed offensive to the authorities. The unwritten rule was that the presidential family and the military were not to be criticized. Media owners exerted another layer of control: firing staff guilty of writing or approving offensive articles. The final layer of control—and the most feared—rested in the military. Various legal measures (PD 1737, PD 1834, and the PCO) empowered the military to detain journalists, for indeterminate periods, for "offenses in the open-ended category of subversion, sedition, rebellion, etc."[12] But despite these layers of control, a few stories critical of the Marcos regime did in fact emerge in the crony media between 1980 and 1982, giving the lie to the widely held notion that the latter were "monolithic."

A July 4, 1982, *Panorama* feature story by Jo-Ann Maglipon exposed the militarization of Davao del Norte, a province in Mindanao, from 1978 to 1981. Titled "Where the Men with Guns Tread Nothing Remains but Charred Remains and the Skeleton of a Village," the story focused on the tribal Atas, who had been intimidated, tortured, and massacred by government troopers in the province. Maglipon was no stranger to militarization; she was arrested in 1974 "on charges of undefined subversion" and was imprisoned for a year.[13]

Other cases of militarization appeared in the magazine in 1982. Staff writer Lorna Kalaw-Tirol wrote an exposé on the government's assault on Church workers in Samar during two months of military operations in the region. Titled "In This Catholic Country, Is it Being Subversive to Live Out Christ's Gospel?," the article appeared in the magazine's November 20, 1982 issue. Tirol's bomba was particularly graphic, describing the troopers' macabre method of instilling fear in the community: "the head of one dead man was displayed in the poblacion, 35 ears attached to it, and dead people were brought to the centers tied to a pole and then dumped into a pit."[14] In "Forty Years after the Fall, Bataan Is Again under Siege,"[15] fellow staff writer Maria Ceres Doyo described how the local population had been subjected to a "nightmarish experience" of "raids, torture, arrests and killings" ever since the military stepped up its counterinsurgency campaign in the region, in September 1981.[16] Like Maglipon, Doyo had had prior brushes with the military. In July 1980 she was interrogated by the military for a story she wrote on Macli-ing Dulag, a Kalinga chief who had been brutally murdered by the military for his activism against the government's Chico Dam project.[17]

By 1982, then, dissenting voices within Menzi's "household" revealed the less than unanimous support that the establishment media had for the Marcos regime. Enmeshed in the growing factionalism within Marcos's national family, the crony press was beginning to mimic the pre-martial-law media's proclivities for strategically "diverse" reporting. *Panorama*'s exposés on worsening militarization in the country could very well have been symptomatic of a vocational awakening in the establishment media. Nonetheless we must consider this belated awakening in light of the instability of the regime. Marcos's health was failing and Imelda had already become a "kind of acting president."[18] Rumors of the dictator's diminishing power may have emboldened reporters to attack the regime. *Panorama*'s bombas against the military—the dictator's core support group—would not go unpunished, however; Marcos may have been ailing, but the military was stronger than ever.

Maglipon, Doyo, and Tirol were "invited" to Fort Bonifacio for interrogation. Other reporters and editors who ran afoul of the military were similarly summoned: *Bulletin Today* columnists Arlene Babst and Ninez Cacho Olivares; *Panorama* editor Domini Torrevillas-Suarez; *Mr. & Ms.* editor Eugenia D. Apostol and staff writer Doris Nuyda; and *WHO* writers Roberto Coloma, Cielo Buenaventura, and Alex Magno.[19] With the exception of Apostol and Nuyda, who worked for the independent magazine *Mr. & Ms.*, the invitees all worked for the Menzi publishing chain.

Military officers subjected the journalists to a battery of questions, including "Why do you write to agitate the mind and arouse the passions? Don't you think that you are being unwittingly used by those who try to subvert the government? Are you familiar with the problem of brainwashing? Do you realize that some of your writings are only a hairline away from subversive writing?"[20]

The officers' questions express a clear prejudice against emotions, a prejudice that is filtered through the military's counterinsurgency tropes ("brainwashing," "subversion"). It is a position that is fully consistent with Marcos's style of political demonology (see chapter 1). This time, however, gendered dynamics factored into the authorities' countersubversive performance. Marcos imagined "the subversive" as a male subject, whereas the officers were dealing mostly with women. No surprise, then, that their mode of intimidation involved asking highly personal questions about the intimate lives of the journalists, who were made to account for their familial relationships and even their religious beliefs. Implicit in this line of questioning were three interrelated propositions: (1) that women are associated with affect and emotion, which they cannot control; (2) that the "normal" woman belongs in the intimate sphere, where passions and intimate relations must be relegated; and (3) that there is something pathological, hence "subversive," about a woman who writes; particularly when she writes news items that bear the mark of her passions. The women journalists thus had to prove that they possessed a proper political-ethical sensorium. Babst summed up her experience thus: "The perceptible objective of the Panel was to intimidate and instill fear in me (as well as all writers of the press) to the point that we will suppress the truth and not freely write or express [our] views on matters of public concern."[21]

In January 1983 twenty-nine journalists filed a petition before the Supreme Court for the prohibition of further military interrogations. Two days before the hearing scheduled for February 1, the military announced that it was filing libel charges against *Panorama* editor Suarez and *Panorama* writers Maglipon, Tirol, and Doyo, as well as *Far Eastern Economic Review* staff writer Sheila Coronel. The libel suits—one of them for a staggering Php 229 million—were in reality superfluous. PD 1834 had made anyone "who shall utter seditious words or speeches, write, publish, or circulate scurrilous libels against the Government of the Philippines" subject to the "penalty of *reclusion perpetua* to death."²² And in any event, the military had no compunctions about extrajudicial killings, as the notorious cases of Demy Dingcong, Kenneth Lee, and Primitivo Mijares had earlier shown.

Dingcong was a *Bulletin Today* correspondent. He was gunned down in his home in Iligan City, Mindanao, in December 1980. Dingcong had alerted the National Press Club of the Philippines (NPC) that he had received death threats in connection with a story he had written about irregularities at Mindanao State University. Dingcong's killer was a PC sergeant who later turned out to be the personal bodyguard of MSU president (and Lanao del Sur governor) Ali Dimaporo.²³ Lee, a reporter for *Depthnews,* had been the victim of "salvaging." His mutilated body was found in Jolo, Sulu, in 1979. As was the case with many summary executions, his killers were never arrested. However, Lee's belongings were later found in the possession of military men. Unlike rank-and-file reporters Dingcong and Lee, Mijares was a media czar—he was a past president of the NPC and had served as chairman of Marcos's Media Advisory Council. The former palace insider precipitously fled to the United States and joined Manglapus's political-exile group, Movement for a Free Philippines. He incurred the full wrath of the regime when he testified before the U.S. Senate Foreign Relations Sub-Committee in 1975 and then went on to write a tell-all book, *The Conjugal Dictatorship of Ferdinand and Imelda Marcos.*²⁴ Shortly after, Mijares was lured back to the Philippines, "where his son was killed before his eyes." Mijares was then tortured and murdered.²⁵

The extrajudicial killings of journalists would in fact escalate from 1983 through 1985. Meanwhile, libel suits, PCOs and the dreaded PD 1834 effectively contained the "quiet revolt" of the establishment media. Former *Bulletin* columnist Antonio Nieva retrospectively assessed the media's "tightrope act" in the New Republic: "Days come when a reading of the climate shows need for extreme caution: storm clouds gathering ahead. . . . Having been in the business this long, the tightrope artist reads the signs fairly well."[26] Signs of a gathering storm were indeed discernable in Imelda's City of Man. The emergence of a new bomba film culture in conjunction with the second Manila International Film Festival (January 24–February 4, 1983) brought into relief the growing fault lines in the national family and triggered organizational activity within the cultural sector.

A New Bomba Film Culture

A February 1983 *Panorama* article describes the feeling of déjà vu then sweeping Metro Manila's movie theaters:

> Flashback: 1970. *Marsha, The Erotic Housewife* was screened at a downtown Manila moviehouse and it became the biggest thing that ever happened to local cinema bugs since *The Ten Commandments*. For demonstration-weary Manilans whose previous encounters with sex on film had been mainly through antiseptic sex-ed films, that American soft porn flick opened the erotic floodgates. . . . As with all post-climax phases, though, there had to be an intermission. Smoking time so to speak. And now, the Second Coming. One Thursday morning, 11 years after the great deluge, eight million Metro Manilans woke up to discover that 99 percent of their 150 plus cinema houses were showing R-rated (For Adults Only) exhibition films in connection with the Second Manila International Film Festival. And it was 1970 all over again, for one whole giddy week.[27]

Though the film industry had occasionally released sexually explicit films in the intervening years, the deluge of sex films at the 1983 Manila International Film Festival (MIFF) gave Manilans pause. Bemused observers flashing back to 1970 could not have missed the uncanny coincidence between the revival of the bomba—both political and cinematic—and the convergence of political trends that loosely reprised the First Quarter Storm. To wit, public outrage over fraudulent elections, the resurgence of strikes and demonstrations, and the escalation of the communist insurgency in the countryside. With the elite opposition's arson-and-bombing campaign still fresh in the public mind and with the moderate Catholic opposition still very active, the political climate in 1983 resembled in many respects the turbulent conditions of the nation on the eve of martial law. But those who read the signs of the Second Coming could not have also missed the profound irony underpinning the outbreak of cinematic bombas in 1983: while the sex-and-violence films of the pre-martial-law era were a "subversive" force associated with the rebelliousness of radical youth, the films of MIFF '83 bore the clear stamp of the regime's cultural patronage. Indeed, the festival was an indicator of the fabulously enhanced stature of the cinema in Imelda's City of Man.

This is how it happened. In January 1981, Marcos signed Executive Order 640-A, which created a Filipino Motion Picture Development Board (Filmboard) to professionalize all workers in the industry, provide soft loans, archive and preserve the national cinema, and organize international film festivals. The board was to be composed of industry representatives, who were to report directly to the chairman of the Cultural Center of the Philippines, Imelda Marcos. In 1982, she organized the first Manila International Film Festival. A fifty-eight-thousand-square-meter film palace was feverishly built especially for the event.

Imelda had originally scheduled the $25 million film center to be completed in two years. In late 1981, however, she impulsively ordered the building to be completed in time for the opening ceremonies of the MIFF, just weeks away. Some seven thousand workers were put to work in round-the-clock shifts. They were paid 45 to 50 pesos a day (roughly $5 to $6).[28] Tragedy hit the building site in the early hours of November 17, 1981.[29] At some point between 2:00 and 3:00 a.m. the ceiling of the main theater collapsed, burying two hundred workers in quick-drying cement. At least seven died instantaneously. Scores of others were seriously injured. The bodies of the dead were never recovered or accounted for and were bulldozed into Manila Bay. The film center—and the tragedy behind it—would in fact become the very symbol of the extravagance of the MIFF.

As conceived by Imelda, the festival was to be "the first in Asia to hold a film competition, film market, film exhibition and film symposia."[30] If the festival was intended to promote Filipino films, it was hardly apparent in the film competition. No Filipino film was entered.[31] Meanwhile, only two local films were screened in the film exhibition module.[32] Local films likewise had a poor showing in the film market module, for which the Philippine Motion Picture Producers Association (PMPPA) entered eighty-six local films. There were no takers.

Two weeks before the festival, Imelda boasted that the MIFF would generate $4 million a day, thus paying for the film center within a week. On day two of the festival, however, MIFF festival director general John J. Litton conceded that the First Lady's estimates may have been unrealistic. Addressing allegations that Imelda had merely used the festival as a pretense to build yet another monument in her City of Man, Litton stated: "The [MIFF] is not the First Lady's festival; it is the Filipino people's festival. It is the Philippines which is at stake."[33]

This brings us back to MIFF '83. As a bread-and-circuses project, Imelda's festival had to do better than its predecessor. Imelda's team thus decided to make the festival a citywide affair (with 157 commercial theaters showing festival films in conjunction with film center screenings), raise the price of admission, and show uncensored films as a "come-on for the mark-up of admission prices."[34]

The strategy proved to be an overwhelming success. After only five hours of screening on opening day, the turnout of moviegoers at the festival's "external venues" had broken box office records. Particularly so in the downtown university belt, where theaters were raking in as much as Php 20,000 on the first screening alone. This was Php 5,000 more than what Metro Manila theaters normally earned in one day.[35] As early as noon, theaters were forced to display Standing Room Only signboards to hold off the crush of juvenile patrons clamoring to get in.

All the commotion centered on three Filipino films, which had been previously banned by the board of censors: Celso Ad. Castillo's *Virgin People,* Artemio Marquez's *Naiibang hayop* (A different kind of animal), and Leroy Salvador's *The Victim.* Also drawing record crowds were two foreign films: *Julia,* featuring Sylvia Kristel (star of *Emmanuelle* and *Lady Chatterley's Lover*), and a German sex comedy called *Joy of Flying.* All five films had one or more elements previously deemed "pornographic" by the Marcos regime: "frontal nudity, masturbation, copulation, rape and sexual violence."[36]

These developments were especially befuddling, given that the New Republic had ushered in the most repressive film censorship system the country had ever seen. In 1981, Marcos yet again revamped the board of censors, which was renamed the Board of Review for Motion Pictures and Television (BRMPT). Marcos appointed Maria Kalaw Katigbak, a former beauty title holder and ex-senator, as chair of the new censorship body. Under Katigbak's leadership, the BRMPT's authority expanded well beyond the rating of films. It now "issued, denied, revoked, or recalled permits of film importers, producers, distributors, broadcasters, and exporters."[37]

The censorship issue had haunted the maiden run of the MIFF the previous year, when industry representatives bemoaned the double standard then being applied to local films. While film imports with politically bold themes and sexually explicit content were being screened at the film center, Filipino exhibition films were banned from the city's theaters.[38] The double standard triggered a panic in the local film industry. What was to stop the regime from showing uncensored foreign films at specialized theaters year-round? If that should happen, the industry stood to lose a sizeable chunk of its audience.

The industry's worst fears were realized just days after the first MIFF ended. On January 29, 1982, Marcos issued Executive Order 770, creating the Experimental Cinema of the Philippines.[39] First Daughter Imee Marcos was named director general. In her first press conference, she stated, "To be frank with you, we simply cannot let this huge building [the film center] go to waste by using it only once a year for two weeks."[40] The ECP, she said, would complement the MIFF by maintaining a year-round schedule of activities, including screenings of the "best of world cinema" and the funding of artistically promising films. The ECP, in other words, was simultaneously an exhibitor of foreign films and a producer of local ones—with government backing.

The creation of the ECP had effectively split the local cinema into two domains: a commercial cinema beleaguered by strict censorship and onerous taxation and a state-supported "parallel cinema" sheltered from those burdens. Marcos's executive order had ensured that the nation's censorship laws would not apply to ECP films—whether imported or produced by the film body. Furthermore, all the ECP's assets, acquisitions, and income were exempt from taxes imposed by the government. Local film producers, on the other hand, were surrendering up to 52 percent of gross receipts to the government—a truly astonishing sum if one considers that in other Asian countries producers paid an average tax of only 10 percent on films.[41]

Litton, the incumbent MIFF director general, was appointed deputy director general of the ECP. The Imelda loyalist was one of the biggest importers of foreign films. Fearing that with Litton on board, the ECP would favor the importation of foreign films, the industry's screen director's guild publicly opposed the creation of the ECP.[42] ECP officials maintained, however, that the importation of films and the screenings of uncensored films were just a means to an end. The ultimate goal was to produce quality films and to help the industry become more viable.

Two films produced by the ECP, *Oro, plata, mata* (Gold, silver, death; Gallaga, 1983) and *Himala* (Miracle; Bernal, 1982), were shown at the festival. The former was entered in the film competition; the latter was honored by being the featured presentation on opening night.[43] But these prestige productions were eclipsed by the sensation stirred by *Virgin People, Naiibang hayop,* and *The*

Victim. Box office receipts indicated that the commercial bombas were simply more popular with festival audiences. *Virgin People* grossed Php 15 million, *Naiibang hayop* Php 13 million. *Oro, plata, mata,* on the other hand, grossed only Php 1.7 million.[44]

Virgin People, Naiibang hayop, and *The Victim* had become highly controversial, not only because they appeared to be the clear winners in the bitter rivalry between the commercial cinema and the ECP but also because these films were reportedly shown with previously cut portions restored. The splicing in of pornographic content at the point of exhibition was a key feature of the pre-martial-law bomba's "subversive" conditions of reception (see chapter 3). The festival saw local film producers and exhibitors reviving this notorious practice, and it didn't take long for the moral guardians of the social order to react to the offense.

On day three of the festival, Marcos stated that he had not been aware of "the irregularities," and vowed to wage a crackdown on the offenders.[45] Marcos's statements piggybacked on the initiatives of the archbishop of Manila, Jaime Cardinal Sin, who stated that the showing of uncensored films at MIFF was corrupting the nation's youth. Sin urged the government to station soldiers and policemen outside cinema houses to keep minors from entering, thereby protecting them from "influences that could be insidious and detrimental." Manila mayor Ramon Bagatsing joined the chorus, vowing to place all theaters "under close watch." Theater owners guilty of violating city ordinances against overcrowding and the entry of minors were to be harshly penalized, he said.[46]

Imelda Marcos took on the moral crusaders—including her own husband. At a press conference held on January 28, Imelda stated that the showing of uncensored films was "part of growing up and meant to elevate public taste."[47] Renewing the discourse of ethical incompleteness, a basic concept in the regime's cultural policy, she claimed that the showing of pornography would "result in a more mature and sophisticated audience."[48] Imelda's statements clearly contradicted Marcos's longstanding "national sexuality" campaign against the bomba film. Imelda's take on the bomba film's capacity to mold tasteful citizens climaxed with the following surprising statement: "For too long, our people had been too sheltered, told what is good or bad." At least for the duration of the festival, people "could see movies previously banned by the censors, and they would be able to judge for themselves."[49] Subtly referencing her role as mother in the national family, she hinted that there was nothing to fear: "Youths who have been inculcated with the proper values and attitudes would not be destroyed by one or two bold movies."[50]

Brocka and fellow New Cinema filmmaker Mike de Leon boycotted the festival and urged cineastes to do the same. Their controversial boycott came on the heels of the public debate over the festival's bomba screenings. As they put it in their press statement:

> The MIFF is encouraging the kind of cynical commercialism which is rampant in the movie industry but which a filmfest is supposed to combat. The deleterious effects of such a policy is [sic] even now apparent. Producers are drawing up plans to make, not serious films tackling serious themes, but more sex-exploitation quickies. We fear that succumbing to crass commercialism in this regard, the MIFF has created a situation which makes a moralistic backlash inevitable—and which would ultimately justify the imposition of more restrictions on freedom of expression in the cinema.[51]

Brocka and Deleon's "crusade" revealed the New Cinema's ambivalent position with respect to the ECP, on the one hand, and the commercial film industry, on the other. Both institutions appeared to shun the New Cinema's commitment to political filmmaking.

In the brouhaha over the festival's bomba screenings, the beleaguered commercial cinema was the fulcrum in the blame game that ensued between his and her loyalists in the national family. From Marcos's camp, Maj. Gen. Prospero Olivas conducted an investigation on the illicit screenings of *Virgin People, Naiibang hayop,* and *The Victim,* and found that "a percentage of the income would go to some people in the festival committee."[52] PMPPA president Marichu Maceda conceded that local producers agreed to cooperate with Entertainment Philippines Corporation, a management firm set up to handle the finances of the MIFF. Local producers agreed to take home only 20 percent of the total gross receipts—instead of the usual 50 percent, she said. For their part, exhibitors agreed to accept only 15 percent.[53] And so, the vilified commercial cinema, which the moral crusaders and even the New Cinema filmmakers had charged with exploiting bombas, was in fact performing a kind of charity work for the MIFF.

From Imelda's camp, festival president Sylvia P. Montes argued that a portion of the box office receipts would go to the "country's disabled and disadvantaged."[54] Montes was a social services minister, and the festival itself was attached to the social services projects of Imelda's Ministry of Human Settlements. The proceeds from the showing of bomba films would thus finance the ministry's "special projects."

Marcos would have the last say in this squabble. Two days before the festival closed, he signed Executive Order 866. The order further expanded Katigbak's censorship powers. Now renamed the Board of Review for Motion Pictures, Television, *and Live Entertainment* (BRMPTLE), the board of censors was given jurisdiction over concerts, plays, even fashion shows. With respect to the cinema, the executive order required all master negatives to be permanently relinquished to the board, which now had the power to destroy censored scenes or films in their entirety.[55]

EO 866 prompted cultural workers to do something they had never done before. On February 11, 1983, thousands of creative people—a number of decorated national artists among them—staged the country's first anticensorship rally. The rally was Brocka's brainchild. He had stressed that the rally "had no political coloration" and that the participants would not involve themselves with human rights, civil liberties, or radical agendas. They would stick to the issue of censorship because that was the unifying theme affecting the cultural community at the moment. Or as de Leon put it, censorship was "the shelling that struck the backyard."[56] More than anything else, the Free the Artist Movement (FTA) rally was intended to prove that "the fractious citizens of culture" could organize.[57]

The upshot of the rally was that Marcos withdrew EO 868. An optimistic Brocka stated, "For me, that's a start. Somehow, they're finally listening; somehow, things can be done."[58] The FTA movement soon expanded to become the Concerned Artists of the Philippines (CAP). This new movement would align itself with the NDF's united front against the Marcos regime. Brocka was named chairman, with journalist and screenwriter Jose F. Lacaba as secretary general. The fight against censorship, though still a cornerstone of CAP's activism, was now broadened to encompass the political and economic issues portrayed by the New Cinema auteurs. What ultimately propelled the movement to let go of its earlier inhibitions was the assassination of Benigno Aquino.

The Aquino Assassination

On August 21, 1983, Aquino returned to the Philippines after three years of self-imposed exile in the United States. Outside Manila International Airport yellow streamers fluttered in abundance (a nod to the 1973 pop song "Tie a Yellow Ribbon Round the Old Oak Tree," about a prisoner returning home). Under the noonday sun twenty thousand people waited to welcome home the most famous figure of the opposition movement. They chanted "Ninoy! Ninoy!"—the moniker by which the politician was affectionately called by friends and supporters. Some time after Aquino's plane landed, a distraught ex-senator, Salvador Laurel, who had organized the welcome rally, called for silence. "I have grave news to tell you," he said to a hushed crowd, "I heard that Senator Aquino has been shot."[59] What the crowd—and the whole shocked nation—would later learn was that Aquino had been killed seconds after disembarking the plane in the custody of three military men.

Aquino, whose 1977 death sentence was reinstated by Marcos in July 1983, knew he was risking his life by returning home. His immediate goal was to organize the opposition for the May 1984 legislative elections; his long-term purpose was to convince Marcos to work toward "national reconciliation."[60]

In June 1983 Aquino presented the essential points of his case before the Subcommittee on Asian and Pacific Affairs of the U.S. House of Representatives. The Philippine economy had deteriorated; so, too, had Marcos's health. The opposition was divided, and many demoralized moderates were now supporting the communist insurgency. Should Marcos die, the military was likely to seize power; "their tactics and the disastrous economic situation could only result in a further slide into violence."[61] Before it was too late, Aquino said he needed to personally convince Marcos to "loosen the reins of authoritarianism and institute crucial national reforms."[62]

Imelda Marcos made a special trip to New York in May to dissuade Aquino from returning. In their meeting she spoke of specific assassination plots and reportedly warned, "Ninoy, there are people loyal to us who cannot be controlled."[63] In July, while attempting to renew his passport at the Philippine consulate in New York, Aquino was advised to delay his trip for one month or until the government had succeeded in "neutralizing" the assassination threat; his request for travel papers was denied. On August 2, Aquino received another warning, this one from Defense Minister Juan Ponce Enrile, who cabled that the military was "convinced beyond a reasonable doubt" of a plot against his life. Once again, Aquino was advised to delay his trip by at least a month.[64]

These warnings coincided with the news that Marcos's health had taken a turn for the worse. On August 5 the *New York Times* reported that Marcos was going into a "three-week seclusion to write books."[65] Indeed, two weeks before Aquino's scheduled return, Marcos had a top-secret kidney transplant.[66] Aquino had heard rumors of Marcos's worsening health from his contacts in Manila; his contacts in Washington had also warned him that the dictator might be using the "seclusion" to reorganize his government.

The succession struggle within Marcos's "household" had devolved into a contest between Imelda Marcos and Defense Minister Enrile. But Enrile had just lost a running battle with Gen. Fabian Ver over military appointments. Ver, who was Marcos's close relative, was now chief of staff of the AFP, commanding general of the PSC and head of the National Intelligence and Security Authority. It had become clear to many palace insiders that an Imelda-Ver alliance had formed, and that these two most powerful figures in the divided Marcos household were poised to seize power.[67] For Aquino, then, coming home had become an even more urgent matter.

Aquino was in Taipei, ready to start the last leg of his return trip, when he received the latest news wire from Manila: General Ver had said that Aquino might be assassinated at the airport. At a press conference just that evening, Aquino had made an announcement that would later cement his status as a "willing martyr" for the opposition: "If my fate is to die by an assassin's bullet, so be it."[68] To his sister, Lupita Kashiwahara, who had arrived days ahead to help coordinate his welcome rally, he entrusted this posthumous message to the Filipino people: "If I die, so be it. But I hope my death will awaken our people to the need to stand up and fight for themselves."[69]

The details of Aquino's tragic journey are now well known. He had traveled with a false passport, under the name of Marcial Bonifacio. The first name stood for martial law, the surname for the camp in which he had been imprisoned for more than seven years. On board with him on China Airlines Flight 811 was his brother-in-law, ABC correspondent Ken Kashiwahara, who would later write a gripping first-person account of the assassination for the *New York Times*. Also on board were a Japanese television crew and a group of journalists from *Time*, UPI, and ABC.[70] "You have to be ready with your hand camera," Aquino is recorded as saying, "because the action can happen very fast. In a matter of three, four minutes, it could be all over and I may not be able to talk to you again." As soon as the plane landed, at 1:04 p.m., an announcement over the plane's intercom instructed passengers to "remain seated." Three soldiers then entered the cabin to collect Aquino. Plainclothes security guards pushed back the newsmen who tried to follow and immediately shut the cabin door. Seconds later, a single shot rang out. Aquino had made it near the bottom of the service stairs when that bullet penetrated his skull from behind, exiting through his chin. This was followed by a torrent of gunfire from the police. A man later identified as Rolando Galman fell dead just a few feet away from Aquino's body. The government would claim that Galman was the assassin and that he was connected to the NPA.

Within minutes of Aquino's death, news of the assassination had traveled the world. But in the Philippines, news broadcasts of the murder were delayed by at least two hours. And when the TV networks finally reported the tragedy, they merely stated that Aquino was "shot."[71] It was through Radio Veritas, a Catholic station, that most Filipinos were first informed about the killing. From 1:00 p.m. to midnight that night, Veritas was on the air to give a running account of what was happening.[72]

That night, Metro Manila was "plunged in darkness"—both literally and figuratively—as a "power blackout was compounded by a news blackout on the assassination and worsened by Marcos' non-appearance on television, spawning rumors of either his impending death or a coup d'état."[73] The next day, *Bulletin Today,* the *Times Journal,* and the *Daily Express* had identical banner headlines: "AQUINO SHOT DEAD." Significantly, the papers contained no editorial comments on the murder.[74] Radio Veritas was far more proactive in following the story, broadcasting from Aquino's home on Times Street, Quezon City, where the ex-senator's body lay in state.

The grieving family chose not to take down the placards and buntings that had been hung the day before the ex-senator's arrival. "Happy Homecoming, Ninoy Aquino," one of them read.[75] The message took on a particular poignancy when Aquino's coffin arrived that morning. At the request of his mother, Doña Aurora

Aquino, the open casket displayed the ex-senator's body in the bloodied white suit that he was wearing when he was killed. His brutally disfigured face had not been touched up "so that the world could see what they had done to my son," she said.[76] Radio Veritas's ongoing broadcasts propelled hundreds of mourners to pay their respects. Within a few days, an estimated one hundred thousand people came to view Aquino's body, "filing by the coffin at a rate of one person every two seconds, twenty-four hours a day."[77]

On August 31 two million Filipinos attended Aquino's funeral—an outpouring of grief that lasted twelve hours. The ex-senator's widow, Corazon Cojuangco Aquino, briefly addressed the mourners gathered at the Santo Domingo Church. The soft-spoken housewife said a few words that powerfully captured her husband's twenty-nine years in politics: "Ninoy, who loved you, the Filipino people, *is now loved in return*."[78] Eliciting thunderous applause, the brief statement contained the dramatic arc of Aquino's career from traditional politician to political prisoner, and from exile to martyr. Indeed, he seemed to have achieved in death what had eluded him in life: the belief of the Filipino people in his "sincerity" as a politician. And it was the funeral's channeling of the visible "proof" of Aquino's "sacrifice" that made even the most jaded cynics believe, as former *Bulletin* columnist Ninez Cacho Olivares later put it, "Because [Aquino] was a politician, [I thought] he may not have had the interests of the Filipino at heart; that he may not have loved his country and our people. I looked at his ashen face, the bullet wound, and the blood all over his shirt. No, Ninoy, I said to myself. I have no more doubts. You loved your country and your people. God be with you, always, wherever you may be."[79]

Collective grief over the assassination had transformed Aquino into a national hero. Expunged forever was Aquino's past as a traditional politician, whose involvement in the LFM and A6LM terror bombings had once raised the question "whether he would be much different from Marcos should he become president."[80]

The transformation of Aquino from symbol of elite politics into icon of the popular struggle against the regime required a "switching of signs" that was made possible by the emergence of an alternative press.[81] Indeed, the sentimental politics of this press amplified the affective dynamics of the "national grief" on display during Aquino's funeral.

National Grief and the Rise of the Alternative Press

Jaime Cardinal Sin's funeral homily presciently articulated the transformative power of the nation's collective grief: "[To Ninoy's challenge] our people are waiting for a reply [from the state]. They wait, no longer as timid and scattered sheep, but as men and women purified and strengthened by a profound communal grief that has made them one."[82] Signs of the mobilizing power of this grief were everywhere, in the placards and T-shirts of the 2 million mourners who followed Aquino's hearse from the Santo Domingo Church to his final resting place, at Loyola Memorial Park. *Ninoy, hindi ka nagiisa* (Ninoy, you are not alone) was the ubiquitous slogan.

Nothing of the funeral was shown on Philippine television.[83] The crony newspapers were just as conspicuously remiss. The nation's collective grief needed to be publicly aired; and the regime's news blackout was not easily forgotten. The recently formed Justice for Aquino, Justice for All movement (JAJA) issued the following statement on media repression shortly after the funeral: "Though two million Filipinos marched in the Aquino funeral and millions more expressed their sympathy throughout the country, media coverage was extremely inadequate. To the media, it was as if the vast numbers of Filipinos crying out for freedom and justice did not exist. . . . Government censors even went to the extent of ordering editors not to use words like "assassination" and "sympathizers" but to substitute more neutral terms like "killing" or "mourners."[84] The statement called for a boycott of the crony press: "Ban the *Bulletin!* Suppress the *Express!* Junk the *Journal!*" It called on news consumers to support *Mr. & Ms., WHO, Business Day, Malaya,* and the *Philippine Times.* These publications had covered the Aquino assassination in ways that recalled the "little tradition" of Philippine protest journalism.

The little tradition was a protest press that emerged in the colonial era. These local publications in the vernacular dedicated themselves to airing popular grievances and thereby set themselves apart from the Manila-centered, English-language, elite-oriented press.[85] An aversion to politics was a basic feature of this tradition, which sought to save the political as a site of aspiration for change.[86] Its ideal reader was a social activist, one who would engage in organizational activity near/against/below the domain of "official politics"; one who would put themselves at risk in order to champion the cause of the "Filipino underclasses."

During martial law the little tradition was upheld by mimeographed newssheets and small independent news publications like *We Forum* (a magazine published by press freedom crusader Jose Burgos), *Ichthys* (a newsletter published by the AMRSP), and *Ang bayan* (the underground news organ of the CPP-NPA).[87] However, this recent iteration of the tradition had a more pronounced sentimental ethos: it addressed socially aware yet culturally privileged audiences, from whom it sought to elicit compassion. Though these publications deployed various epistemological frameworks (liberalism, liberation theology, and Marxism, respectively) to compel their imagined readers to take political action, "true feeling" was always part of the equation. The litmus test of sentimental politics for their privileged readers was identification with the pain of the oppressed. Indeed, these publications staked their moral power on the pain of the oppressed. Consequently, their national allegories made a melodramatic imaginary an essential feature of social analysis. This imaginary, the product of an affective rationality, holds that to truly apprehend the "national question," it is necessary to "interrupt cognition, to test a view against feeling's higher truth."[88]

After the Aquino assassination, *Business Day, Malaya, Mr. & Ms.*, and the tabloid *Philippine Times* were at the forefront of a mode of sentimental publicity not unlike the protest press of years past; only this time, their stories were dedicated to channeling national grief. They actively perpetuated Aquino's martyr image; a passage from *Mr. & Ms.* is representative: "Gazing at his blood-soaked chest and his wounded face still bearing its bullet-marks, . . . a grief stricken people were actually gazing not only at Ninoy Aquino but at themselves, bloodied and wounded by a long history of colonial domination, still suffering from foreign and native oppression."[89]

In melodramatic language that clearly instantiates the discursive power of national allegory, the statement presents Aquino's slain body as a conduit to national self-understanding: to encounter Aquino's body is to experience, at a deeply personal level, the nation's long struggle with colonialism and neocolonialism. In this account, Aquino's figure becomes a prismatic "surface" that brings the macroprocesses of state repression and neocolonialism into sharp focus. But as a vital "prop" in this dramaturgical process, Aquino's wounded body ceases to be the indexical trace of a historical figure. It becomes instead a discursive mirror, reflecting and refracting the social realities reported by the alternative media. This mirroring was subversive to the extent that it demanded acts of heroism borne out of—and purified by—national grief. As a letter to the editor of *Malaya* put it, "If we are not willing to die, I am afraid we will be responsible for the death of another, and still another, Ninoy. *For God's sake, for once in our lives, let's be Marcial Bonifacio.*"[90] Not Benigno Aquino, but Marcial Bonifacio. Not the elite opposition leader calling for "national reconciliation" but the "willing martyr" whose death was now compelling the Filipino people to place themselves in a new revolutionary scenario.

That the alternative press was characterizing Aquino as a martyr was less a case of "literary overkill" than an allegorical channeling of the "meaningful politics" described by Ileto. An alternative to politics as usual, this alterative politics had "remained the minor partner of a politics defined as colonial, national, central and elite." As a buried epistemology, this meaningful politics centered on the veneration of the dead, and worked to mobilize a radical patriotism colored by intensely personal feelings. We have seen this at work in

the immediate aftermath of the 1978 stolen elections, when protestors sang the nationalist song *Bayan ko* (My country)—the haunt-
ing lyrics of which "evokes deep pity for a suffering motherland."[91]
It was through the melodramatic signs and symbols of this "other
politics," then, that the alternative press turned Aquino's public
image "inside-out."[92]

But the alternative press's calls for bravery on the part of the
culturally privileged reader gets clawed back to the much safer
ground of sentimental politics. Aquino's inside-out image is just
that—an image. Aquino, the historical person, has to die in order
to become a quasi-religious icon that mediates both the suffering
of the Filipino underclasses and the compassionate leadership of
the culturally privileged. In death he mediates the pain of the oppressed *and* the social responsibility of the privileged, without fully
embodying either. The sentimental politics of the alternative press
offers a solution to the suffering of the popular classes: the sacrifice of the privileged. But this sacrifice is confined to the aesthetic,
which emerges as a healing space for an intimate public.

Scenes and stories of national grief activate an aesthetic fascina-
tion in the sentimental reader. For such a reader, the slain body
of the martyr occasions an aesthetic encounter, not with an object
of beauty, but with an object of true feeling. Aquino's "sacrifice"
enjoins the reader to feel the ethical imperative toward social
transformation. And in heeding the injunction to perform national
grief, the reader experiences the sublime thrill of the sentimental
text: the feeling of belonging to a community of pain marked by a
"fantastic transpersonal intimacy." Aquino's image, which hovers
both beyond and within the political, thus "renders a seam at the
place where *the political* exists as an intimate sphere to one side of
politics."[93] Aquino's sentimental reinvention as a "willing martyr,"
in short, has purified the political sphere as a space of optimism to
one side of politics as usual.

Malaya, Mr. & Ms., and the *Philippine Times* were the beneficiaries of a dramatic shift in public confidence as the populace embraced JAJA's call for a media boycott. Almost overnight, Filipinos

were driven to the alternative media "in search of news that the controlled media refused to print."[94]

Malaya was an offshoot of the opposition journal *We Forum,* which had printed a series of articles questioning Marcos's war record. This directly led to the magazine's closure by the authorities, in December 1982.[95] The NPC and the International Press Institute publicly denounced the *We Forum* closure, prompting Marcos to order the temporary release of its publisher and several staff writers from detention. The group proceeded to reinvent *Malaya,* which was then a limited-circulation Tagalog-language weekly. The day after the Aquino assassination, *Malaya* ran the full text of Aquino's arrival statement—the speech he intended to read at his welcome rally—and issued ninety thousand copies instead of its usual fifteen thousand. Public demand for news on the killing was so intense that Burgos had to mobilize his entire family to produce extra editions.[96] By 1984, *Malaya* had become the "first opposition daily in twelve years."[97]

Mr. & Ms. released a "Ninoy" supplement on the week following the assassination. The day after the funeral, the magazine came out with a second special edition with "numerous photos of the unprecedented event and reprints of previously inaccessible wire agency stories." Publisher-editor Eugenia Apostol was one of the women journalists "invited" to Fort Bonifacio for interrogation by the military in 1982. Other women journalists harassed by the military became regular contributors to subsequent special editions of *Mr. and Ms.*[98]

In September 1983, almost a full year before the commission appointed to investigate the assassination issued its formal report, the *Philippine Times* ran a story implicating the military in the Aquino assassination. In retaliation, soldiers closed down the tabloid on September 29 and two days later arrested its publisher-editor, Rommel Corro.[99] Corro was charged with sedition under PD 1834. He was released only in November 1984, after the Supreme Court ruled in favor of his wife's petition for bail and for habeas corpus. Many, however, felt that a "facilitating factor" was the fact that the findings of the Agrava Fact-Finding Board "coincided with the contents of the *Philippine Times* story."[100] But Corro's case was an exception. Other journalists were arrested without hope of a fair trial. Furthermore, in 1984 alone, a total of five journalists were the victims of extrajudicial killings in the hands of the military: *Mindaweek* reporter Alex Orcullo, *Philippine Post* reporter Geoffrey Siao, *Mindanao Observer* publisher Jacobo Amatong, Radio DXCP commentator Florante Castro, and *Manila Business Weekly* reporter Noe Alejandrino.[101]

Even *Veritas,* a weekly publication created by Jaime Cardinal Sin and bankrolled by the Bishops-Businessmen's Conference, was constantly harassed. Its editor, Felix Bautista, received death threats almost weekly. The harassment peaked when the Agrava board was preparing to release its findings, in August 1984.[102] The board's majority report accused Ver and several other military men of plotting the Aquino assassination. Bautista's staff managed to secure an advance copy of the report, which hit the newsstands minutes after the report was submitted to President Marcos.[103]

The NPC's Committee to Protect Writers nonetheless found that the "Philippine press [was] in some respects freer . . . than at any time since the imposition of Martial Law in 1972."[104] Notwithstanding the harassment of journalists, a true oppositional press now existed for the first time in over a decade, and it enjoyed broad support from middle-class Filipinos—the captive audience and intimate public of the new alternative media.

Chapter 6

THE NEW POLITICS, LINO BROCKA, AND PEOPLE POWER

After the Aquino assassination, the streets of Manila erupted with angry demonstrations almost every day. An estimated 265 demonstrations took place from August 1983 to February 1984.[1] The rallies saw two powerful groups, the Catholic Bishops' Conference and the business class, belatedly joining the protest movement. However, at this juncture, the NDF represented the "biggest, best-organized and most militant force within the broad anti-Marcos movement."[2] It, too, embraced the "new politics" emerging in the streets—a "pressure politics" that eschewed elections in favor of public performances of "an analytically powerful and political rage."[3] However, behind the scenes, the NDF's vanguardist practices threatened to undermine the newfound solidarity of the anti-Marcos movement.

The Vanguardism of the Radical Left

Three days after the Aquino assassination, the CPP issued the following statement:

> The former Senator and we had our differences over how to bring about the downfall of the Marcos fascist regime. . . .

But our objectives—to end the hated regime—run parallel to each other. In many ways, his efforts and ours complemented each other as we fought a common enemy of the Filipino people. The party and the entire Filipino people recognize Aquino's immense contribution to the struggle against the regime. His example and sacrifice leave all of us a concrete lesson: that all forces must unite, persist in all forms of struggle against it, bring about its downfall at the earliest possible time, and attain the Filipino people's national and social liberation.[4]

Noting Aquino's "example and sacrifice," the CPP became an active participant in the construction of Aquino's martyr image in the alternative media. The party's calls for unity among the various factions of the anti-Marcos movement must be taken with a grain of salt, however. The party had always maintained a "united-front" policy, but that policy was hardly straightforward.

When the NDF was created, in 1973, the CPP made alliance with any anti-Marcos group contingent on that group's acceptance of the party's armed revolution.[5] In 1977, however, the NDF softened the "shrill Maoist syntax" of its united front policy, emphasizing instead the creation of a "democratic coalition government" based on the principle of political pluralism.[6] By the time of the Aquino assassination, this position had attracted a large number of political moderates, including businessmen, lawyers, doctors, journalists, and liberal politicians. By 1984 the NDF would lay claim to fifty thousand full-time organizers operating in two-thirds of the country's provinces. The NDF had over 1 million members in its constituent organizations—the labor group May First Movement (KMU), the Christians for National Liberation (CNL), the Nationalist Youth (KM), the League of Filipino Students (LFS), the Movement of Philippine Peasants (KMP), the Women against Marcos Boycott (WOMB), the Movement of Free and Unified Women (SAMAKANA), the Nationalist Health Association (MASAPA) and the Association of Nationalist Teachers (KAGUMA), among others—with a mass base of an additional 10 million.[7]

Meanwhile, the NPA was gaining dramatically in the countryside. The U.S. Department of Defense noted that the NPA had an estimated guerrilla strength of ten thousand and was "active in nearly all areas of the country." Government casualties were higher than ever, making 1983 the "most active year in the long-standing government-insurgent struggle."[8] It bears emphasizing that for the CPP, the NDF's united front work was primarily aimed at supporting the war in the countryside.[9]

Some CPP cadres secretly described the NDF's united-front policy as *bahay-pera-frente* (house-money-front). The term captured the party's "tendency to use middle class contacts for financial support and shelter without building relationships of mutual interest and trust."[10] Meanwhile, CPP cadres actively sought to micromanage the popular organizations making up the NDF's base among the masses. The party held that the struggle for state power claimed strategic priority; all other "micro" causes—such as women's rights, minority rights, and environmental rights—were to be treated as subservient to it.[11] Consequently, the party's relationship with cause-oriented groups tended to be "top-down, hierarchical, even patriarchal." The CPP sought to influence the NDF's constituent organizations from within through clandestine party cells; it also used a political-officer system to exact discipline from without. Though the party did in fact provide much-needed guidance and infrastructural support to popular forces during the darkest days of martial law, its subsequent efforts to control popular organizations produced a reverse effect: "from being instruments of popular empowerment," so-called party-influenced organizations within the NDF had become "mere 'transmission belts' of party policies and directives."[12]

These "undemocratic" features of the NDF were acutely felt in May 1985, during the disastrous founding congress of the Bagong Alyansang Makabayan (BAYAN) or New Patriotic Alliance. The congress sought to "unify and consolidate the leadership of popular organizations."[13] However, National Democrats pressed for more seats for organizations representing laborers, farmers, students, the urban poor, fishermen, and teachers, arguing that these organizations far outnumbered those of the other factions. By the second day of the congress, the Social Democrats and the Liberal Democrats walked out, charging National Democrats with conspiring "to increase the electors in favor of the dominant (Left) forces."[14] An atmosphere of paranoia had thus derailed the BAYAN congress. Opponents feared that the CPP was using the NDF's main strength—the strength of numbers—to dictate the terms of the protest movement.

To rival BAYAN, Social Democrats and Liberal Democrats created a new opposition coalition, Bansang Nagkaisa sa Diwa at Layunin (BANDILA), or Nation United in Spirit and Purpose. BANDILA rejected the armed struggle of the CPP and saw itself as an "alternative mass-oriented opposition" shunning both the "patronage politics of the traditional Right" and the "overcentralized vanguardism of the extreme Left."[15]

The parliament of the streets bore clear marks of the divided opposition. On August 21 (the anniversary of the Aquino's assassination) and September 21 (marking the declaration of martial law), separate demonstrations took place. The rivalry between BAYAN and BANDILA manifested itself in the colors of the banners: red for National Democrats, yellow for Social Democrats and Liberals. The "monochrome rallies" were a far cry from the inclusive—and literally colorful—mass actions immediately after the assassination.

The climate of mutual distrust and hostility rending the opposition movement negatively impacted those whom BAYAN and BANDILA had both claimed to champion—the Filipino masses. Torn between the vanguardism of the NDF and the patronage politics of the elite and middle-class opposition, marginalized Filipinos had to bargain with both camps in their struggles against the Marcos dictatorship. The activism of New Cinema filmmaker Lino Brocka powerfully captured the embattled position of these non-elite actors.

Lino Brocka, Political Activist

In the heady days just after the assassination, Lino Brocka quickly became a beloved figure of the new politics. The New Cinema filmmaker was one of the core members of JAJA. He had entered the protest movement at a time when the various factions of the anti-Marcos movement were still by and large supportive of one another. National Democrats routinely attended prayer rallies set up by rival Social Democrats; the latter, in turn, were willing to overlook their longstanding enmity with the communists to support NDF demonstrations. And venerated politicians like Diokno and Tañada legitimized the new "pressure politics" of JAJA. Indeed, it was Diokno who coined the term, arguing that mass actions were the most expedient method for pressuring Marcos to institute crucial reforms, or even better, to step down from power.[16]

Brocka was so taken by the concept of "pressure politics" that in the next two years he devoted himself entirely to protest work. He stopped making movies; he became penniless. The righteous indignation buoying JAJA was enough to sustain him. But even during the protest movement's early days, the filmmaker harbored doubts about the sincerity of the traditional politicians in the movement. "Politicians are using Ninoy for their own ends," Brocka was wont to tell close associates. But thinking that JAJA's "great numbers" were the movement's "biggest weapon against the giant Marcos," he held his anger in check.[17]

Brocka was a member of BAYAN. He felt an immediate connection with the NDF's many popular organizations—labor, peasant, and urban-poor groups—whose grievances he sympathetically portrayed in his "socially relevant" melodramas. As he would put it to his fellow New Cinema filmmakers, they were *"mga kauri natin"* (of our class).[18] When many moderates abandoned the coalition, Brocka remained a steadfast BAYAN supporter.

Brocka's loyalty to BAYAN earned him a reputation as a leftist activist. But only four years earlier, in 1981, Brocka was "rabidly anti-Left." At the time, Brocka was the executive director of the

Philippine Educational Theater Association (PETA), an activist group that performed politically oriented plays. It had come to his attention that a CPP cell had infiltrated the organization. Brocka called a meeting. The session quickly devolved into an inquisition, as Maglipon recounts:

> One artist broke down. Feeling he had to protect the others, he spoke up: "If there was a group, it [did not intend] to manipulate [PETA members]." But Lino would not be deterred in his mission. His grilling trudged on, prying out names, activities, culpability. He wanted this fellow now to confess all. It got so scary two boys walked out while one girl vomited. . . . When it seemed no one could breathe anymore, [PETA actress Cecilia Garrucho] remembers crying out: "Stop it! What do you want? His blood?" Only then did Lino stop.[19]

Brocka's communist witch hunt was driven by paranoia. As Garrucho later conceded, "it was the time of living dangerously." The year 1981 was indeed a terrible one, when heightened militarization saw a dramatic escalation of preventive arrests, disappearances, and salvagings. It was also the year when PETA began taking exposure trips to the countryside. But Brocka hardly needed to be convinced that poverty and militarization were real. He simply did not see the CPP-NPA as serving the best interests of the popular classes. His loathing for the communists was not based on his objection to the CPP's political doctrines; rather, it stemmed from his own melodramatic code of right and wrong: "His was a right and wrong that the modern world no longer sees much of: a code of moralisms . . . spreading its clamps over behavior both private and public, impervious to change in clime and era, wary of explanations, disdainful of compromise."[20]

In Brocka's moral code, the *sincerity* of political leaders claiming to champion the poor mattered more than the substance of conservative, moderate, and radical viewpoints. Doubtful that the CPP's armed struggle was directly benefiting the poor, Brocka was equally distrustful of liberal, Church, and business groups in the protest movement. To be sure, Brocka was unclear about the political differences between National Democrats and Social Democrats, and needed CAP colleague Jose Lacaba to explain. Brocka remained perplexed: "'So what am I?' 'That depends,' [Lacaba] answered. 'What do you want to happen in this country?' Without a by your leave, Lino answered, 'Oh, I just want to bomb Malacañang, the MIFF, etc.' So then [Lacaba] said to him, 'You are an anarchist.' At which, illumined, Lino went around that whole day telling friends, 'Now I know what I am. I am an anarchist! That's what Pete said, that I'm an anarchist!'"[21]

Maglipon's account makes much of Brocka's political naïveté. It is a disarming profile of the activist, whose antics call to mind the childish rebelliousness of the student activists during the First Quarter Storm. But given the privileged place accorded the performance of national grief in the postassassination rallies, Brocka's highly emotive and personal brand of activism was an asset to the broad-based protest movement.

Brocka saw himself as belonging to the popular classes and wore his lack of political expertise as a badge of honor. He was known to preface his public speeches with the disclaimer, "I am not a political scientist nor am I an economist. I do not have the expertise to debate with World Bank scholars and lawyers of multinationals." His nonexpert status was more than compensated by his readiness to translate his personal convictions into action. And frequently such action conformed to the dissidents' performances of abjection and nonnormative conduct during the First Quarter Storm. We see this at work in the following vignette from Maglipon:

> The gang had gathered in front of [the censor's] office to protest the no-show of *Dear Sam, Yours Truly, Juan,* the anti-bases documentary that the censor had decreed was "injurious to the prestige of the Republic of the Philippines." Ishmael Bernal kept pushing Lino to speak, but Lino kept declining. . . . But as he looked up at the sun beating down, he saw this TV

cameraman atop a roof. Without warning, he waved him down, then let loose instructions like a hotshot movie director: "Close-up! Close-up, okay? Close-up!" Then . . . he screeched, "Hey M——! You son of a bitch! Fag! Come down at once! We both are going to J——. Your code name there is Mafia."[22]

Brocka was performing a textbook political bomba. His target was Manuel Morato, who in 1986 replaced Katigbak as the chief of censors. Brocka, it must be pointed out, was very open about his homosexuality. The prudish Morato, however, was not. Alluding to an underground gay club (J——) to which they were both frequent customers, Brocka was publicly outing the censor. In Brocka's activism, as in his films, passion dominates intellectual debate, and it is the language of the street, not the refined discourse of the public sphere, that begs to be heard.

As an activist, Brocka's melodramatic performative style was conspicuously at odds with the urbane style of the rallies then taking place in Makati, Manila's financial district. Consider the incongruity between the above scene and the activism of the business community:

> These mass actions included religious masses and prayer rallies, marches and demonstrations, confetti and noise barrages, and other innovations such as window shopping at Rustan's (the premiere department store reportedly owned by Imelda Marcos), "pasyalan" (strolling) along Ayala Avenue, *jogging for justice.* . . . Even Filipino humor found its way early into the protest movement. Leaflets were distributed inviting the public to a dog show at Ugarte Field during the march of professionals on November 11, 1983. Pet owners were asked to dress up their dogs in Ninoy shirts and to give them "*a leisurely stroll for justice.*"[23]

The window-shopping strolls and jogs for justice in the financial and upper-class residential district of Makati could not have been further removed from the diegetic worlds of Brocka's films. The sharp contrast between the business class's mass actions (patterned after socially approved elite pastimes) and the sordid, sensational confrontation in the preceding vignette is equally jarring. The dog show rally in particular underscores the elitist ethos of the Makati demonstrations, which excluded the popular classes (who could hardly afford the luxury of lap dogs).[24]

The Makati "lifestyle" rallies, however, were a response to the climate of austerity imposed by the regime following a shocking economic scandal in late 1983. Shortly after the Aquino assassination, an IMF team discovered that the Central Bank of the Philippines had overstated the country's dollar reserves by $500 to $600 million.[25] The news triggered a financial panic. Investors spirited dollars abroad at the calamitous rate of $5 million a day.[26] Keenly aware that the economic crisis was directly linked to the political instability of the regime, business groups used the lifestyle rallies to pressure Marcos into instituting reforms. Ironically, however, the economic activities of these elites exacerbated the crisis. In the weeks after the Aquino assassination the flight of capital from the Philippines reached an estimated $700 million—a substantial portion of which represented exits in the black market.[27] Brocka was outraged by the business class's practice of engaging in capital flight, a tactic he saw as hurting the poor.

Maglipon provides another tableau that illustrates Brocka's fundamental loyalty to the popular forces marginalized by the elite and middle-class sectors of the protest movement:

> One day Lino Brocka had to give a lecture on national issues to an audience that happened to be Makati-rich. . . . The many times his fame has pushed him into rich company, he came out civilized enough—the fellow was an excellent conversationalist. . . . For a good hour, he was getting all these remarks from a [perfumed] audience about the lazy peasant and the thieving poor. Soon, his nose began to bleed. . . . That went on and on, the bleeding and the lecturing—until it was

time to go. [Later, his doctor] exclaimed: "You've burst an artery! Your blood pressure shot up too high! More of this and you could have died!"[28]

Brocka's style of debate consisted of equal parts melodrama (in the order of the popular cinema's hyperemotionality) and sentimentality (in the order of the alternative press's promotion of compassionate politics). Meanwhile, the business class used disinvestment and capital flight as political weapons and communicated to foreign lenders their doubts about the competence of the regime. The popular classes were the big losers—in a sense, collateral damage—in the business community's assault on the regime. Such tactics discomfited Brocka, whose emotional attachment to the peasantry and the lumpenproletariat often rubbed up against elite perceptions of the popular classes as politically apathetic, hence insignificant. But as Brocka himself would learn, the popular classes had no safe haven in the NDF. Indeed, they were prey to the regime's crackdown on the vanguardist methods of the CPP-NPA.

In January 1985, Brocka was arrested for participating in a jeepney drivers' strike.[29] Brocka, along with fellow New Cinema filmmaker Behn Cervantes (*Sakada*), were among the 151 protesters arrested that day. They had come to the demonstration in Cubao, a bustling section of Metro Manila, to show CAP's solidarity with the jeepney drivers, who belonged to cause-oriented groups affiliated with the NDF.

The drivers were demanding a rollback in oil and gasoline prices—issues far removed from CAP's agendas.[30] The regime nonetheless singled Brocka out as one of the strike leaders. He was slapped with the dreaded Preventive Detention Action (PDA)—and only a presidential pardon could release him.[31]

Metro Manila vice governor Ismael Mathay accused Brocka and Cervantes of intimidating drivers and commuters into joining the strike, even setting up barricades. "Join us and be part of the bloody revolution," the two men reportedly shouted.[32] These allegations may have been influenced by Brocka's reputation—an unfounded one at that—as a leftist. It is indeed ironic that the man who only four years earlier had gone on a witch hunt to rid PETA of CPP infiltrators was being accused of coercing the drivers to adhere to CPP directives.

Many of the NDF's demonstrations were in fact "command demonstrations" mobilized by the party as retaliation for state attacks against the NPA. These demonstrations complemented the hidden war in the countryside by providing a dramaturgical space for the CPP to "harvest" popular outrage against the repressive regime. In order to recruit more supporters for its insurgency campaign, the CPP was "inclined to *accelerate* demonstrations, in so-called 'outrage rallies,' when government seemed least forthcoming or most aggressive."[33] For Brocka, whose connection to the underground Left was tenuous at best, the strike was a glaring reminder of how the marginalized classes—in this case, underpaid jeepney drivers and poor commuters—were collateral damage in the CPP's efforts to make the NDF's mass actions serve insurgent—as opposed to legal, political—ends.

After eighteen grueling days, Marcos agreed to release Brocka and his group. The decision came after European and American film artists and celebrities sent letters to the dictator protesting Brocka's incarceration. At the time of his release, Brocka was especially emotional. He had been recently informed that not all the protesters at the jeepney drivers' strike had been as fortunate as he. Three bodies were fished out of the city's great river, the Pasig, just days earlier. They were among the countless strikers reported missing after the rally. "Now, more than ever, I'm dying to get to the next rally. The only way to fight them is to continue fighting them. You just don't give up—*now I have more personal reasons,*" he said.[34]

Brocka's brief though suspenseful incarceration overlapped with the controversy over his latest film, *Bayan ko: Kapit sa patalim* (My country: Seize the blade). Shown at the main competition in Cannes in May 1984, the film featured footage of postassassination rallies. Fearing that the film would be banned by the regime, Brocka preemptively smuggled the film to its French coproducers (Stephan

Films). For the next few months, CAP's political activities centered on having the film released in the Philippines—without cuts. The regime was willing to negotiate. They would allow an abridged version of the film to be shown if Brocka agreed to a For Adults Only classification. Brocka and CAP refused to compromise.

On November 6, 1985, *Bayan ko* was shown to the public—with no cuts. Significantly, the film explicitly parallels the plight of the popular classes with the ongoing mass actions of the opposition movement. For its "underclass" protagonists, it becomes increasingly clear that in these desperate times, their survival depends on the success of the protest movement.

Bayan ko: Kapit sa patalim

Bayan ko follows the downward spiral of two laborers, Turing (Philip Salvador) and Luz (Gina Alajar), who live *kapit sa patalim* (clutching the knife)—the vernacular expression for a desperate existence—in the polarized atmosphere of Manila after the Aquino assassination.[35] It is a conjugal drama that allegorically captures the options for empowerment open to the urban poor, who must choose between the patron-client relations of the old politics, the mass action strategy of the new politics, and that age-old option derided by elites as endemic to the political unreliability of the poor—violent crime.

Early in the film, we see Luz and Turing at work in a cramped shop, the Jefferson Printing Press, where gender-specific jobs are clearly demarcated and closely monitored. The shop is not unlike a family. It is a small operation that is paternalistically run by Mr. Lim (Nomer Son) and his wife, Sally (Lorli Villanueva).

A party commemorating the company's twenty-seventh anniversary powerfully encapsulates the patron-client relationships that have structured Turing and Luz's workplace. Mr. Lim opens the festivities with a thanksgiving speech. Despite an industry recession, the printing press has managed to survive another year, he says. He commends the employees for their hard work and in an awards ceremony, Mrs. Lim hands out small gifts as tokens of the company's appreciation.

The banners, balloons, speeches, and gifts call to mind a campaign rally. To borrow Xavier's terms, the scene prods the spectator to take an "analytical posture"—to perceive in the loaded iconography of the Lims' thanksgiving ceremony a "signalization" of "another scene" that is the national context as a whole.[36]

Mr. Lim's promise to keep the company going in the face of an industry crisis and Sally Lim's munificent gesture toward the company's most loyal subjects allegorize the benevolence of the elite and the loyalty of clients—the ideal qualities of the parties engaged in the patronage system. Both must abide by mutually recognized rules and expectations: patrons are duty bound to lend money during lean times and to act as sponsors in community rituals; clients are expected to prove their loyalty by freely accepting the low wages and lack of benefits characteristic of their indentured service. The notion of mutual reciprocity softens the social hierarchy underpinning the exchange of favors between "parties unequal in status, wealth and influence." But as Quimpo points out, there will always be those who "resist or try to break out of these unequal relationships," hence the nation's long history of popular rebellions. These rebellions are not simply aberrations, as proponents of elite politics would lead one to believe. The problem is that "in times of social tension the aberrations become too numerous."[37]

Turing's emotional breakdown at the company party presents one such aberration. Upstairs, in the Lim home, Mr. and Mrs. Lim are personally entertaining the company's wealthy clients, family, and friends. English dominates their discourse, and it is Sally's pretentious talk (about a new fad diet) that fills the soundtrack. Guests are plied with "imported" whiskey and are served fancy hors d'oeuvres. Downstairs, in the courtyard, rank-and-file employees are served cheap beer and barbecue. An inebriated Turing wanders upstairs and helps himself to the refreshments denied his crew. Sally Lim accosts him for his rude behavior. "I told the crew that you and

Mr. Lim are nice people," Turing says, to remind Sally of her obligations. "And *since this party is for everyone,*" he says pointedly, "I said that you wouldn't think poorly of me if I came up."[38]

The confrontation with Mrs. Lim ends badly for Turing. He makes a spectacle of himself as he physically resists Hugo (Paquito Diaz), the foreman, who is trying to pacify him. Luz, who had tried to intercede, gets the brunt of Turing's anger. Turing explodes: "The problem with you is that you always try to henpeck me. *I get criticized when I am too servile, and I get the same when I'm too assertive.* When do I ever do anything right?" The statement speaks volumes, not just about Turing and Luz's less than perfect domestic relations, but also about the popular classes whom he is clearly meant to personify. Elite and middle-class perceptions of people like Turing seem to oscillate between the two extremes of docility and brutishness—qualities that moderates and radicals alike have used to justify their own paternalistic or vanguardist (or both) stances toward the Filipino masses.

Turing's masculinity is in crisis. His sense of emasculation stems from two intervening factors. Luz hails from a privileged background. She was a student activist before martial law, and had been disowned by her well-to-do family for her radical beliefs. Her estrangement from her family, we learn, was not helped by her marriage to the *"hampas lupa"* (dirt-poor) Turing. Repeated references to her well-off father (now in exile in the United States) underscore Turing's inability to provide for Luz "as a real man should." Turing and Luz also desperately want a child. Luz, who in Turing's words "has a weak womb," has had several miscarriages—owing in no small part to the harsh realities of their meager existence. Their childless marriage is yet another glaring reminder to Turing of how he has failed as a man.

Not long after Turing's shameful outburst at the company party, however, Luz and Turing learn that she is expecting. In a scene reminiscent of the opening sequence of Brocka's *Tinimbang ka ngunit kulang* (see chapter 3), official portraits of Ferdinand and Imelda Marcos dominate the mise-en-scène as a community clinic nurse exhorts the couple to take stronger measures to avoid another miscarriage. Dwarfed by the portraits and striking a deferential posture, Turing and Luz make a pact to see the pregnancy through, whatever it takes.

The community clinic exists in a continuum with the Jefferson Printing Press: these institutions capture the "vertical chains of patron-client relationships" extending all the way from the top—from no less than the mother and father of the national family—to the lower-order surrogates of this paternalistic system. At every turn in Luz's difficult pregnancy, Turing must appeal to patrons for assistance. Naturally, he applies to Mr. Lim to grant Luz maternity leave. The "benevolent" patriarch of the printing press agrees to grant her a leave—but not a paid one. Later, when Turing can no longer pay for the expensive prenatal medications prescribed by the community clinic, he appeals once again to Mr. Lim for help. The latter seizes the opportunity to force Turing to prove yet again his loyalty to the company. Management, Mr. Lim informs Turing, has got wind that the workers are organizing a union. In exchange for a cash advance of a few pesos, Turing signs a waiver guaranteeing he will not join.

Brocka sympathetically portrays the fledgling workers' union as an alternative "family" to Luz and Turing. The union is being organized by Ka Ador (Venchito Galvez) and Aling Fely (Aida Carmona), the company's two oldest employees and hence father and mother figures to the younger workers. Ka Ador is politically inexperienced but tries in his own fashion to explain to Turing the necessity of organizing: "You know how it is, when we workers get to drinking together, we end up airing our heartaches (*"sama ng loob"*). *We think that we should do more than just share our heartaches with each other.* It is time for us to act. Our situation at the printing press will only change if we workers unite, if we join forces. In this way, we can protect our rights."

Ka Ador's speech uses the vernacular *sama ng loob* to refer to workers' grievances. The expression captures the emotive and highly personal qualities of the "meaningful politics" of the popular classes. Referring to the human core of each person, the term *loob* captures the workers' sense that the abuses at the press have hurt them fundamentally. The expression signals the failure of the related concepts *utang ng loob* (debt of gratitude) and *hiya* (saving face) to ensure the integrity of the personal ties binding patrons and clients in a patrimonial society. But as Ka Ador intuits, it is necessary to translate feelings of being wronged into a political program of action. And the end of his speech indicates that he now possesses enough knowledge of Marxist ideology to know that collective action is the answer. But Turing has already signed away his rights to join the union and it is with profound shame (*hiya*) that he reveals this to his crewmates.

Focused as it is on Luz and Turing's conjugal drama, the film asks the spectator to connect Turing's beleaguered masculinity—his desire to be a man—with the workers' struggle to "protect their rights." The film is elliptical about the work conditions at the press, but the formation of the union marks a critical break in the diegesis. Before Ka Ador's meeting with Turing, Hugo is shown rebuking tardy workers. He lightly castigates some of Turing's crewmates for napping or playing cards during their lunch break—this appears to be the extent of his powers as the foreman. But as soon as the union enters the picture, an atmosphere of paranoia and mutual distrust stifles work relations at the press. The workers are not allowed to speak to each other on the floor; and Hugo's previously infantalizing demeanor toward the workers becomes markedly more brutal. When Turing's coworker Willie (Ariosto Reyes) is unjustly terminated following a *personal* altercation with Hugo, Ka Ador and Aling Fely begin organizing the union's first strike.

Hugo pays a visit to Turing, inviting him to join the strikebreakers. Luz entreats her husband not to join. A heated argument ensues, ending with Turing hitting his wife. Luz's "accident" leads to the premature birth of their baby, and the frail infant is placed in intensive care. Like the millions of workers in the great city, Turing and Luz are uninsured. Each day in the hospital drives the couple deeper and deeper in debt.

Because patron-client relationships are all he has ever known, Turing appeals to "patrons" at the hospital to discharge Luz and the baby. But as the "acting officer" of the private hospital makes abundantly clear, the hospital will not bend its rules for "someone like him." The hospital will not discharge his wife and child unless he can come up with the money. Agitated, desperate, he physically assaults his would-be patron, even as he pathetically begs to work for free at the hospital in exchange for forgiveness of his debt. As he is being taken away by private guards, he tries in vain to remind the hospital authorities of their social obligation to "clients" such as himself. "I'm only trying to work something out with you—to reach some sort of agreement," he says. The scene marks the inherent instability of patron-client relations and the failure of the linchpin of the system—personal bargaining mechanisms—to resolve disputes between parties of unequal status and power.

Pushed against the wall, Turing feels he has no other choice but to accept Hugo's proposition. He joins the strikebreakers. In a highly emotional encounter, Willie spits on Turing, yelling, "Traitor!" That night, hired goons come to intimidate Ka Ador's crew. Something goes horribly wrong, however, and the episode turns into a massacre. Though Turing literally jumps the fence to help his former mates, it is too late. Ka Ador has been fatally shot; many others have been wounded.

In Brocka's film, the doomed strike is told in flashback. The film actually begins with Turing watching an anti-Marcos rally. There he spots Willie among the demonstrators. The two former coworkers renew old ties. Willie asks Turing to forgive him for the harsh words he had said to him at the strike. A deeply shamed Turing bids his friend farewell. It is then that the film narrates the intertwined stories of Turing and Luz's unraveling marriage and the failed strike. After the scene depicting Ka Ador's death, the film brings us back to Turing and Willie at the rally. The repetition of their leave-taking becomes a highly symbolic parting of ways. Willie's participation in the demonstration suggests that his faith in the union has expanded to a belief in the mass-action strategy of the protest movement. It is a different path than the one that awaits the apolitical Turing.

The anti-Marcos rally in this scene operates like a hall of mirrors, absorbing and refracting Ka Ador's union and the doomed strike. Indeed, the film begins with a parade of banners, each held aloft by swarms of protesters marching toward the camera. The color of the banners—red—signals that this is an NDF rally. This cue is corroborated by the fighting slogans of the National Democrats: Workers Unite in Struggle for National Freedom and Democracy; Bring Down the U.S.-Marcos Dictatorship.

The banners allow the NDF to articulate what Ka Ador had been ill equipped to say to Turing when he was trying to recruit him. The actuality footage of the rally enables the micro struggle of Ka Ador's union to be absorbed by the broader struggle of the many groups in the NDF. If, as Ka Ador had earlier suggested, it is necessary to transform the workers' feelings of discontent into political action, then these organizations are modeling the highly disciplined and ideologically informed mass action that results when the emotions of the marginalized are properly harnessed toward the performative ends of the new "pressure politics."

Nested in the film's strike flashback, however, is a markedly different rally. The footage comes by way of a shock cut. From closely framed shots of the ragtag picket line of Ka Ador's crew, the film abruptly cuts to a crane shot of a massive JAJA rally. We see hundreds of thousands of demonstrators jogging along Roxas Boulevard, all sporting yellow T-shirts bearing the silk-screened image of Ninoy Aquino. The yellow shirts and banners, the joggers' recourse to the "lifestyle" activism of the business class, the English-language discourse of the demonstrators ("We are calling on you to resist the attacks of the military and the police"), and the "noise barrage" filling the diegetic soundtrack signal the rally's elite and middle-class orientations.

Standing apart from the political spectacle on the street, Turing listens to the diegetic strains of "Bayan ko" flooding the scene. We hear his thoughts on the demonstration via internal monologue.

He asks himself, "But what can a *demo* accomplish? Would I get some money if I joined? Would a *demo* solve my problems?"

Significantly, the two monochrome rallies—the red and the yellow—are alien spectacles to Turing. They simultaneously signal and efface the vanguardist aspirations of National Democrats, as well as the paternalistic dynamics of the moderate opposition. To these rival factions, rallies were a means of winning over people like Turing to their disparate visions of—and competing leadership claims over—the anti-Marcos struggle. If the old politics integrated the popular classes into the political arena as individuals (through personal, remunerative agreements), then the new politics used the parliament of the streets to harvest the popular will of the oppressed; it integrated them as masses through the careful stoking of their discontent.

But Turing clearly cannot comprehend the value of such stage-managed mass actions. He interprets such performances as a kind of exhibitionism. For the politically apathetic Turing, demonstrators wishing to be heard and seen are no better than supplicants waiting for a miracle. He cannot wait for a miracle; he has to make one happen.

In a crucial sequence, we see his final rejection of the parliament of the streets in favor of a more immediately rewarding, albeit dangerous, path. The sequence begins with Turing cryptically announcing to his wife that he is "going to make a miracle happen." The film cuts to Turing driving his jeepney down a dark alley. Over his shoulder and through the windshield, we see yellow-shirted protesters frolicking in the streets. From his perspective inside the dark cab, the protestors look like a vaguely sinister mob. His interior monologue highlights his alienation from them. "Go on, make more noise, so you'll be heard, so you'll be noticed," Turing's inner voice mockingly says.

He navigates the city's red-light district in search of Lando (Raoul Aragon), his childhood friend. For the desperate Turing, Lando might be his last hope.

Earlier in the film, a chance encounter reunites the two old friends. The meeting comes at a critical juncture for Turing, who has begun to resent the moral superiority of his "henpecking" wife.

To assert his masculinity, he agrees to go out with Lando, who takes him to a girlie bar. Lando, he discovers, is something of a gangland boss. He has done well for himself in the "buy and sell" trade. Thereafter, his meetings with Lando become more frequent. He even agrees to shelter Lando from the cops after one of Lando's robberies goes wrong. All this further estranges him from Luz.

Turing's search for Lando ends in a dark pact. Lando had earlier attempted to enlist Turing in a heist—in exchange for getting Lando's crew through the tight security of the Lim compound, Turing could walk away with a third of the take. Turing had earlier refused. The situation has changed, he now explains to Lando.

He leads Lando's crew into the Jefferson Printing Press. Nervous, sweating profusely, he helps Lando and his stooge, Boy Echas (Rez Cortez), pillage Mr. Lim's office. Later, we see Boy Echas helping himself to food in the upstairs kitchen of the Lim home. Sally Lim is awakened by the muffled sounds of the burglars and is calling the police. Mr. Lim is out gallivanting with Hugo, and Sally's vulnerable family unit is without male protection. Meanwhile, in an act of extreme vandalism, Boy Echas defecates on the kitchen floor.[39] The dark comedy of the scene is abruptly cut short by the sound of gunshots outside. The police have shot the driver of the getaway car and have surrounded the house. To protect themselves, Lando and Turing hold Sally and her children hostage.

In her yellow nightgown (signaling the elitist pretensions of her middle-class habitus), Sally Lim's image synthesizes the patron-client ties of the old politics and the sentimental paternalism of the new middle-class politics. Turing, who has been marginalized by the former and is chary of the latter, does not conceal his contempt for Sally. She beseeches him: "I have never done you wrong, Turing. How can you do this?"

Parallel editing reveals Luz at the hospital, listening to a radio broadcast of the unfolding hostage situation in the Lim household. The announcer states that Turing has agreed to be interviewed by a TV crew. The film abruptly cuts to a frontal shot of a newsman's camera. An off-screen voice asks Turing to name his demands.

His face bleached by the bright lights of the television crew, Turing demands the release of his wife and child from the hospital. His language then becomes progressively incoherent. Here, the mise-en-scène once again takes on an allegorical register: we cut to a crowd massed before the display window of an electronics store, watching multiple images of Turing on a bank of television screens. "The strikers should be given justice," he haltingly says. "All I ask is to be given a proper job, so I can get my wife and child.... And I demand amnesty.... And, I demand that Mr. Lim be thrown in jail—and be starved—so that he can experience the hardship that befell all the workers here."

The presence of the media in the unfolding hostage drama puts Turing in a profoundly ironic situation. "Go on, make more noise, so you'll be heard, so you'll be noticed," he had earlier said about the protesters in the street. Choosing a criminal path over legitimate political action, he ends up a notorious felon on live television—seen and heard by millions. Placed in an extraordinary situation, Turing finds himself *performing* a new identity, as an activist.

Throughout the film, Turing has made plaintive demands for justice. His appeals have fallen on the deaf ears of his patrons. He has been slow to learn that the personal ties of the old politics were insufficient and slower still to learn the importance of massing his grievances with those of others fighting for the same thing—"a little justice," as Aling Fely poignantly says to the television crew in the succeeding scene. But his actions this night have negated his legitimate demands for justice. To the many viewers watching the hostage drama on television, particularly the elite classes, Turing is no more than a common criminal.

Shortly after the interview, Luz enters the hostage drama. The police grant Luz the privilege of speaking to her husband in private. Unbeknownst to the couple, however, Luz is a decoy. While Luz convinces Turing to surrender, a SWAT team breaks into the Lim home. In the chaos that ensues, Mrs. Lim is fatally shot by Lando. The SWAT team counterattacks, killing Lando and Boy Echas. As Turing is hauled away by the police, the camera follows his point of view. In the crowd, he spots Hugo, who gives him the finger. The crass gesture, which would have been mildly offensive—even comical—under other circumstances, triggers Turing's fatal downfall. In their brief exchange of looks, Turing "misrecognizes" the foreman as the personification of all the structural injustices that have conspired to rob him of his "manhood." Enraged, he tries to grab a policeman's gun. The police shoot him down. The film ends with an extended shot of Luz, holding her dead husband as reporters savagely swarm around her.

In a 1984 press release written in conjunction with the film's screening at the Cannes festival, Brocka stated, "My wish is that this modest but hopefully clear film—as contained as it may be in its ambitions and the facilities of production—will help the audience to feel the pulse of the boiling blood of politically unprepared characters such as Turing."[40] *Bayan ko* is "modest" and "contained" to the extent that it is a low-budget film that adheres to the melodramatic conventions of the popular cinema. But as a national allegory, *Bayan ko* is a complex analysis of the dysfunctional nature of the patronage system underpinning the old politics. And though the film shows the mass action strategy of the new politics to be on the rise, Turing's allegorical trajectory suggests that far too many of the popular classes are still "politically unprepared" to see beyond the immediate satisfaction—at whatever cost—of their demands for personal justice. How would these marginalized Filipinos be integrated into the opposition's dream of a more "authentic, popular, pluralist democracy"? How would such a democracy avoid the vanguardism and paternalism of the radical and elite forces behind the opposition? These are the questions that Brocka's national allegory poses, but leaves unanswered.

People Power

Bayan ko's antihero had mistakenly thought that proponents of the new politics were waiting for a miracle to happen. As it turns out, that "miracle" was not too far from happening. In February 1986 the long struggle against the dictatorship culminated in people power, a phenomenon that has been widely attributed to elite and middle-class agitation against the hated regime.[41] Though elite leadership did in fact create a highly organized opposition movement, and though intraelite competition had indeed set the clock ticking for the momentous events of February 22 through 25, the lower classes had a critical role to play in the mass actions that led up to Marcos's ouster. Indeed, as Quimpo has recently argued, the popular classes were the critical mass at the people power demonstrations.[42] How did the popular classes assume this historic role? This is perhaps the biggest puzzle behind people power; and Brocka's national allegory provides some essential insights that will allow us to begin tackling the question.

Bayan ko highlights the irreconcilability of the two dominant perceptions of the lower classes. Turing's own description of his predicament (being accused of being either too aggressive or too docile), captures the ambivalent position of these marginalized Filipinos, who are seen as either "potentially violent and socially disruptive" or "essentially conservative, having similar aspirations to those in the middle class." But what these mutually exclusive perceptions tend to ignore is the class hostility that even the most conservative of the marginalized have for the elite and the middle class. As Michael Pinches's prescient study of the urban poor rightly predicted in 1985, "the manner and authority with which . . . opposition parties attempt to harness the class hostility that exists among them is crucial."[43] And so it was for the 1986 popular revolt.

As a national allegory, *Bayan ko* presents the ambivalent political characteristics of the urban poor as having been grounded in the old politics and having important implications for the new. Turing's initial rejection of the parliament of the streets may be attributed to his "conservative" aspirations for a better life, which he pursues through the patron-client ties of the old politics. Failing to attain the bare minimum of justice in this dysfunctional system, he belatedly—and blindly—converts to the new politics when he finds himself becoming a media activist. His melodramatic demise, how-ever, underscores the crucial importance of political "priming"—the careful transformation of class hostility into an analytically power-ful and organized *mass* action. As a bellwether for the 1986 popular revolt, *Bayan ko* thus advances the important point that it falls on the opposition movement to mobilize people like Turing—the "re-serve army" of the anti-Marcos struggle. And here, the methods and tactics of the new politics will be crucial. But what Brocka's allegory failed to anticipate was the persistent pull of *elections* for both elite and popular forces within the anti-Marcos struggle.

Already divided by the BAYAN-BANDILA split, proponents of the new politics became even more polarized in November 1985, when Marcos announced snap presidential elections. A year earlier, the broad anti-Marcos movement organized a boycott of the May 1984 legislative elections. But the opposition's boycott consensus collapsed when several moderates, including Cardinal Sin and Corazon Aquino, decided to participate in the elections.[44] The ral-lies of the opposition candidates drew large crowds, and Corazon, who gave "simple monotone accounts of her husband's life and death," quickly emerged as an effective campaigner.[45] The opposi-tion candidates won 60 of 183 contested legislative seats—15 of the 21 in Manila. The gains made by the moderates who had jumped ship to embrace the 1984 elections had considerably weakened the antielection position of the street parliamentarians, so that by the time Marcos made his announcement for snap elections, only the radical Left remained to champion the new politics.

In the lead-up to the February 1986 presidential elections, Cora-zon Aquino had become so popular—even to the masses—that the CPP's party organ, *Ang bayan,* had to concede, "Although con-vinced that a boycott is correct and conforms to principles and mo-rality, many antifascists and progressives among the middle forces are worried that by boycotting they may be isolating themselves from the people."[46]

To salvage what was left of the new politics, some BAYAN leaders made overtures toward the Aquino camp. They offered organizational support in exchange for the presidential contender's adoption of some of BAYAN's "nationalist and pro-people" positions. But the National Democrats had irreversibly alienated themselves from the Aquino camp when the CPP gave the following assessment of the candidate: "well meaning though she may be, she is either politically naïve or she has not transcended her own comprador-landlord class background."[47] Aquino's campaign handlers rejected BAYAN's proposition, prompting BAYAN to issue a boycott manifesto. The manifesto reinforced the irreconcilability of the old and new politics: "Boycott expresses the people's determination to struggle against the U.S.-backed dictatorship, relying not on sham elections, but persevering mainly in direct combative forms of mass struggles."[48]

By then, however, Aquino's campaign was enjoying a groundswell of support, and BAYAN's calls for "direct mass struggles" became oddly anachronistic as the new politics suddenly seemed like a thing of the past.

Candidate Cory's campaign hinged on the careful elision of her elite status; and indeed, it highlighted her inexperience as a politician. And through emotional appeals to the "meaningful politics" of the popular classes, she was able to woo the masses from the sinking ship of the NDF's ideologically based mass-action politics:

> Drawn by her simplicity and sincerity, crowds of hundreds of thousands all over the country waited for hours to catch a glimpse of her and hear her talk about the agonies she and her family went through during Ninoy's incarceration. The tale of woe which she used to the hilt proved to be highly effective . . . the masses wept and identified with her and her sufferings under the dictatorship, and pledged to protect and support this valiant woman who had very gallantly taken up the cudgels for them.[49]

Highly emotional and certainly "pro-poor," Aquino's melodramatic style on the campaign trail seemed to be cut from the same cloth as Brocka's social melodramas. In her campaign speeches, Cory, the "sincere" neophyte politician, presented herself as having the best interests of the popular classes *at heart,* and as someone seeking only just retribution from an "evil" regime. "I don't seek vengeance, only justice, not only for Ninoy but for the suffering Filipino people. Here I am asking for your help to topple the Marcos regime. . . . Join me in my crusade for truth, justice and freedom."[50]

The melodramatic cultural politics of the postassassination rallies had clearly supplied the language and symbols of the Aquino campaign. Significantly, however, the campaign made few concrete promises on behalf of the popular classes. Aquino had magnanimously promised to open Malacañang to all visitors, and made vague references to land reform, long a cornerstone of the dictator's populist rule. However, when a court ordered Hacienda Luisita, her family's vast sugar estate, to be redistributed to its laborers, she condemned the episode as an instance of "political harassment." She made no moves to substantively incorporate land reform into her platform; and even as many liberal oppositionists had followed BAYAN's lead to press for the removal of the U.S. bases, she "insisted on keeping her options open." Indeed, candidate Cory made no "class-based promises of social reform, which would have offended her wealthy supporters, nor nationalist pledges, which would have alienated the Americans."[51]

Moderates who supported the Aquino campaign harbored no illusions that the election would be fair and honest; nor did they expect a significant transformation of Philippine society should their candidate be elected. Their elite and middle-class positions circumscribed their limited aspirations. At best, they perceived the election as a democratic opening that could be used to strengthen the opposition's ranks. For their part, radicals fretted over the CPP's boycott policy. The leftist nationalist Epifanio San Juan, Jr., warned National Democrats against confusing tactics (boycott) and goals (mass mobilization): "We know the limits of the elite politicians and forces . . . given their history. But the question is how do you maximize—not shut out—even the tiniest openings to reach the widest number of people and raise the level of consciousness and organizing in spite of the regime's restrictions? To confuse the maximum goal of the nationalist democratic program with the tactical goals of the present alignment of forces is to act as a 'vanguard' leading your sect to the swamps."[52]

For seventeen years the CPP had patiently chipped away at the dictator's power base and had been amply rewarded. Indeed, 1985 had yielded spectacular political and military successes; the party, its army, and its legal front could "legitimately claim to be a national political force with broad-based, grassroots support."[53] Why indeed slow down this momentum and possibly lose large sections of their mass base to the party's tactical allies? San Juan's views were not substantially different from those of Jose Maria Sison. From his prison cell at Fort Bonifacio, the CPP founder issued a statement rejecting a "maximum" boycott. He recommended that National Democrats take a "critical" position: limiting their involvement in the election but nonetheless allowing opposition candidates to seek votes from their organized mass base.[54]

Days before the election, the CPP leadership heeded Sison's recommendations. The party's executive committee ordered cadres and legal organizations to redirect their energies to preventing election fraud. So unpopular was the party's boycott position, however, that some regional party committees had not waited for the central committee's instructions and urged their organized supporters to vote for Aquino. On election day, February 7, the overwhelming voter turnout amounted to a popular rejection of the party's "vanguard" position. CPP leaders were stunned by the rejection. In one Manila municipality considered to be a communist stronghold, 70 percent of the membership of the party-led unions disobeyed party orders and voted.[55]

As expected, however, the election was "stolen." It was stolen not once, but twice; and all before the eyes of a U.S. team that had come for the express purpose of monitoring the election. Indeed, the CPP did not anticipate the role that U.S. "observers" would play in what was to become the decisive showdown between the dictator and the opposition.

Though the Reagan administration supported Marcos, the State Department and a majority in the U.S. Congress supported Aquino.[56] Both camps agreed that the election had to be fair. To that end, Republican senator Richard G. Lugar organized (and headed) a bipartisan U.S. delegation to observe the election. In addition, the U.S. government secretly contributed $1 million to the National Citizens' Movement for Free Elections (NAMFREL), an independent poll watchers' group, and also backed Radio Veritas. The secret donations, it was hoped, would strengthen the two moderate organizations' efforts as electoral watchdogs.[57]

On election day, these watchdogs, along with the 850 foreign journalists who had flown to Manila to cover the polls, found more than the usual levels of fraud and terrorism. In Metro Manila, Tarlac, and most of the opposition's strongholds, massive disenfranchisement took place: citizens found their names scratched off the voting lists; and NAMFREL would later estimate that over a million eligible voters were unable to cast their votes.[58] Electoral violence, which in the 1984 elections was largely confined to remote areas (where it could not be documented by foreign media), took place in Makati—where foreign observers and the international press were headquartered. Media images of poll watchers being physically assaulted by the KBL's goons circulated around the world. The lapse was a clear indication of how Marcos's heretofore invisible political machine was sputtering; he simply *had* to "cheat in ways that U.S. observers and the international press could plainly see."[59]

Though the election brought out the worst of the old politics (electoral fraud and violence), the mediating presence of foreign observers brought out the best in the popular classes who had supported the election. Many of them believed that the Americans had pushed Marcos into the election, and so they expressed considerable goodwill toward both the Lugar delegation and the foreign media.[60] They *performed* their democratic aspirations for these observers. The common sight of hundreds of ordinary, mostly poor, civilians forming human shields to protect ballot boxes powerfully allegorized the continuing faith of the popular classes in the electoral process. And as fraud and violence escalated at the polls, these national allegories became especially vivid. As Gemma Almendral puts it, "The mass turnout of vigilant, determined, and angry citizens disproved the contention of skeptics that 'nothing positive will come out of the February 7 polls' . . . the election afforded the people an appreciation of the value of moving together as one in pursuit of a common goal."[61]

Something of the new politics, in short, had entered the old. This was the important lesson that the 1986 election would leave for the National Democrats, who had effectively shut themselves out of the climaxing struggle against the regime: that a formal democracy could still unite the Filipino people against the Marcos dictatorship.

The feeling of popular unity against the regime peaked when the election was once more stolen during the official counting of the ballots by COMELEC. In a dramatic moment captured on live television, thirty computer workers, mostly young frightened women, walked out after witnessing the padding of Marcos's votes.[62] The women sought refuge in a nearby church, where a crowd had quickly gathered to show their support. Lugar's delegation rushed to the scene, where even the most conservative among them became convinced that Marcos had cheated.[63]

The delegation issued a damning report on the conduct of the polls; but Reagan, a longtime friend of Marcos, announced that both sides committed fraud. The U.S. president's televised statement caused an uproar in the Philippines. Aquino sharply rebuked Reagan and called on the Filipino people to take part in a civil-disobedience campaign in protest of the "Reagan-Marcos connivance." In clearly melodramatic tones, the CBCP declared, "A government that assumes or retains power through fraudulent means has no moral basis. . . . If such a government does not of itself freely correct the evil it has inflicted on the people, then it is our serious moral obligation as a people to make it do so."[64]

The election fallout saw millions of Filipinos—the popular classes, elites, and the middle class—united once again in an emotional outpouring of righteous indignation not seen since the Aquino assassination. On February 16, 1986, 2 million people gathered at Luneta Park, chanting, "Cory is our president." The so-called People's Victory Rally culminated with Aquino issuing instructions for her civil disobedience campaign. She called for a boycott of the pro-Marcos media. Banks and companies with crony ties were to be boycotted as well.[65]

As was the case at the height of the economic crisis in 1984, elites acted without fear that the economic repercussions of the civil-disobedience campaign would result in anarchy in the streets. Mass anger, as Vincent Boudreau points out, was "reliably mass *base* anger, linked to organized leadership and discipline." The unity of purpose temporarily synthesizing the "summits" and "bases" of the revived opposition hinged on an unstated promise that the struggle would end in a "post-dictatorship golden age of just social and economic relations."[66]

The dramatic trigger for the decisive events of February 22–25 came not from the opposition between the elite and the middle class, however, but from the military. In the early evening of February 22, Juan Ponce Enrile and Fidel Ramos declared their defection from the Marcos regime. With them at Camp Aguinaldo were five hundred loyal followers of the Reform the Armed Forces Movement (RAM).

Some backstory is in order. After Enrile lost to Imelda and General Ver in the succession struggle, he found an ally in General Ramos, whom Marcos had also passed over in favor of Ver. Since at least 1983, Enrile had been recruiting young graduates of the Philippine Military Academy and mid-level officers disgruntled by the massive corruption and deprofessionalization of the armed forces; these officers would form the core of RAM.[67] When the snap election was announced, RAM declared its goal to "bring back the armed forces to its rightful place—the center."[68] RAM officers forged ties with moderate cause-oriented groups to establish trust. Secretly, however, its leaders and Enrile were organizing a coup d'état. They had planned to attack Malacañang on February 23, but the coup plot was discovered. Fearing for their lives, the defectors held a press conference at Camp Aguinaldo and pleaded for mass support.

The public's initial reaction was lukewarm—far too many Filipinos regarded the military with fear and loathing. But when Cardinal Sin implored on Radio Veritas for civilians to protect the rebels, things quickly changed. "These two gentlemen need our help," Sin said in his broadcast. "They need food and support. *People, please come.*"[69] And they did.

The four-day revolt saw millions of ordinary citizens forming a human barricade along the city's main artery, Epifanio de los Santos Avenue (EDSA). They came to stop the regime's tanks headed for the rebel camps (Camp Aguinaldo and Camp Crame). Women and children handed out flowers to pro-Marcos soldiers; priests and nuns flashed religious images to shame the rebels into lowering their guns. The military's human-rights violations were temporarily forgotten; and in a striking reversal of roles, unarmed civilians came to protect armed soldiers. Indeed, they provided the "defense in depth" that had been part of Enrile and RAM's coup strategy.[70] When, on day two of the revolt, General Ver finally gave orders for a frontal assault on the rebel camps, the regime quickly discovered that they had missed their chance to quell the revolt; the majority of soldiers deployed at EDSA had by then defected.

The EDSA revolt brought out the organized leadership and discipline of the opposition movement—a testament to the continued importance of the new politics, despite the opposition's swing back to the ingrained habits of the old (elections). Crucially, the millions of demonstrators gathered along EDSA comported themselves according to the codes of conduct developed in the opposition's mass actions. Priests and nuns shepherded demonstrators to form well-ordered campgrounds, even forming a food brigade that would serve as the crowd's life support system.[71] Nuns stood at the front lines—a strategy used to pressure police into practicing restraint during the postassassination rallies and now used "for maximum emotional impact" upon M-14-toting officers and oncoming tanks.[72]

But the crucial thing was to control the pent-up emotions of the demonstrators and to prevent class hostilities from devolving into a riot. Once again, experienced street parliamentarians drew on the nonviolent praxis of the new politics. When an enraged crowd threatened to storm Malacañang and began harassing soldiers guarding the palace gates, a priest calmed the mob: "These soldiers are our brothers! They are Filipinos like us!"[73] For the most part, however, the demonstrations were peaceful and most accounts of the EDSA revolt highlight the protestors' performance of highly sentimental acts meant to literally disarm the regime's troops. Pedrosa's description is representative:

> It was a unique protest. At one point, a mother stopped a soldier to say how much he resembled her son. Would the soldier shoot his mother, she asked. Another group of protesters sang native drinking songs and passed drinks to the soldiers, who were persuaded to join in the tumultuous clapping of hands. There were scenes upon scenes, but each Filipino who participated in that unbelievable show of people power employed every ounce of charm and humor available to make it impossible for the soldiers to reach for their guns and fire. . . . All motives, political or otherwise, had fused into indefinable courage.[74]

Though moderate cause-oriented organizations (notably, church groups) coordinated the defenses and restrained violent elements within the demonstration, the masses were the foot soldiers, so to speak, in this popular revolt. This brings us back to an essential point raised by Brocka's *Bayan ko:* the ambivalent political characteristics of the masses. By now it should be clear that between the "conservative" and "socially disruptive" poles of their political aspirations lay a middle ground—one that expressed their desire for empowerment in the face of an elite-dominated formal democracy and the centralized conformity imposed by the Left. Far from being apolitical, they seized the vote *and* the exercise of mass action—to be seen and heard, and to have their political will taken seriously.

Accounts of the EDSA revolt tend to emphasize the unexpected outbreak of people power during those four fateful days in February 1986. The common view that a spontaneous force had toppled the dictator does not hold up against the evidence outlined in the last three chapters that the 1986 rebellion was the culmination of a long and bitter struggle against the regime. The massive presence of the popular classes at EDSA had been "primed" by the numerous mass actions that took place since 1983; and their melodramatic actions during the four-day revolt confirmed the power of the new politics to transform personal understandings of social injustice into a politically viable expression of resistance against the Marcos regime.

But we should not be too quick to romanticize the EDSA revolt. The patronage dynamics of an elite-dominated formal democracy and the undemocratic features of the CPP-NPA have survived the fall of the dictator and continue to pose limits on the political activities of the popular classes. And indeed, the "golden age of just social and economic relations" has yet to come. Brocka's homage to the anti-Marcos protest movement continues to provoke. And the question—how to integrate the masses into a truly popular democracy—while still unanswered, benefits from retrospective analyses of the Marcos era. The 1986 popular revolt set an important precedent, and the popular classes, now well seasoned in the democratic possibilities of both the old and the new politics know they have powerful recourse to the legacy of the Marcos era—people power.

Conclusion

THE FORCE OF
NATIONAL ALLEGORY

I was there.

I was fifteen years old, just a month shy of finishing my second year of high school, when people power happened. The morning after Jaime Cardinal Sin went on the air ("People, please come!"), our home was a scene of confusion. I remember: my mother ordering us to pack wet washcloths ("in case there'll be tear gas"), my father making hurried plans on the phone ("Hello? Hello, Boy! Are you and Charo going to EDSA?"), my older brother and his young family glued to the television (the new baby was fast asleep), and my other two younger siblings and I bickering as we were wont to do when agitated, confused or feeling put out (all of which I remember feeling at the time).

We three younger kids had grown up during the dictatorship— my sister was born during the First Quarter Storm, in 1970; I was born a year later; and my younger brother was born three days before martial law was declared (his premature birth was induced because my mother's obstetrician was fleeing the country). We were still children, really, with nothing to prepare us for the sublime thrill—the heady mixture of terror and euphoria—of heeding Cardinal Sin's call.

Nobody in my family had ever been to a demonstration. Though my parents were NAMFREL volunteers, and though they counted several prominent leaders of the elite opposition among their "church friends," my father had a long enough history with the regime to mark him as something of a turncoat. He was Imelda Marcos's dressmaker—her couturier, as his old passport listed his occupation.

In Ramona Diaz's documentary *Imelda: Power, Myth, Illusion* (2003), my father gets to recount how he was often given just twenty-four hours to produce the ternos she was famous for wearing. They were truly beautiful dresses. Those ternos, like the modernist architecture of the Cultural Center of the Philippines, were part of the visual iconography of the regime and its beguiling national symbolic.

I remember how my father was often roused out of bed in the middle of the night because "Madame wants her fitting now." But he couldn't complain. Our family's material comfort was paid for by those command fittings. Truth be told, Imelda's patronage allowed my father, the talented son of a schoolteacher, to rise out of poverty and obscurity, buy a home in Makati, and send his children to elite schools (Cory Aquino's youngest daughter was my classmate and Imelda's niece was one of my closest friends growing up).

In my childhood home, traces of Ferdinand and Imelda Marcos were everywhere. There was a blown-up color photograph in our upstairs hallway of Imelda wearing one of my father's creations. And the president was always on television, interrupting our favorite shows to explain his letters of instruction to the people. I had my first taste of "national discipline" when I was about six years old: I was caught telling a lie and was quickly chastised by mother with, "Do you want the president to get angry with you?" Oh, the irony of that scene.

My family's disillusionment with the regime came gradually and painfully, like a slow death. Around 1981 or 1982, my father had a professional falling out with Imelda, who ended their seventeen-year creative partnership to search for "fresher talent." Meanwhile, the Philippines was hit with a spectacular economic crisis, and we had to put our house on the market. After the Aquino assassination, my family, too, grieved. Like so many others trying to get the "real picture," we switched from *Bulletin Today* to *Malaya*. One night in 1984, we were driving along EDSA when a news bulletin came on the radio about the financial crisis. My father, who very rarely talked about politics at home, suddenly wailed, "Why won't someone kill that man?" Turning to me, he said, "I don't understand you young people. *Why aren't you doing anything?*" My father is not a demonstrative man, nor is he impulsive. The desperation in his voice was very real and gave me pause.

We came very close to fleeing the country in 1985, but something held my father back. He went to church every day. He and my mother got very active with NAMFREL. For the snap elections, their poll-watching duties included checking voter's registration lists for anomalies. For two days, my whole family stayed up all hours poring over those lists (we found many, many instances of single-family households claiming thirty residents or more). Yes, something made my father stay put—a sense of political optimism he couldn't account for, but nonetheless felt.

In Diaz's documentary, he owns up to his political inaction all those years he was beholden to Imelda: "As many as there were people who hated the couple, there were also those people like us who [really] *didn't know anything about the political situation.* We were all too charmed by the couple. When I realized that I was taken for a ride it was too late" (emphasis added). The interview ends there, quite unceremoniously.

But on February 23, 1986, my father did take political action. He packed his wife and three teenage children in the family car and took them to EDSA. He did the same thing the next day, and the next, until it was all over.

When I tell my students that I stood in front of the tanks, I feel a rush of pride. *I was there.* Those three words can hardly convey the sense of accomplishment—the sense of ownership, even—that so many of us feel when we think about people power. Those four days were so impactful for me that I've spent the better part of the last thirty years trying to understand how it all happened and what it all means. This book has been the product of that life's work.

I've given you my father's arc, and mine as well, as an allegory of how political action (and inaction) is shaped as much by rational things like political knowledge (or lack thereof) as by nonrational things like political emotion (or lack thereof). It is shaped as much by structural determinants (for example, the "accident" of being born poor in a Third World country) as by individual agency. If you are a perceptive reader—cognitively and affectively perceptive—you may have sensed in my confessions some of the themes covered in this book: Marcos's national symbolic, the sentimental politics of the elite opposition, and the melodrama of people power. You may have sensed as well that these themes cohere around the complex dynamics of political knowledge, political emotion, and political action.

The world has changed so much since 1986; it thus behooves us to put this case study in perspective. Let's start with the changing fortunes of the Third World.

The story of Marcos's democratic revolution is a microcosm of the story of the Third World as a political coalition: both were products of a specific ideological-political conjuncture that ran its course. The period of euphoria when it seemed that Third World struggles for national liberation would lead to a tricontinental revolution was railroaded by the collapse of communism, the realization that the wretched of the earth were not unanimously revolutionary, and the recognition that international geopolitics and the global economic system obliged even socialist regimes to seek a détente with transnational capitalism.[1]

In East and Southeast Asia, successful capitalist industrialization generated new social forces that undercut traditional Left strategies, resulting in the delinking of nationalism from socialism. If, in the 1970s, peasant uprisings and radical student movements were the dominant forms of opposition for the Left, by the mid-1980s, insurgent and extraconstitutional challenges to existing power relations fell out of favor. Concomitantly, Left political claims have been restricted to more reformist—as opposed to revolutionary—goals.[2]

Except in the Philippines. The Philippines has been the one notable exception in a regional pattern of remarkable capitalist development. In Thailand, Singapore, and Indonesia, economic growth kick-started by authoritarian rule has been a source of national pride, undercutting socialism's potential appeal. Only in the Philippines, where the richest 20 percent receive 12.4 times the share of the poorest 20 percent, has the Left remained resilient.[3] National Democrats, who have long blamed imperialism and globalization for the nation's social inequities, have successfully projected themselves as genuine nationalists. And though the 1986 boycott campaign pushed the Left into a protracted internal crisis, the recent escalation of CPP-NPA guerrilla activity has breathed new life into the National Democratic struggle. The CPP's armed struggle is now one of the world's longest-running insurgencies, claiming forty-three thousand lives. The longevity of the struggle is a powerful indicator of the "depth of popular opposition not just to Marcos's authoritarian rule, but also to elite rule in general."[4]

So, coming back to the story of Marcos's democratic revolution: how did the then-fashionable discourse of Third World liberation and the Left's genuine nationalism play into Marcos's hands?

In chapter 1, we saw how Marcos effectively co-opted the Left's insurgent and extraconstitutional forms of dissent, principally through his command of political spectacle and his astute manipulation of the media. Reconstructing the First Quarter Storm from Lacaba's reports for the *Philippines Free Press*, reveals how the Fanonian ideal of liberatory violence was enacted in the national allegories performed by young radical students in defiance of the authorities and for the benefit of the national news media. Their "parliament of the streets" constituted a juxtapolitical space of political contestation, and their medium of dissent—passionate and hyperembodied performances of radical subalternity—seemed to open up a new and exciting space of political action. But Marcos's mass-mediated countersubversive "war" was itself a national allegory, one that "otherized" the young dissidents even as it appropriated the anticolonial politics of the radical Left. As captured in the propaganda film *The Threat—Communism,* the dictator had powerful recourse to the Cold War discourse of defensive nationalism and the U.S. technique of the covert spectacle to legitimize the rise of a martial-law state in the Philippines.

In chapter 2, we examined how the New Society and the ideology of national discipline sought to effect an "internal revolution" by regimenting social conduct and recalibrating the mental dispositions of the populace. The cultural policy of the regime seemed to obey the Foucauldian concept of "liberal government," in that it valorized ethico-aesthetic exercises as instrumental to the production of self-monitoring and self-regulating subjects committed to the development agendas of the New Society. Marcos's internal revolution uncannily echoed the colonial discourse of white love, as articulated by the U.S. policy of benevolent assimilation, and then later reimagined as modernization. These discourses hinged on training cultural subjects to recognize their ethical incompleteness and to subject themselves to an "apprenticeship of obedience."

As a national allegory rehearsing the regime's cultural policy, the Marcos romance brought to the fore the profound tensions between the cultural paternalism of white love/modernization and the anticolonial populism of cultural liberation, the other pole of the regime's cultural policy. Mimicking the Fanonian concept of cultural rehabilitation, the latter emphasized the psychoaffective treatment of colonial subjects and the therapeutic correction of their subalternity. Within the melodramatic universe of the Marcos romance, Imelda Marcos allegorized these competing discourses, which simultaneously called for the hegemonic normalization of the popular classes into tasteful citizens and the revaluation of the identities and cultural practices of disempowered Filipinos. These irreconcilable cultural policy agendas underpinned a melodramatic cultural policy that also instrumentalized folk culture for commercial exploitation.

In chapter 3, we saw how the regime's highly ambivalent cultural policy played out in the cinema that was undergoing profound changes. Occasioned by the discursive overflow between the sex and violence flooding the nation's screens and the excesses of the nation's violent and—at least for Marcos, libidinous—political culture, Marcos instituted a national sexuality campaign against the bomba film to reestablish boundaries between the intimate and public spheres and to protect the heteronormative ideology of the national family. But the ambivalent combination of strict censorship and Imelda's efforts to create a world-class national cinema enabled the production of national allegories that would indeed gain world attention as powerful forms of media activism. Lino Brocka's early career and the sentimental politics of his *Tinimbang ka ngunit kulang* (Weighed and found wanting, 1974), reveal how the legacy of the First Quarter Storm loomed large over the cinematic activism of New Cinema auteurs and their national allegories of political repression in the New Society. These three chapters leave us with some insights about the interrelationships between political knowledge, political emotion and political action.

During the First Quarter Storm, strong pathos and sensational expressionism marked the dissidents' melodramatic political action, which acquired moral clarity through melodrama's power to reveal those social contradictions that can only be apprehended by one's affective reason. The same can be said for Marcos's countersubversive performance, which was no less melodramatic. However, the young dissidents used melodrama's emotional excess to shock the citizen-spectator out of their habituated perceptions of politics and thereby gain a sharper picture of moral injustice, while Marcos's red-scare tactics exploited the distress and moral outrage occasioned by the young dissidents' national allegories and projected them onto the specter of the "subversive." This demonized cipher, the product of melodrama's affective conditioning, was the pretext for Marcos's own national allegory of heroic rescue and return.

The Marcos romance substitutes the political spectacle of revolution with a spectacular fantasy of romantic fulfillment. A long-standing trope of the culture industry, the love plot "makes erotic, normal and personal" all the cruel disappointments and "impossible promises of democracy under capitalism."[5] When yoked to the hegemonic operations of a postcolonial cultural policy, the love plot gains the added function of defusing revolutionary threats by containing them within a national symbolic premised on the redemptive—if painful—power of love. This was the case with the

Marcos romance, which presents Imelda as the symbol of the ethical incompleteness of the popular classes, whose quest for the good life is divinely rewarded—but not without considerable suffering. As strikingly illustrated in her self-styled performances as the People's Star, Imelda turned the suffering of the colonial/subaltern subject into an amnesiac spectacle: something meant to be aesthetically contemplated, but ultimately transcended, and thereby forgotten. The spectacle of Imelda occasions a sentimental bargain with the popular classes, who are trained to accept suffering as something that has to be endured. Ferdinand and Imelda's love plot thus lends to the New Society's cultural policy a sentimental dimension: it names the subjective impacts of colonial-popular struggle and then delivers a plot of its ultimate transcendence. These two operations make up the "promise and premise of sentimental politics."[6]

The New Cinema shares the sentimental politico-aesthetic of the Marcos romance. Take Brocka's national allegory in *Tinimbang ka,* which, like Imelda's fraught performance as the People's Star, takes up the sentimental form to deliver a simplified account of subaltern identity. Within sentimental culture, simplicity is paradoxically the mark of someone's depth of being; it signals the subaltern's profound grief in defeat and in struggle. There is no better symbol of the "simple suffering" of the popular classes than the image of the insane vagrant Kuala. But like the Marcos romance, *Tinimbang ka* delivers the sentimental text's optimistic message of transcendence: the belief that the subaltern *survives* despite the enormity of her struggles. The film's final image, of Kuala's child—safe in the arms of the enlightened/sensitized middle-class hero, Junior—powerfully evokes this survival subculture.

Critiquing the cultural backwardness of the folk *and* social cleansing in the New Society, all while generating a tale of the folk's resilience and survival, the film tries to have it both ways: "bargaining with the memory of [colonialism] and tinkering with the hardwiring of national optimism."[7] But what ultimately brands its national allegory with the mark of sentimentality is how it turns an aesthetic experience—the audience's shared consumption of the pain of the folk—into a juxtapolitical forum where a pain community is constructed, not through simultaneous collective struggle, but in a transformed mentality.[8]

The ideal of liberal empathy animates the sentimental politics of the New Cinema auteurs: the belief that by reading and deciphering their national allegories the audience will gain a collective consciousness of collective pain. But this model of cultural politics is not without its limitations, and Berlant's insights are instructive here. Insofar as "entertainment is the condition under which [the sentimental] scene of critique finds its expression; the guise of 'feeling' as a thing distinct from and superior to public sphere norms . . . requires the modern sentimental text's central moments of instruction and identification to appear only as sublime ephemera." The sensitive/enlightened reader must thus look for punctuated events—the knowing glance, the telling gesture, and so on—that "shape the fragile temporal material of feeling and memory that make an entertainment text also a 'serious' one that requires the exercise of compassion and empathy." Indeed, the ability to read critically becomes more than a marker of distinction; it emerges as a conduit to an emotional humanism. National allegories, especially those that bear the lowly cultural status of "entertainment," require this critical faculty from their viewers who must be able to discern the "serious film" within the genre film. But here's the rub: the conventions and repetitions of the sentimental text "provides alibis for the privileged, who, seeing the impacts of inequality and injustice are trained into demonstrating and identifying with a sense of overwhelming helplessness about how to [intervene]."[9] And so, all the sentimental reader seems to have to show for her critical labor and her good intentions—all she has agency over—seems to be her haunted feelings.

This brings us to the story of people power and the big question with which we began: how do changes in feeling bring about structural social change? Sentimental politics is limited by the way it privatizes political action. What is required is precisely the movement away from the private performance of political emotion to real-world organizing and resistance.

In chapters 4, 5, and 6 we saw how the regime's disastrous development initiatives set in motion the long struggle against authoritarian rule that was shaped by two competing models of resistance: the equation of democracy with elections by oppositional elites and the grassroots struggles of popular forces for social justice. As a national allegory of "democracy from below," Cervantes's *Sakada* (1976) encapsulates the unstable alliances between marginalized groups, Church activists, and the radical Left—forces fighting for popular empowerment and a more egalitarian democracy. Adhering to an "elite democracy" model of resistance, oppositional elites used human-rights activism to press for the restoration of competitive elections. However, their moral crusade was preempted by Marcos's showy gestures at political normalization. I revisited the legislative elections of 1978, in which Benigno Aquino, Jr., emerged as a media star. As we have seen, the stolen election prompted Aquino and an elite minority to pursue a bombing campaign from 1978 to 1982. Lacking a mass base, the campaign backfired: not only did it fail to secure power-sharing arrangements between the elite opposition and the regime, it also justified further militarization in Marcos's Philippines.

This critical juncture saw an upsurge of protest journalism in the establishment press—a trend conditioned by a mounting succession crisis in Marcos's political household. Enmeshed in the growing factionalism in the national family, the crony press mimicked the pre-martial-law media's proclivities for strategically "diverse" reporting. Meanwhile, Imelda's City of Man hosted the second Manila International Film Festival (1983), which saw the emergence of a state-supported bomba film culture as a bread-and-circuses diversion from the succession crisis. These developments marked the convergence of political trends that uncannily reprised the First Quarter Storm and Marcos's countersubversive performance: electoral violence, urban terrorism, and leftist agitation. But the full effect of the "second coming" would come in August 1983, with the assassination of Benigno Aquino, Jr.

Blending the "little tradition" of Philippine protest journalism and the "meaningful politics" of the oppressed, publications like

Malaya and *Mr. & Ms.* transformed Aquino from a symbol of elite politics into an icon of the popular struggle against the regime. The sentimental publicity of the alternative press helped engender a new politics centered on cause-oriented groups and popular mass action. But as we have seen, the dramatic revival of the parliament of the streets from 1983 to 1985 belied the class tensions that divided the anti-Marcos movement.

In the immediate postassassination period, a strong "united front" spirit animated the rallies that engulfed Manila daily; but less than a year later, hegemonic contests between a vanguardist Left and a paternalist elite opposition further marginalized their mass base. The lines of conflict and collusion between these factions of the anti-Marcos struggle generated an atmosphere of mutual distrust that stifled the new politics.

Lino Brocka's extrafilmic activism encapsulates the struggle of the popular classes to navigate the new politics. As captured in Jo-Ann Maglipon's journalistic account of the filmmaker's work in the Justice for Aquino, Justice for All movement, Brocka's identity as a street parliamentarian was clearly driven by a melodramatic imaginary. His participation in the protest movement was not anchored in a political ideology, but in the meaningful politics of the popular forces. As a national allegory of the nation on the cusp of people power, *Bayan ko* (My country, 1985) presents valuable insights into the stubborn inertias of elite politics that proved to be especially pertinent to the unfolding of people power.

The new politics was undermined by the powerful pull that elections continued to hold on both the elite and popular sectors of the opposition. Regaling crowds with stories of personal hardship and woe, Corazon Aquino emerged as a media star during the 1986 presidential election cycle. "Cory magic," as we have seen, hinged on wooing the masses from the ideologically based mass-action politics of the radical Left.

The media's interventions into the many popular struggles leading up to people power encapsulated the push-pull dynamic at the heart of melodrama. On the one hand, New Cinema films like *Sakada* and the corpus of investigative journalism emerging from the crony press instantiated the melodramatic impulse to move audiences to feel moral outrage against the regime. But on the other hand, these texts instantiated melodrama's tendency to locate moral agency in the retributive actions of traditional figures of political authority: the Church, the vanguard of the radical Left, and the paternalistic figures of elite democracy. These texts, in short, begged questions of cultural leadership and very often confined the popular classes to the position of a "reserve army" that was up for grabs in the rivalry between the various factions of the anti-Marcos movement.

Driving the sentimental publicity of the alternative media was a fantasy of transcending—of purifying—the dirty domain of politics. Within this fantasy, the citizen emerges not as a subject of politics (someone who is empowered or disempowered) but as a subject of feeling (someone whose political actions are determined by their ability to feel compassion for the less fortunate). And as the alternative press's coverage of national grief attests, sentimental publicity sees transactions of pain and recognition as the best means of purifying the political. However, there were limits to the alternative press's sentimental-utopian fantasy.

While the alternative media evinced optimism for social change, such optimism was also marked by a fear of too much change. For National Democrats and elite oppositionists alike, ceding control of the protest movement to the other side was already "too much change." The alternative media were thus locked in the paradoxical situation of sentimental publicity, in which "political dissatisfaction runs up against affective commitments not to risk much change while witnessing the need for it." Confining political action to the healing space of the aesthetic was the implicit solution to this dilemma, as strikingly shown in the alternative media's participation in national grief. That episode of high sentimental drama perfectly captures Berlant's point that in sentimental politics "political failure foments not revolution but the reproduction of wistful fantasy that things might be otherwise."[10]

For the alternative media's subjects of feeling, the prospect of a people's democracy under the CPP-NPA was the ultimate specter of "too much change." When severed from sentimental stories of suffering, struggle, and transcendence, "the masses"—as a political-ideological concept—cannot but inspire for the privileged readers of *Malaya* and *Mr. & Ms.* similar feelings of fear and loathing as those inspired by the specter of the "subversive" in Marcos's countersubversive national allegory. Both are products of melodrama's affective conditioning (Marcos's political demonology and the CPP's Marxist dogma, respectively).

As tellingly captured in Brocka's extrafilmic activism and allegorized in *Bayan ko,* the affective conditioning at the heart of melodrama renders its cultural politics still incomplete. Sentiment, pathos, and affect are indeed integral to channeling the desires, fears, and political aspirations of disempowered groups; but to truly engage their moral outrage requires a politics of "dirty hands"—political work beyond the privatized space of the aesthetic. In order to become a positive force for sociocultural change, melodrama must be harnessed toward the pedagogical and performative drives of national allegory: the revelation of the facts of oppression, the emotional channeling of a perceived good, and the extra-aesthetic performance of collective identification and communal action.

The melodramatic imaginary that galvanized people power was based on a perceived good: the promise of a more participatory and equitable democracy. All the actors in that drama saw the elimination of dictatorship as the crucial step toward the fulfillment of this promise. Not long after the euphoria of the 1986 popular revolt had dissipated, however, the economy entered a protracted crisis as the oligarchy was restored to its position of power. Structural-adjustment programs marked by deregulation, privatization, and trade and investment liberalization—compounded by "booty capitalism"—have proven the lack of fit between the "globalizing" values and agendas of neoliberalism and the patrimonial habits of thought enshrined in Marcos's national family.

The gap between rich and poor, far from narrowing in the post-Marcos era, has widened considerably.[11] And far from being eliminated by the demise of the regime, corruption has been on the rise: the government lost an estimated $48 billion to corruption over the past twenty years, exceeding the country's $40.6 billion foreign debt.[12]

In January 2001, EDSA 2—a sequel to people power—took place in the Philippines as another popular uprising ousted President Joseph Estrada, who had amassed $70 to $80 million in just three years in power. But less than four months later, Estrada loyalists attacked Malacañang in a show of armed force. Sadly, the majority of these loyalists, like the "foot soldiers" of EDSA 1, also came from the popular classes. The incident was defused. Two years later, however, military rebels staged a coup to force then-president Gloria Macapagal Arroyo from power, the latest in a series of failed coups that had bedeviled the government since 1986. These social convulsions—fed by various iterations of people power—have made it difficult to perpetuate the romantic mystique of the 1986 EDSA revolution. Especially with respect to the actions of pro-Estrada groups during EDSA 2, it is glaringly apparent that large numbers of the popular classes remain vulnerable to the stubborn inertias of patronage politics. At the same time, however, the last two decades have seen the emergence of powerful countertrends to these reactionary developments. National Democrats are moving forward with the NDF's vision of popular democracy, with growing numbers of cause-oriented organizations joining the alliance. Significantly, the "new politics" of the Left is no longer limited to mass actions, but now includes electoral struggle; and the once powerful pull of the CPP's brand of Marxism has given way to "democracy from below," as instantiated by the political activities of nongovernmental organizations, people's organizations, and new political parties actively opposing elite politics.

People power and its aftereffects have left the Philippines with two valuable lessons: democratic social change requires political emotion, political knowledge, *and* political action; and the deepening of democracy requires more than the removal of dictatorship—it requires the transformation of an elite-dominated formal democracy into a truly participatory and egalitarian one. The nation awaits new national allegories of this transformation.

Abbreviations

AFP	Armed Forces of the Philippines
AMRSP	Association of Major Religious Superiors of the Philippines
ASTA	American Society of Travel Agents
A6LM	April Sixth Liberation Movement
BANDILA	Bansang Nagkaisa sa Diwa at Layunin (A Nation United in Spirit and Purpose)
BAYAN	Bagong Alyansang Makabayan (New Patriotic Alliance)
BCC	Basic Christian Community
BCMP	Board of Censors for Motion Pictures
CAP	Concerned Artists of the Philippines
CBCP	Catholic Bishops' Conference of the Philippines
CCP	Cultural Center of the Philippines
COMELEC	Commission on Elections
CPP	Communist Party of the Philippines
ECP	Experimental Cinema of the Philippines
EDSA	Epifanio de los Santos Avenue
Filmboard	Filipino Motion Picture Development Board
FTA	Free the Artist Movement
JAJA	Justice for Aquino, Justice for All
KBL	Kilusang Bagong Lipunan (New Society Movement)
KM	Kabataang Makabayan (Nationalist Youth)
KMU	Kilusang Mayo Uno (May First Labour Movement)
LABAN	Lakas ng Bayan (People Power)

LFM	Light-a-Fire Movement
MFP	Movement for a Free Philippines
MIFF	Manila International Film Festival
MOWELFUND	Movie Workers Welfare Foundation
NAMFREL	National Citizens' Movement for Free Elections
NASUTRA	National Sugar Trading Corporation
NDF	National Democratic Front
NICA	National Intelligence Coordinating Agency
NPA	New People's Army
NPC	National Press Club of the Philippines
PANAMIN	Presidential Assistant on National Minorities
PC	Philippine Constabulary
PCO	Presidential Commitment Order
PDA	Preventive Detention Action
PDSP	Partido Demokratiko Sosyalista ng Pilipinas (Philippine Socialist Democratic Party)
PETA	Philippine Educational Theater Association
PHILEX	Philippine Exchange Commission
PHILSUCOM	Philippine Sugar Commission
PMPPA	Philippine Motion Picture Producers Association
PSC	Presidential Security Command
RAM	Reform the Armed Forces Movement
RPN	Radio Philippines Network
TFD	Task Force Detainees of the Philippines
ZOTO	Zone One Tondo Organization

Notes

Introduction: The Power of Political Emotions

1. Lauren Berlant's work on "public feelings," "intimate publics," and "national sentimentality" is very relevant to my project. See esp. Berlant, "The Epistemology of State Emotion," in *Dissent in Dangerous Times,* ed. Austin Sarat (Ann Arbor: University of Michigan Press, 2005), 46–78.

2. Deborah Gould provides a useful genealogy of this anxiety from within the field of sociology. See Gould, "On Affect and Protest," in *Political Emotions: New Agendas in Communication,* ed. Janet Staiger, Ann Cvetkovich, and Ann Reynolds (New York: Routledge, 2010), 18–44.

3. Lauren Berlant, "The Subject of True Feeling: Pain, Privacy, and Politics," in *Cultural Pluralism: Identity, Politics, and the Law,* ed. Austin Sarat and Thomas R. Kearns (Ann Arbor: University of Michigan Press, 2001), 49–84. See also Berlant, *The Female Complaint: The Unfinished Business of Sentimentality in American Culture* (Durham: Duke University Press, 2008).

4. Berlant, "Epistemology of State Emotion," 51, 49, 54.

5. See Joyce L. Arriola, "Scripting the Filipino Story through Media Images: Official and Popular Notions of Nation during the Marcos Years," *Pilipinas: Journal of Philippine Studies* 44 (2005): 33–48; Rolando B. Tolentino, "Marcos, Brocka, Bernal, City Films and the Contestation for Imagery of Nation," *Kritika kultura* 19 (2012): 115–38.

6. Jonathan Beller, *Acquiring Eyes: Philippine Visuality, Nationalist Struggle, and the World-Media System* (Quezon City: Ateneo de Manila University Press, 2006).

7. Bobby Benedicto, "Queer Space in the Ruins of Dictatorship Architecture," *Social Text* 31, no. 4 (Winter 2013): 25–47.

8. Lauren Berlant, *The Anatomy of National Fantasy: Hawthorne, Utopia, and Everyday Life* (Chicago: University of Chicago Press, 1991).

9. Frantz Fanon, "The Pitfalls of National Consciousness," quoted in ibid., 21; emphasis added.

10. See Alfred McCoy, "An Anarchy of Families: The Historiography of State and Family in the Philippines," in *An Anarchy of Families: State and Family in the Philippines,* ed. McCoy. (Quezon City: Ateneo de Manila University Press, 1998), 1–32; Vicente Rafael, "Patronage and Pornography: Ideology and Spectatorship in the Early Marcos Years," *Comparative Studies in Society and History* 32, no. 2 (1990): 282–304; Rolando Tolentino, "Postnational Family/Postfamilial Nation: Family, Small Town and Nation Talk in Marcos and Brocka," *Inter-Asia Cultural Studies* 4, no. 1 (2003): 77–92.

11. Ismail Xavier, *Allegories of Underdevelopment: Aesthetics and Politics in Modern Brazilian Cinema* (Minneapolis: University of Minnesota Press, 1997), 8, 3, 5.

12. Ibid., 8–9.

13. Representative texts are Renato Constantino, *Dissent and Counterconsciousness* (Manila: Erehwon, 1970); William Pomeroy, *American Neo-colonialism: Its emergence in the Philippines and Asia* (New York: International Publishers, 1970); Amado Guerrero [pseud. for Jose Maria Sison], *Philippine Society and Revolution,* 4th ed. (Hayward, CA: Philippine Information Network Service, 1996).

14. Arriola, "Scripting the Filipino Story," 36.

15. Ferdinand E. Marcos, *Tadhana: The History of the Filipino People* (Manila: Marcos Foundation, 1976).

16. Jürgen Habermas, *The Structural Transformation of the Public Sphere: An Inquiry into a Category of Bourgeois Society,* trans. Thomas Burger and Frederick Lawrence (Cambridge, MA: MIT Press, 1989).

17. Lauren Berlant, "Intimacy: A Special Issue," *Critical Inquiry* 24, no. 2 (Winter 1998): 284.

18. For an overview of this debate, see Ben Singer, *Melodrama and Modernity: Early Sensational Cinema and its Contexts* (New York: Columbia University Press, 2001).

19. Matthew Buckley, "Introduction," *Modern Drama* 55, no. 4 (Winter 2012): 431.

20. See, for example, Elisabeth Anker, "Villains, Victims and Heroes: Melodrama, Media and September 11," *Journal of Communication* 55, no. 1 (2005): 22–37; Matthew Buckley, "Refugee Theater: Melodrama and Modernity's Crisis," *Theatre Journal* 61, no. 2 (2009): 175–90.

21. Peter Brooks, "The Melodramatic Imagination" in *Imitations of Life: A Reader on Film and Television Melodrama,* ed. Marcia Landy (Detroit: Wayne State University Press, 1991), 64.

22. Linda Williams, "Mega-melodrama! Vertical and Horizontal Suspensions of the 'Classical,'" *Modern Drama* 55, no. 4 (2012): 524, 530.

23. Anker, "Villains, Victims," 23.

24. Buckley, "Refugee Theater," 176.

25. Singer, *Melodrama and Modernity,* 39.

26. Aristotle, quoted in ibid., 44.

27. Williams, "Mega-melodrama!" 525. See also Anker, "Villains, Victims," 24–26.

28. Buckley, "Refugee Theater," 186.

29. Ibid., 188.

30. Ana Lopez, "The Melodrama in Latin America: Films, Telenovelas, and the Currency of a Popular Form," in Landy, *Imitations of Life,* 597; emphasis in original.

31. Ibid., 604.

32. Sheetal Majithia, "Rethinking Postcolonial Melodrama and Affect," *Modern Drama* 58, no. 1 (Spring 2015): 1–23. The quote is from Michael Hardt, "What Are Affects Good For?"; quoted in Majithia, 7.

33. Susan Dever, *Celluloid Nationalism and Other Melodramas: From Post-Revolutionary Mexico to* fin de siglo *Mexamérica* (New York: State University of New York Press, 2003), 9.

34. Reynaldo Ileto, "The Past in the Present Crisis," in *The Philippines after Marcos,* ed. R. J. May and Francisco Nemenzo (London: Croom Helm, 1985), 13, 15.

35. Christine Gledhill, "Speculations on the Relationship between Soap Opera and Melodrama," *Quarterly Review of Film and Video* 14, no. 1 (1992): 108.

36. Berlant, "Subject of True Feeling," 53.

37. Berlant, *Female Complaint,* 110–11.

38. Berlant, "Subject of True Feeling," 53.

39. Berlant, *Female Complaint,* 40.

40. Ibid., 36.

41. Ibid., 56.

42. Ibid., 41.

43. Majithia, "Rethinking Postcolonial Melodrama," 1.

44. Gould, "Affect and Protest," 29, 30.

45. Berlant, *Female Complaint,* 65.

46. Gould, "Affect and Protest," 30.

47. Berlant, "Epistemology of State Emotion," 52.

48. Berlant, "Subject of True Feeling," 54.

49. Jose F. Lacaba, *Days of Disquiet, Nights of Rage: The First Quarter Storm and Related Events* (Manila: Salinlahi Publishing House, 1982).

50. Frantz Fanon, *The Wretched of the Earth,* trans. Constance Farrington (New York: Grove Press, 1963), 36, 210.

51. Nathan Gilbert Quimpo, *Contested Democracy and the Left in the Philippines after Marcos* (New Haven: Yale Southeast Asia Studies, Monograph 58, 2008), 53.

Chapter 1: The First Quarter Storm

1. Philip Shabecoff, "Protest Movement in the Philippines Widening Rapidly," *New York Times,* March 3, 1970, p. 10.

2. Proclamation No. 1081 Proclaiming a State of Martial Law in the Philippines; reprinted in Ferdinand E. Marcos, *The Democratic Revolution in the Philippines,* 2nd ed. (Englewood Cliffs, NJ: Prentice-Hall International, 1979), 335–51.

3. Ferdinand E. Marcos, "Today's Revolution: Democracy" (1971); reprinted in Marcos, *Democratic Revolution,* 1.

4. "Today's Revolution" was completed on September 17, 1971, one year and fourteen days before the declaration of martial law.

5. Shabecoff, "Protest Movement," 10.

6. F. Marcos, *Democratic Revolution,* 25.

7. Ibid., 9, 26.

8. Ibid., 35.

9. Ibid., 26.

10. Ibid., 10.

11. Tillman Durdin, "Philippine Communism," *Problems of Communism* (May–June 1976), 41.

12. Jose F. Lacaba, "The January 26 Confrontation: A Highly Personal Account," *Philippines Free Press,* February 7, 1970; reprinted in Lacaba, *Days of Disquiet,* 63.

13. In Filipino folktales, the crocodile appears as a symbol of avarice.

14. Jose F. Lacaba, *Days of Disquiet, Nights of Rage: The First Quarter Storm and Related Events* (Manila: Salinlahi Publishing House, 1982), 74.

15. All quotes in this paragraph are from ibid., 79.

16. Ibid., 80; emphasis added.

17. Robin Blackburn, "The Philippines: Rebirth of the Revolution," *Nation* 211 (December 1970): 585.

18. CPP, "Rectify Errors and Rebuild the Party," mimeograph, 1968; quoted in David Rosenberg, "Communism in the Philippines," *Problems of Communism* (September–October 1984), 34. Sison's CPP had broken away from the Philippine Communist Party, the Partido Komunista ng Pilipinas (est. 1930) and distinguished itself from its predecessor by insisting that the nation's only viable revolutionary path was armed struggle—a people's war.

19. The Huks began as an anti-Japanese resistance movement during World War II. After the war, the guerrillas remobilized in a peasant uprising (1946–57), which was effectively put down by the government with military assistance from the United States.

20. The essay appeared in the *Philippine Collegian,* the student newspaper of the University of the Philippines, on January 8, 1970.

21. Gregg Jones, *Red Revolution: Inside the Philippine Guerrilla Movement* (Boulder: Westview, 1989), 29.

22. Justus M. van der Kroef, "Philippine Communist Theory and Strategy: A New Departure?" *Pacific Affairs* 48, no. 1 (1975): 182.

23. Lacaba, *Days of Disquiet,* 69–71.

24. Vicente Rafael, *White Love and Other Events in Filipino History* (Quezon City: Ateneo de Manila University Press, 2000), 156.

25. Jose F. Lacaba, "The January 30 Insurrection," *Philippines Free Press,* February 7, 1970; reprinted in Lacaba, *Days of Disquiet,* 81.

26. Ibid., 83.

27. Ibid., 87.

28. Ibid., 19; emphasis in original.

29. The Philippine flag has two equal horizontal fields, blue and red. In peacetime, the blue field lies above the red.

30. F. Marcos, *Democratic Revolution,* 27; emphasis in original.

31. Ibid., 27, 29.

32. For a detailed account of the trial, see Raymond Bonner, *Waltzing with a Dictator: The Marcoses and the Making of American Policy* (New York: Vintage, 1988), 12–13.

33. Ibid., 45–47. The U.S. media contingent was on hand to cover the visit of Vice President Hubert Humphrey, the highest-ranking U.S. official to attend the inaugural.

34. Valenti to Johnson, memorandum, July 1, 1966; cited in Bonner, *Waltzing with a Dictator,* 47.

35. Arthur Schlesinger, "On Heroic Leadership and the Dilemma of Strong Men and Weak People," cited in Richard Slotkin, *Gunfighter Nation: The Myth of the Frontier in Twentieth-Century America* (New York: Atheneum, 1992), 501–3.

36. J. Hoberman, *The Dream Life: Movies, Media, and the Mythology of the Sixties* (New York: New Press, 2003), 33.

37. Figures are from UNESCO, "The Philippines," in UNESCO, *World Communications: Press, Radio, Television, Film* (Paris: UNESCO, 1964): 246–48.

38. I shall discuss the Philippine uptake of "modernization" as a Cold War ideology in chapter 2.

39. Hoberman, *Dream Life,* 39.

40. Daniel J. Boorstin, *The Image; or, What Happened to the American Dream* (New York: Atheneum, 1962), 258.

41. Jean Baudrillard, *Simulacra and Simulation* (Ann Arbor: University of Michigan Press, 1994), 6.

42. Hoberman, *Dream Life,* 39.

43. Michael E. Latham, *Modernization as Ideology: American Social Science and "Nation Building" in the Kennedy Era* (Chapel Hill: University of North Carolina Press, 2001), 2.

44. Quoted in Hoberman, *Dream Life,* 44.

45. W. W. Rostow; cited in Latham, *Modernization as Ideology,* 21–22.

46. Michael Rogin, "'Make My Day!': Spectacle as Amnesia in Imperial Politics" *Representations* 29 (Winter 1990): 115.

47. Fred Block; cited in Rogin, "Make My Day!," 115.

48. Ibid.

49. Slotkin, *Gunfighter Nation,* 3; emphasis in original.

50. Hoberman, *Dream Life,* 46–48, 59, 64, 69.

51. Rogin, "Make My Day!," 103.

52. Ibid., 103, 107.

53. Ibid., 106.

54. Michael Rogin, *Ronald Reagan, The Movie, and Other Episodes of Political Demonology* (Berkeley: University of California Press, 1987), 44–80.

55. Ibid., xiii, 237.

56. Rogin, "Make My Day!," 116.

57. Jonathan Schnell; cited in ibid., 115.

58. Rogin, "Make My Day!," 116.

59. For a detailed history of the collaborative efforts of national elites and Washington to defeat the Huks, see William Pomeroy, *The Philippines: Colonialism, Collaboration, and Resistance* (New York: International Publishers, 1992).

60. Bonner, *Waltzing with a Dictator,* 50.

61. Alex Campbell, "The Lawless and Corrupt Philippines," *New Republic* 160 (1969): 15.

62. Bonner, *Waltzing with a Dictator,* 53. The $3.5 million went into building the Cultural Center of the Philippines, the bastion of New Society cultural policy, which I shall examine in chapter 2.

63. Bonner, *Waltzing with a Dictator,* 78–79.

64. *Manila Times,* September 16, 1971; cited in Justus M. van der Kroef, "The Philippine Maoists," *Orbis* 16, no. 4 (1973): 917.

65. Radio Peking, December 30, 1970; cited in van der Kroef, "Philippine Maoists," 915.

66. *Manila Chronicle,* June 26, 1972; *Far Eastern Economic Review,* June 24, 1972, 11; both cited in van der Kroef, "Philippine Maoists," 893.

67. *Manila Chronicle,* June 28, 1972; cited in van der Kroef, "Philippine Maoists," 893n3.

68. Eduardo Lachica, *The Huks: Philippine Agrarian Society in Revolt* (New York: Praeger, 1971), 9; emphasis Lachica's.

69. Jones, *Red Revolution,* 59. See also Bonner, *Waltzing with a Dictator,* 79–80; van der Kroef, "Philippine Maoists," 915–16.

70. Based on interviews conducted with former top officials of the CPP-NPA in 1988, Gregg Jones reveals that Sison had in fact ordered the bombings in the belief that the nation needed a "well-timed, traumatic incident to spark the great upheaval that would lead to an early Communist victory." See Jones, *Red Revolution,* 60–65.

71. Oscar Villadolid, "Marcos Celebrates behind Barred Gates," *New York Times,* September 19, 1971; cited in van der Kroef, "Philippine Maoists," 916.

72. F. Marcos, televised address, August 21, 1971, footage in the Philippine Information Agency film archives.

73. Summary in *Philippines Free Press,* September 23, 1972; cited in Bonner, *Waltzing with a Dictator,* 95, 97.

74. Bonner, *Waltzing with a Dictator,* 97–98.

75. The film was produced by the National Media Production Center in 1971 and is archived at the Philippine Information Agency. No other metadata is available.

76. In June 1969 military personnel discovered a secret tunnel in Tarlac Province, Luzon. It proved to be a goldmine, yielding a cache of documents outlining the creation of the CPP-NPA earlier that year. The discovery propitiously coincided with the annual congressional budget hearings for the severely underfinanced Armed Forces of the Philippines. Hoping to secure a larger share of the national budget, the AFP published the captured documents under the title *So the People May Know.* South East Asia Treaty Organization, "The Maoist Communist Policy of the Philippines," SEATO Short Paper no. 52, Bangkok, September 1971; cited in Van der Kroef, "Philippine Maoists," 906.

77. The photographs, which were among the documents captured by the AFP in 1969, depict CPP cadres in an educational trip to the People's Republic of China.

78. Rogin, *Ronald Reagan,* 50, 68.

79. For an excellent analysis of these stock tropes, see Ella Shohat and Robert Stam, *Unthinking Eurocentrism: Multiculturalism and the Media* (London: Routledge, 1994), 137–70.

80. Rogin, "Make My Day!," 107.
81. Jones, *Red Revolution*, 68.
82. Rogin, "Make My Day!," 117.
83. Francis T. Underhill, quoted in Bonner, *Waltzing with a Dictator,* 93.
84. Ibid., 97.
85. Proclamation 1081, the long document spelling out the justifications for martial law was dated September 21. Marcos, who was superstitious about the number 7, backdated the document to reflect a number divisible by 7, his lucky number. See ibid., 101–2n.
86. I shall analyze this rivalry in terms of the Marcos romance in the next chapter.
87. "Marcos Is Said to Admit Spy Activities," *Washington Post,* July 16, 1986, A19; cited in Richard Kessler, *Rebellion and Repression in the Philippines* (New Haven: Yale University Press, 1989), 116–21.
88. Rogin, *Ronald Reagan*, 77.

Chapter 2: Social Conduct and the New Society

1. Roman Dubsky, "The Institutionalizing of Social Conduct and the New Society of the Philippines," *Philippine Journal of Public Administration* 18, no. 2 (April 1974): 127–45.
2. Ferdinand E. Marcos, *Notes on the New Society of the Philippines* (Manila: Marcos Foundation, 1973), 45.
3. Michael E. Latham, *Modernization as Ideology: American Social Science and "Nation Building" in the Kennedy Era* (Chapel Hill: University of North Carolina Press, 2001), 23.
4. David Rosenberg, "Liberty versus Loyalty: The Transformation of the Philippine News Media under Martial Law," in *Marcos and Martial Law in the Philippines,* ed. David Rosenberg (Ithaca: Cornell University Press, 1979), 149.
5. Raymond Bonner, *Waltzing with a Dictator: The Marcoses and the Making of American Policy* (New York: Vintage, 1988), 116.
6. Ibid., 116–17.
7. Latham, *Modernization as Ideology*, 4.
8. Samuel P. Huntington, *Political Order in Changing Societies* (New Haven: Yale University Press, 1968), 4.
9. Bonner, *Waltzing with a Dictator,* 123–24.
10. Ferdinand E. Marcos, *An Ideology for Filipinos* (Manila: Marcos Foundation, 1980), 64.
11. Ferdinand E. Marcos, *In Search of Alternatives: The Third World in an Age of Crisis* (Manila: Marcos Foundation, 1980), 34.

12. Ibid., 37.

13. Frantz Fanon, *Wretched of the Earth,* trans. Constance Farrington (New York: Grove Press, 1963), 99, 315.

14. F. Marcos, *Notes on the New Society,* 85.

15. F. Marcos, *In Search of Alternatives,* 50–51.

16. Fanon, *Wretched of the Earth,* 36–37.

17. Vicente Rafael, *White Love and Other Events in Filipino History* (Quezon City: Ateneo de Manila University Press, 2000), xii.

18. While U.S. history textbooks typically devote pages to the Spanish-American War and only a paragraph or two to the Philippine conflict, the staggering violence of that war cannot be overemphasized. The Philippines lost sixteen thousand men in combat (against four thousand U.S. casualties), while another two hundred thousand Filipinos died from war-related hunger or disease. See Luzviminda Francisco, "The Philippine-American War," in *The Philippines Reader: A History of Colonialism, Neocolonialism, Dictatorship and Resistance,* ed. Daniel B. Schirmer and Stephen Rosskam Shalom (Boston: South End Press, 1987), 19; Bonner, *Waltzing with a Dictator,* 29.

19. See, for example, Dean C. Worcester, *The Philippines Past and Present,* 2 vols. (New York: Macmillan, 1914), 2:921–22, 938.

20. Rafael, *White Love,* 20.

21. Quoted in Paul A. Kramer, "The Pragmatic Empire: U.S. Anthropology and Colonial Politics in the Occupied Philippines, 1898–1916" (Ph.D. diss., Princeton University, 1998), 149–50.

22. Quoted in Rafael, *White Love,* 21.

23. Rafael is here quoting the 1900 Philippine Commission in *Report of the Philippine Commission to the President* (Washington, D.C.: U.S. Government Printing Office, 1900–1901), 1:4–5; Rafael, *White Love.*

24. Rafael, *White Love,* 22.

25. William Howard Taft, The Philippine Islands: An Address Delivered Before the Chamber of Commerce of the State of New York (New York: 1904), 6–9; cited in Rafael, *White Love.*

26. Woodrow Wilson, *Constitutional Government in the United States* (New York: Columbia University Press, 1921), 52–53; cited in Rafael, *White Love.*

27. Fanon, *Wretched of the Earth,* 63.

28. See Ferdinand E. Marcos, *Five Years of the New Society* (Manila: Marcos Foundation, 1978), 181–85.

29. Dubsky, "Institutionalizing of Social Conduct," 134–35.

30. Marcos, *Ideology for Filipinos,* 69.

31. Jose Maria Crisol, *Towards the Restructuring of Filipino Values* (Manila: Office of Civil Relations, Philippine Army, n.d.), 47, quoted in McCoy, "Anarchy of Families," 16–17.

32. Jacques Donzelot, *The Policing of Families*, trans. Robert Hurley (New York: Pantheon, 1979), 6–7.

33. Michel Foucault, "Governmentality," in *The Foucault Effect: Studies in Governmentality*, ed. Graham Burchell, Colin Gordon, and Peter Miller (London: Harvester Wheatsheaf, 1991), 93.

34. F. Marcos, *Five Years*, 184.

35. Fanon, *Wretched of the Earth*, 210, 218.

36. F. Marcos, *Five Years*, 177–78.

37. Tony Bennett, *The Birth of the Museum: History, Theory, Politics* (London: Routledge, 1995), 18.

38. F. Marcos, *Notes on the New Society*, 69.

39. Bennett, *Birth of the Museum*, 24.

40. Foucault, "Governmentality," 93, 95. See also Tony Bennett, *Culture: A Reformer's Science* (London: Sage, 1998), 69.

41. F. Marcos, *Notes on the New Society*, 70.

42. Ibid., 120.

43. Ibid., 77.

44. Constantino C. Tejero, "Imelda's Role as Patroness of the Arts," *Philippine Daily Inquirer*, August 4, 2003, G2.

45. See Talitha Espiritu, "The Marcos Romance and the Cultural Center of the Philippines: The Melodrama of a Therapeutic Cultural Policy," *Journal of Narrative Theory* 45, no. 1 (Winter 2015): 141–62.

46. Toby Miller and George Yúdice, *Cultural Policy* (London: Sage, 2002), 1.

47. Toby Miller, *The Well-Tempered Self: Citizenship, Culture, and the Postmodern Subject* (Baltimore: Johns Hopkins University Press, 1993), xii.

48. Miller and Yúdice, *Cultural Policy*, 9

49. Christine Gledhill, "Speculations on the Relationship between Soap Opera and Melodrama," *Quarterly Review of Film and Video* 14, no. 1 (1992): 108.

50. Miller and Yúdice, *Cultural Policy*, 12, 9.

51. George Yúdice, "For a Practical Aesthetics," *Social Text* 25–26 (1990): 136.

52. Lucrecia R. Kasilag, "The Cultural Center of the Philippines: Its Role in the Development of National Culture" (paper presented at the National Conference on Enhancing the Development of Our National Culture, National Library, Manila, 7–9 April, 1980), 2.

53. Ilenea Maramag, *Official Primer of the Cultural Center of the Philippines*, souvenir program (Manila: Cultural Center of the Philippines, 1969).

54. Tejero, "Imelda's Role," G2.

55. Vicente Rafael, "Patronage and Pornography: Ideology and Spectatorship in the Early Marcos Years," *Comparative Studies in Society and History* 32, no. 2 (1990): 282–304.

56. Quoted in Raymond Bonner, *Waltzing with a Dictator: The Marcoses and the Making of American Policy* (New York: Vintage, 1988), 19.

57. Kerima Polotan, *Imelda Romualdez Marcos* (New York: World Publishing, 1969).

58. Nancy Armstrong, "The Rise of Domestic Woman," cited in Bennett, *Culture,* 80.

59. Carmen Navarro Pedrosa, *The Untold Story of Imelda Marcos* (Manila: Bookmark, 1969).

60. Carmen Navarro Pedrosa, *Imelda Marcos: The Rise and Fall of One of the World's Most Powerful Women* (New York: St. Martin's Press, 1987), 16–49.

61. Luciano Carlos and Emanuel Borlaza. *Iginuhit ng Tadhana.* VHS. Directed by Mariano Torre, Jose De Villa and Conrado Conde. Manila: Sampaguita Pictures, 1965.

62. Laura Mulvey, "Visual Pleasure and Narrative Cinema," in *Film Theory and Criticism,* ed. Gerald Mast, Marshall Cohen, and Leo Braudy (London: Oxford, 1992), 803–16.

63. Hartzell Spence, *Marcos of the Philippines* (New York: World Publishing, 1982), 240.

64. Miller and Yúdice, *Cultural Policy,* 12.

65. Pedrosa, *Imelda Marcos: Rise and Fall,* 86–88.

66. Polotan, *Imelda Romualdez Marcos,* 184.

67. Miller and Yúdice, *Cultural Policy,* 7, 9, 15.

68. Terry Eagleton, *The Ideology of the Aesthetic;* cited in Yúdice, "For a Practical Aesthetics," 132.

69. Miller and Yúdice, *Cultural Policy,* 11.

70. Quoted in Miller and Yúdice, *Cultural Policy,* 7.

71. Pedrosa, *Imelda Marcos: Rise and Fall,* 91.

72. Bonner reveals that Imelda was diagnosed as "manic depressive" and was treated with tranquilizers and lithium. Bonner, *Waltzing with a Dictator,* 55.

73. Pedrosa, *Imelda Marcos: Rise and Fall,* 91–92.

74. Rafael, "Patronage and Pornography," 283.

75. Mulvey, "Visual Pleasure," 811.

76. Rafael, "Patronage and Pornography," 290 ; emphasis added.

77. Pedrosa, *Imelda Marcos: Rise and Fall,* 94, 104.

78. Kerima Polotan, "The Men, the Method," *Philippines Free Press,* April 5, 1969, 59–60.

79. Pedrosa, *Imelda Marcos: Rise and Fall,* 106.

80. For a detailed architectural analysis of the building, see esp. Gerardo Lico, *Edifice Complex: Power, Myth and Marcos State Architecture* (Manila: Ateneo de Manila University Press, 2003), 89–90; 105–6.

81. Cultural Center of the Philippines, "A Special Presentation on the Occasion of the Inauguration of the CCP," program notes, 1969.

82. I am here alluding to Tony Bennett's insights on the ethico-aesthetic functions of cultural institutions in general, which he describes, following Foucault, as "technologies of the self." See Bennett, *Birth of the Museum,* 24.

83. Laurajane Smith, *The Uses of Heritage* (London: Routledge, 2006), 305.

84. Lico, *Edifice Complex,* 70, 74–75.

85. Quoted in Nick Joaquin, "A Stage for Greatness," *Philippines Free Press,* September 30, 1969, p. 73.

86. Ma. Elena H. Abesamis, "Cultural Center Fare Program," *Sunday Times Magazine* (Philippines), March 23, 1969, p. 27.

87. Cultural Center of the Philippines, brochure, 1966, quoted in Lico, *Edifice Complex,* 41.

88. Abesamis, "Cultural Center Fare Program," 27.

89. F. Marcos, *Five Years,* 172.

90. In reconstructing these discussions, I am relying on unpublished symposium documents archived in the National Library, Manila.

91. Julian E. Dacanay, "The State of Research on Cultural Development in the Philippines," unpublished manuscript prepared for UNESCO Division for Cultural Development, Manila, Ateneo de Manila University Institute of Philippine Culture, 1973, pp. 1–2.

92. Leonidas V. Benesa, "Do We Have a Cultural Policy?," paper presented at the Symposium on Cultural Policy of the Philippines, Cultural Center of the Philippines, December 11, 1972, pp. 1–4.

93. Article IV, section 9, paragraphs (2) and (3). The relevant passages appear unchanged in the "new" constitution of the Philippines, ratified in 1973. See Jose M. Aruego, *The New Philippine Constitution Explained* (Manila: University Book Supply, 1973).

94. Jose D. Ingles, "The Cultural Policy of the New Society," paper presented at the Symposium on Cultural Policy of the Philippines, December 11, 1972, pp. 1–2.

95. Fanon, *Wretched of the Earth,* 224–25.

96. Ingles, "Cultural Policy," 2.

97. See Talitha Espiritu, "Native Subjects on Display: Reviving the Colonial Exposition in Marcos' Philippines," *Social Identities* 18, no. 6 (Fall 2012): 729–44.

98. Philippines, National Media and Production Center, *The Marcos Revolution: A Progress Report on the New Society of the Philippines,* (Manila: NMPC, 1980), 169.

99. Bonner, *Waltzing with a Dictator,* 245.

Chapter 3: National Discipline and the Cinema

1. Ferdinand Marcos to Board of Censors for Motion Pictures, Manila, Letter of Instruction no. 13; reprinted in *Official Gazette,* October 9, 1972, p. 7955.

2. Project Development Institute, "Feasibility Study: Philippine National Cinema Values Formation Program," unpublished study, October 1991, pp. 8–9; ASEAN, Committee on Culture and Information, Working Group on Film, "The Film Industry in the Philippines," in *ASEAN Country Reports on Film* (Manila: Office of Media Affairs, 1983), 26.

3. A. Roces, "The Bakya Mentality," *Manila Times,* March 12, 1965, quoted in John Lent, *The Asian Film Industry* (Austin: University of Texas Press, 1990), 158.

4. Guillermo C. de Vega, *Film and Freedom: Movie Censorship in the Philippines* (Manila: Board of Censors for Motion Pictures, 1975), 32–33

5. Community feeling particular to cinema spectatorship; see Ella Shohat and Robert Stam, *Unthinking Eurocentrism: Multiculturalism and the Media* (London: Routledge, 1994), 103.

6. Namely, the Dalisay, Life, and Center theaters. Lina Flor, "Problems of the Philippine Movie Industry," *Fookien Times Yearbook,* 1961, p. 223.

7. De Vega, *Film and Freedom,* 34–35.

8. Ibid., 34.

9. Clodualdo del Mundo, "Philippine Cinema: An Historical Overview," *Asian Cinema* 10, no. 2 (Spring/Summer, 1999): 29–66. See also Nicanor Tiongson, "The Filipino Film Industry," *East-West Film Journal* 6, no. 2 (1992): 23–61.

10. ASEAN, Committee on Culture, "Film Industry in the Philippines," 25–26.

11. Philippines Project Development Institute, feasibility study, 8.

12. De Vega, *Film and Freedom,* 44

13. Bienvenido Lumbera, "Problems in Philippine Film History," in *Readings in Philippine Cinema,* ed. Rafael Ma. Guerrero (Manila: Experimental Cinema of the Philippines, 1983), 75.

14. Ibid., 76.

15. ASEAN, Committee on Culture, "Film Industry in the Philippines," 27.

16. Russell Johnson, "Is the Philippines Next?," *Liberation,* November 1970, p. 27; cited in Justus M. van der Kroef, "The Philippine Maoists," *Orbis* 16, no. 4 (1973): 902.

17. Robin Blackburn, "The Philippines: Rebirth of the Revolution," *Nation* 211 (December 1970): 583.

18. David Wurfel, *Filipino Politics: Development and Decay* (Ithaca: Cornell University Press, 1988), 103.

19. *Philippines Free Press,* March 28, 1953, p. 34; cited in McCoy, "Anarchy of Families," 14.

20. U.S. Embassy, Manila, confidential report, November 8, 1965; cited in Raymond Bonner, *Waltzing with a Dictator: The Marcoses and the Making of American Policy* (New York: Vintage, 1988), 25.

21. R. H. Leary, "President's Progress," *Far Eastern Economic Review,* November 4, 1966; cited in ibid., 25.

22. Carmen Navarro Pedrosa, *Imelda Marcos: The Rise and Fall of One of the World's Most Powerful Women* (New York: St. Martin's, 1987), 105.

23. William C. Rempel, *Delusions of a Dictator: The Mind of Marcos as Revealed in His Secret Diaries* (Boston: Little, Brown, 1993), 84.

24. Jose Veloso Abueva, "The Philippines: Tradition and Change," *Asian Survey* 10, no. 1 (1970): 62.

25. Blackburn, "Rebirth of the Revolution," 583.

26. Rempel, *Delusions of a Dictator,* 84.

27. Marcos would name a palace auditorium Maharlika Hall, a major highway Maharlika Highway, and even sought to change the country's name to Maharlika. Bonner, *Waltzing with a Dictator,* 17.

28. Marcos filed a claim with the U.S. government, stating that the organization had eighty-three hundred members. Had the claim been accepted, all the men would have been entitled to back pay and benefits from the U.S. government. Marcos also claimed to have been the recipient of at least thirty awards, medals, and citations, including the Congressional Medal of Honor. This would have made him the most decorated Filipino soldier in history. Bonner, *Waltzing with a Dictator,* 14–17. See also Charles C. McDougald, *The Marcos File: Was He a Philippine Hero or Corrupt Tyrant?* (San Francisco: San Francisco Publishers, 1987).

29. Rempel, *Delusions of a Dictator,* 76.

30. Beams's screen credits include *Wild Wheels* and a bit part in the television show *The Name of the Game.* Ibid., 79–80.

31. Bonner, *Waltzing with a Dictator,* 67.

32. Rempel, *Delusions of a Dictator,* 83.

33. The full transcript of Beams's tape was published in Hermie Rotea, *Marcos' Lovey Dovie* (Los Angeles: Liberty Publishing, 1983).

34. Rempel, *Delusions of a Dictator,* 86.

35. Beams claimed to have received death threats from Marcos's hired goons. She also claimed that U.S. diplomats offered to give her $100,000 for her audiotapes. Bonner, *Waltzing with a Dictator,* 68.

36. Rempel, *Delusions of a Dictator,* 86; Bonner, *Waltzing with a Dictator,* 67–68.

37. Pedrosa, *Imelda Marcos: Rise and Fall,* 121.

38. Marcos never forgave editors of the *Graphic.* When martial law was declared, they were among the hundreds of journalists arrested by the military.

39. For the full text of the speech and a thorough account of the political rivalry between Marcos and Aquino, see Manuel F. Martinez, *The Grand Collision: Aquino vs. Marcos* (Hong Kong: AP&G Resources, 1984).

40. Quoted in Rempel, *Delusions of a Dictator,* 50–51.

41. Ferdinand Marcos, personal diary, February 3, 1970; quoted in ibid., 51.

42. De Vega, *Film and Freedom,* 36.

43. Ibid., 37.

44. De Vega, "A Look at Film Censorship," *Fookien Times Yearbook,* 1974, p. 339.

45. De Vega, *Film and Freedom,* 38.

46. De Vega, "Film Censorship," 339.

47. De Vega, *Film and Freedom,* 38.

48. Lauren Berlant and Michael Warner, "Sex in Public," *Critical Inquiry* 24, no. 2, Intimacy (special issue, Winter 1998): 553; emphasis in the original.

49. Ibid., 554–55.

50. Ibid., 549.

51. De Vega, *Film and Freedom,* 43.

52. Ibid., 44.

53. "New Role in the New Society: A Great Challenge Faces Philippine Movie Industry," *Philippine Panorama,* October 14, 1973, p. 10.

54. De Vega, "Film Censorship," 339.

55. Imelda Romualdez Marcos, "Film as Art," Filipino Academy of Movie Arts and Sciences Awards, Manila, April 21, 1974; reprinted in *The Compassionate Society and Other Selected Speeches,* ed. Ileana Maramag (Manila: National Media Production Center, 1976), 58–59.

56. De Vega, *Film and Freedom,* 45.

57. Board of Censors for Motion Pictures, Guidelines on Film and Television Production and Exhibition, brochure July 9, 1975, pp. 1–2; emphasis in original.

58. Ibid., 2–3; emphasis in original.

59. Vicente Rafael, *White Love and Other Events in Filipino History* (Manila: Ateneo de Manila University Press, 2000), 156.

60. Ibid., 152.

61. Frantz Fanon, *The Wretched of the Earth*, trans. Constance Farrington (New York: Grove Press, 1963), 36.

62. Gustave Le Bon, *The Crowd: A Study of the Popular Mind* (1895; repr., New York: Viking, 1960). See Gould's instructive overview of the collective behavior school in Gould, "On Affect and Protest," in Staiger, Cvetkovich, and Reynolds, *Political Emotions*, 20–23.

63. Gould, "Affect and Protest," 21.

64. Ibid., 24.

65. I am here drawing from Gould's explication of affect as a "structure of feeling." Ibid., 32.

66. Tiongson, "Filipino Film Industry," 30.

67. Joel David, *The National Pastime: Contemporary Philippine Cinema* (Manila: Anvil, 1990), 17.

68. Lent, *Asian Film Industry*, 167.

69. Bienvenido Lumbera, *Pelikula: An Essay on Philippine Film, 1961–1992* (Manila: Cultural Center of the Philippines, 1992), 30.

70. Filipino film historians hail this group as the auteurs of the New Cinema. Representative works are Brocka's *Maynila sa kuko ng liwanag* (Manila in the claws of light, 1975), *Insiang* (1976), *Jaguar* (1979), *Bayan ko: Kapit sa patalim* (My country: Seize the blade, 1985), and *Orapronobis* (Fight for us, 1989); Bernal's *Pagdating sa dulo* (In the end, 1971), *Nunal sa tubig* (Speck in the water, 1976), *Manila by night* (1980), *Relasyon* (Affair, 1982), *Himala* (Miracle, 1982), and *Broken Marriage* (1984); Castillo's *Pagputi ng uwak, Pag-itim ng tagak* (When the crow turns white, when the heron turns black, 1978); Eddie Romero's *Ganito kami noon, paano kayo ngayon?* (This is how we were, how are you now?, 1976); Diaz-Abaya's *Brutal* (1980), *Moral* (1982), *Karnal* (1983); de Leon's *Batch '81* (1982), *Kisapmata* (In the blink of an eye, 1981), and *Sister Stella L.* (1984); and Gallaga's *Oro, plata, mata* (Gold, silver, death, 1982) and *Virgin Forest* (1984). See Tiongson, "Filipino Film Industry," 31–43.

71. Lent, *Asian Film Industry*, 173.

72. Zenaida Latorre, film review, *Sixteen*, June 1970, quoted in Agustin L. Sotto, "Filmography," in *Lino Brocka: The Artist and His Times*, ed. Mario Hernando (Manila: Cultural Center of the Philippines, 1993), 245.

73. Luis Francia, "Philippine Cinema: The Struggle against Repression," in *Film and Politics in the Third World*, ed. John D. H. Downing (New York: Praeger, 1987), 214.

74. In the predominantly Catholic society of the Philippines, abortions are illegal. The 1930 Revised Penal Code of the Philippines, which remains in effect today, mandates imprisonment for a woman who undergoes an abortion, as well as for any person who assists in the procedure.

75. Mario Hernando, "Lino Brocka: Director in Control, Blending Popular Entertainment, Realism and Social Comment," in Hernando, *Lino Brocka,* 42.

76. Fanon, *Wretched of the Earth,* 212.

77. The festival was initiated in 1976 by the Philippine Motion Picture Producers Association (PMPPA), a professional organization created in 1963 (initially as an industry response to the lack of government support for local films).

78. MOWELFUND was set up in 1974 by Joseph Estrada, a former action star, who at the time, was mayor of San Juan. For information on MOWELFUND's programs, see Philippine National Cinema Values Formation Program, 1991, appendix 2.

79. "New Role in the New Society," 10.

80. Philippine National Cinema Values Formation Program, feasibility study, 1991, pp. 8–11.

Chapter 4: Popular Struggles and Elite Politics

1. Alex Campbell, "The Lawless and Corrupt Philippines," *New Republic* 160 (1969): 16–17.

2. Quoted in Alfred W. McCoy, "An Anarchy of Families: The Historiography of State and Family in the Philippines," in McCoy, *Anarchy of Families,* 7.

3. Benedict Anderson, *The Spectre of Comparisons: Nationalism, Southeast Asia and the World* (London: Verso, 1998), 201–2.

4. McCoy, "Anarchy of Families," 7.

5. A high-profile example is the case of ex-president Corazon Cojuangco Aquino (1986–90). A local battle for political legacy had led her cousin Eduardo "Danding" Cojuangco, Jr., into a long-term alliance with Marcos. Fostering a lifelong estrangement between the two cousins, this internal family dispute was further compounded by Corazon's marriage to Benigno Aquino, Jr.

6. J. Maravilla, "Upsurge of Anti-Imperialist Movement in the Philippines," *World Marxist Review* vol. 8, no. 11 (November 1965): 59.

7. Frank H. Golay, *The Philippines: Public Policy and National Economic Development* (Ithaca: Cornell University Press, 1961), 71–72. See

also Gary Hawes, *The Philippine State and the Marcos Regime: The Politics of Export* (Ithaca: Cornell University Press 1987), 28–30, 89–90.

8. Paul D. Hutchcroft, *Booty Capitalism: The Politics of Banking in the Philippines* (Ithaca: Cornell University Press, 1998), 28–30.

9. David Wurfel, *Filipino Politics: Development and Decay* (Ithaca: Cornell University Press, 1988), 152.

10. Ricardo Manapat, *Some Are Smarter Than Others: The History of Marcos' Crony Capitalism* (New York: Aletheia Publications, 1991), 85.

11. Paul D. Hutchcroft, "Oligarchs and Cronies in the Philippine State: The Politics of Patrimonial Plunder." *World Politics* 43, no. 3 (1991): 414–50.

12. Jose Veloso Abueva, "Ideology and Practice in the 'New Society,'" in Rosenberg, *Marcos and Martial Law*, 66.

13. Rigoberto D. Tiglao, "The Consolidation of the Dictatorship," in *Dictatorship and Revolution,* ed. Aurora Javate de Dios, Petronilo Daroy, and Lorna Kalaw-Tirol (Manila: Conspectus, 1988), 38. See also Lela Garner Noble, "Politics in the Marcos Era," in *Crisis in the Philippines: The Marcos Era and Beyond,* ed. John Bresnan (Princeton: Princeton University Press, 1986), 90.

14. Hawes, *Philippine State,* 83–84.

15. Joseph Lelyveld, "Workers in Richest Sugar Region Are Still Untouched by Boom," *New York Times,* November 11, 1974, p. 7.

16. The Association of Major Religious Superiors of the Philippines (AMRSP) is a permanent organization representing Catholic priests and nuns. It was established in 1971 to study structural injustices in the Philippines. The Association of Major Religious Superiors, *The Sugar Workers of Negros* (Manila, 1975); cited in Hawes, *Philippine State,* 85.

17. Republic of the Philippines, National Wage Commission, *The 1977 Sugar Industry Study* (Manila, n.d.); cited in Hawes, *Philippine State,* 84.

18. "The Philippines: Powder Keg of the Pacific," *Time,* September 24, 1979.

19. John M. Meenahan, "When Sweetness Goes," *Veritas,* October 27, 1987, p. 17.

20. Noble, "Politics in the Marcos Era," 93.

21. Hawes, *Philippine State,* 97.

22. Tiglao, "Consolidation of the Dictatorship," 61.

23. See Youngblood's summary of the crony-controlled press in Robert L. Youngblood, "Government-Media Relations in the Philippines," *Asian Survey* 21, no. 7 (1981): 711–12.

24. For an overview of the ownership structure of the broadcasting sector, see John Lent, *Broadcasting in Asia and the Pacific: A Continental*

Survey of Radio and Television (Philadelphia: Temple University Press, 1983), 183.

25. "Martial Law and Its Consequences," in *The State of the Philippine Press: Report of the National Press Club Seminar Committee,* ed. Renato Constantino (Manila: Foundation for Nationalist Studies, 1983), 19.

26. Juan Miguel's description meshes with the *New York Times* report. See Lelyveld, "Richest Sugar Region."

27. Exemplary works illustrating the Philippine uptake of liberation theology are Antonio Lambino, "Justice and Evangelization: A Theological Perspective," in Pedro S. Achútegui, ed. *On Faith and Justice: Contemporary Issues for Filipino Christians,* Loyola Papers 5 (Manila: Loyola School of Theology, Ateneo de Manila University, 1976); Carlos H. Abesamis, *Salvation: Historical and Total* (Manila: JMC Press, 1978); Catalino G. Arrevalo, "The Task of the Church: Liberation and Development," in *The Filipino in the Seventies,* ed. Vitalino R. Gorospe and Richard L. Deats (Manila: New Day, 1973), 233–83.

28. Robert L. Youngblood, *Marcos against the Church: Economic Development and Political Repression in the Philippines* (Ithaca: Cornell University Press, 1990), 70–71.

29. Association of the Major Religious Superiors of the Philippines (AMRSP) to the Catholic Bishop's Conference of the Philippines (CBCP), January 12, 1974; cited in ibid., 85.

30. Carl Lande, "The Political Crisis," in Bresnan, *Crisis in the Philippines,* 132.

31. Bernard Wideman, "Philippines' Tough Line on Strikes," *Far Eastern Economic Review,* November 14, 1975, pp. 47–48.

32. Francisco Nemenzo, "The Left and the Traditional Opposition," in May and Nemenzo, *Philippines after Marcos,* 54.

33. Tiglao, "Consolidation of the Dictatorship," 59.

34. Nemenzo, "Left and the Traditional Opposition," 54.

35. Pablo Tariman, "The Theater Odyssey of Behn Cervantes," *Philippine Star,* 7 November 7, 2010, http://www.Philstar.com.

36. See Talitha Espiritu, "Performing Native Identities: Human Displays and Indigenous Activism in Marcos' Philippines," in *The Routledge Companion to Global Popular Culture,* ed. Toby Miller (New York: Routledge, 2015), 417–25.

37. Martha Winnacker, "The Battle to Stop the Chico Dams," *Southeast Asia Chronicle* 67 (October 1979): 22–29.

38. Joel Rocamora, "The Political Uses of PANAMIN," *Southeast Asia Chronicle* 67 (October 1979), 17.

39. *Panamin News* 1, no. 3 (October 1976).

40. Francisco F. Claver to President Ferdinand E. Marcos, April 25, 1975; reprinted in Francisco E. Claver, *The Stones Will Cry Out: Grassroots Pastorals* (Maryknoll, NY: Orbis Books, 1978), 135–45.

41. Sheilah Ocampo, "Breaching a Dam of Despair," *Far Eastern Economic Review*, June 13, 1980, p. 23.

42. Richard Vokey, "Assault on the Peaks of Power," *Far Eastern Economic Review*, June 13, 1980, p. 24.

43. Winnacker, "Stop the Chico Dams," 28–29.

44. Bernard Wideman, "Cracking Down on Dissent," *Far Eastern Economic Review*, February 6, 1976, p. 12.

45. For an overview of these urban development projects, see Walden Bello, David Kinley, and Elaine Elinson, *Development Debacle: The World Bank in the Philippines* (San Francisco: Institute for Food and Development Policy, 1982), 108–20.

46. Youngblood, *Marcos against the Church*, 112.

47. Francisco F. Claver, "Who's Afraid of the Basic Christian Communities?," *Solidarity*, no. 95 (1983): 26.

48. Tiglao, "Consolidation of the Dictatorship," 60.

49. "Trining Herrera, ZOTO Head Tortured," news release from the National Office of Mass Media, Manila, May 6, 1977; cited in Youngblood, *Marcos against the Church*, 152.

50. *Bulletin Today*, December 12, 1974, pp. 1, 5; cited in Youngblood, *Marcos against the Church*, 151.

51. Amnesty International, *Report of an Amnesty International Mission to the Republic of the Philippines, 22 November–5 December, 1975* (London: n.p., 1977), 6; cited in Mark Thompson, *The Anti-Marcos Struggle: Personalistic Rule and Democratic Transition in the Philippines* (New Haven: Yale University Press, 1995), 72.

52. TFDP to the ARMSP, April 25, 1974, "To All Major Superiors Men and Women," cited in Youngblood, *Marcos against the Church*, 159.

53. TFDP, *Political Detainees Update*, May 3, 1985; cited in Youngblood, *Marcos against the Church*, 154.

54. The technique was named for the bridge connecting Imelda Marcos's home province of Leyte with neighboring Samar. On Lacaba's imprisonment and torture, see Bonner, *Waltzing with a Dictator*, 167.

55. Task Force Detainees, *Political Detainees Update*, August 15, 1982, pp. 3, 6; cited in Youngblood, *Marcos against the Church*, 152.

56. Abueva, "Ideology and Practice," 51.

57. Thompson, *Anti-Marcos Struggle*, 73.

58. "Promises, Promises in Manila," *New York Times*, August 25, 1977, p. 18.

59. Kit G. Machado, "The Philippines in 1978: Authoritarian Consolidation Continues," *Asian Survey* 19, no. 2 (February 1979): 132.

60. Gregorio Brilliantes, "More than a Martyr of the Bourgeoisie: Ninoy and the Left," *National Midweek,* September 24, 1986, p. 10.

61. Rodney Tasker, "A Political Star Is Reborn," *Far Eastern Economic Review,* March 24, 1978, p. 10.

62. Ibid., 11.

63. Thompson, *Anti-Marcos Struggle,* 76.

64. Carl Lande, "Philippine Prospects after Martial Law," *Foreign Affairs* 59, no. 5 (Summer 1981): 1159–60.

65. Machado, "Philippines in 1978," 133.

66. Bonner, *Waltzing with a Dictator,* 238.

67. Rosalinda Pineda-Ofreneo, *The Manipulated Press: A History of Philippine Journalism since 1945* (Manila: Solar, 1986), 142.

68. Thompson, *Anti-Marcos Struggle,* 74. See also Gregg Jones, *Red Revolution: Inside the Philippine Guerrilla Movement* (Boulder: Westview, 1989), 115.

69. The account of Tañada's symbolic gesture and the protestors' dramatic reaction is from Bonner, *Waltzing with a Dictator,* 240.

70. James B. Reuter, "Death in Manila," April 1978 (typescript); cited in Youngblood, *Marcos against the Church,* 122.

71. Bonner, *Waltzing with a Dictator,* 240; Joaquin G. Bernas, provincial superior, Philippine Province of the Society of Jesus, "Arrest, Investigation and Death of Teotimo Tantiado, 17," April 25, 1978 (typescript); cited in Youngblood, *Marcos against the Church,* 122.

72. Emmanuel S. de Dios, "The Erosion of the Dictatorship," in Javate de Dios, Daroy, and Kalaw-Tirol, *Dictatorship and Revolution,* 72.

73. See Yosi Shain and Mark Thompson, "Role of Political Exiles in Democratic Transition: The Case of the Philippines," *Journal of Developing Societies* 6 (1990): 71–86.

74. Thompson, *Anti-Marcos Struggle,* 84.

75. See, for example, Jose De Vera, "Media, Business Offices Marked for Bombing—PC," *Bulletin Today,* December 30, 1979, pp. 1, 10; Jose De Vera, "Link M'lapus Group to Urban Terror Scheme," *Bulletin Today,* December 31, 1979, pp. 1, 10.

76. April 6th Liberation Movement, *The Philippine Struggle* (Manila: Filipino Information Service, 1981), 60.

77. Sheilah Ocampo, "Marcos Wins on All Fronts," *Far Eastern Economic Review,* February 15, 1980, pp. 13–14.

78. Cited in Clark D. Neher, "The Philippines in 1980: The Gathering Storm," *Asian Survey* 21, no. 2 (1981): 264.

79. Pedrosa, *Imelda Marcos: Rise and Fall,* 163.

80. "Baffrey Links Student to Plot," *Bulletin Today,* October 20, 1980, p. 16.

81. C. C. Rosales, "Cancel ASTA Public Sessions," *Bulletin Today,* October 21, 1980, p. 1.

82. "Philippines: No to Marcos," *Time,* November 30, 1980, http://www.time.com.

83. Thompson, *Anti-Marcos Struggle,* 92.

84. Youngblood, *Marcos against the Church,* 62; Noble, "Politics in the Marcos Era," 107.

85. Thompson, *Anti-Marcos Struggle,* 92.

86. Amnesty International, USA, *"Disappearances": A Workbook* (New York: Amnesty International, 1981), 66.

87. Ibid., 63.

88. Youngblood, *Marcos against the Church,* 154.

89. Amnesty International, *Report of an Amnesty International Mission to the Republic of the Philippines, 11–28 November 1981* (London: Amnesty International, 1982), 19–20.

90. Task Force Detainees, *Political Detainees Update,* May 31, 1985, p. 9.

91. Tiglao, "Consolidation of the Dictatorship," 57.

92. Youngblood, *Marcos against the Church,* 155.

93. The following cases of militarization are drawn from Renato Constantino, *State of the Philippine Press,* 19.

Chapter 5: The Media and the Second Coming of the First Quarter Storm

1. National Media Production Center, *Annual Report 1981* (Manila: National Media Production Center), 4.

2. Raymond Bonner, *Waltzing with a Dictator: The Marcoses and the Making of American Policy* (New York: Vintage, 1988), 311.

3. Marcelo B. Soriano, *The Quiet Revolt of the Philippine Press* (Manila: WE Forum, 1981), 4.

4. The full text of Magsanoc's article is quoted in ibid., 4–8.

5. David Wurfel, "The Succession Struggle," in May and Nemenzo, *Philippines after Marcos,* 19.

6. Metro Manila was created in 1975 by Presidential Decree 1396, which merged four cities and thirteen municipalities into one city.

7. Stephan Haggard, "The Political Economy of the Philippine Debt Crisis," In *Economic Crisis and Policy Choice,* ed. Joan M. Nelson (Princeton: Princeton University Press, 1990), 227–28.

8. Kit G. Machado, "The Philippines 1978: Authoritarian Consolidation Continues," *Asian Survey* 19, no. 2 (February 1979): 131–40.

9. Henry Kamm, "Creating a Dynasty in the Philippines, *New York Times Sunday Magazine,* May 24, 1981, SM4; Wurfel, "Succession Struggle," 21.

10. David Rosenberg, "Liberty vs. Loyalty: The Transformation of the Philippine News Media under Martial Law," in Rosenberg, *Marcos and Martial Law,* 153; John Lent, *Broadcasting in Asia and the Pacific: A Continental Survey of Radio and Television* (Philadelphia: Temple University Press, 1983), 177.

11. Amado Doronila, "The Media," in May and Nemenzo, *Philippines after Marcos,* 197, 200.

12. Ibid., 201. On the self-censorship of editors and publishers, see also Rosalinda Pineda-Ofreneo, *Manipulated Press: A History of Philippine Journalism since 1945* (Manila: Solar, 1986), 154–56.

13. H. S. Beltran, "The Persecution of Journalists," *Diliman Review* 31, no. 3 (May–June 1983): 24.

14. Cited in Republic of the Philippines, Supreme Court decision, September 28, 1984, GR no. L-6992; retrieved from http://philippinelaw.info /jurisprudence/grl62992-babst-et-al-v-national-intelligence-board-et-al .html.

15. During World War II, Philippine-American forces made their last stand in the Bataan peninsula before surrendering to the Imperial Japanese Army.

16. Ibid.

17. Ma. Ceres Doyo, "Was Macli-ing Killed Because He Damned the Chico Dam?," *Panorama,* June 29, 1980; reprinted in National Press Club, ed., *The Philippine Press—Under Siege,* vol. 2 (Manila: National Press Club, Committee to Protect Writers, 1985), 13–19.

18. Mark Thompson, *The Anti-Marcos Struggle: Personalistic Rule and Democratic Transition in the Philippines* (New Haven: Yale University Press, 1995), 108.

19. Pineda-Ofreneo, *Manipulated Press,* 151; Beltran, "Persecution of Journalists," 19–20; Joel C. Paredes, "Martial Law Evils Still Dominate Local Media," in *Philippine Mass Media: A Book of Readings,* ed. Clodualdo del Mundo (Manila: Communication Foundation for Asia, 1986), 157.

20. Arlene Babst, affidavit, January 15, 1983, annex A, Republic of the Philippines Supreme Court decision, September 28, 1984, GR no. L-6992.

21. Ibid.

22. "Full Text of PD 1834," *Malaya,* May 23–29, 1980, pp. 1, 6.

23. Paredes, "Martial Law Evils," 154.

24. Primitivo Mijares, *The Conjugal Dictatorship of Ferdinand and Imelda Marcos* (San Francisco: Union Square Publications, 1975).

25. Thompson, *Anti-Marcos Struggle,* 69.

26. Nieva was served a PCO in April 1983 for his activities with the labor group Kilusang Mayo Uno (KMU). He was eventually released from detention following agitation by the NPC. His statement about the media's "tightrope act" was delivered at the director's meeting of the Confederation of Asian Journalists, held in Manila in 1984. Paredes, "Martial Law Evils," 155.

27. Randy V. Urlanda and A. C. Lee, "It's Alarming to Think What the Next MIFF Might Bring," *Panorama,* February 13, 1983, p. 30.

28. Cristina P. del Carmen, "The Cultural Edifice Turns into a Tombstone," *WHO,* January 9, 1982, p. 28.

29. Contemporaneous news accounts are sparse in detail. The following description is drawn from del Carmen's account. For a retrospective account on the film center tragedy, see Talitha Espiritu, "House of Horror," *Manila Chronicle,* November 14, 1993, p. 32.

30. "Primer on the Manila International Film Festival," *Starwatch,* January 19, 1982, p. 7.

31. "No RP Entry in Tilt," *Starwatch,* January 19, 1982, p. 6.

32. The film *PX* (Brocka, 1982) was screened, by invitation only, on January 27. The film *Kisapmata/In the Blink of an Eye* (de Leon, 1981), which had won several awards in the recently concluded Metro Manila Film Festival, was selected to close the festival.

33. "The Manila Film Fest: Paying for High Stakes," *Starwatch,* January 19, 1982, p. 2.

34. Metro Manila vice governor Ismael Mathay, Jr., quoted in Al S. Mendoza, "A Festival of Porno Flicks," *Philippine Panorama,* February 13, 1983, n.p.

35. "Uncensored Films Break Box Office Records," *Times Journal,* January 28, 1983, p. 1.

36. Ibid.

37. Luis Francia, "Philippine Cinema: The Struggle against Repression," in *Film and Politics in the Third World,* ed. John D. H. Downing, 209–18 (New York: Praeger, 1987), 212.

38. Mario Hernando, "The Experimental Cinema of the Philippines: Will It Help Make Filipino Films?," *WHO,* March 13, 1982, p. 24.

39. The new film body rendered the extant Filmboard inoperative, having absorbed all its functions. The ECP, which was attached to the Ministry of Tourism, effectively disengaged the state-supported cinema from the jurisdiction of the Cultural Center of the Philippines.

40. Hernando, "Experimental Cinema," 25.

41. Nicanor Tiongson, "The Filipino Film in the Decade of the 1980s," in *The Urian Anthology, 1980–1989,* ed. Tiongson (Manila: Antonio P. Tuvera, 2001), xviii.

42. Albert Aragon, "The Controversial, Complicated, Celebrated ECP: Two Views," *WHO*, October 6, 1982, p. 24.

43. The film was also the ECP's official entry to the Berlin Film Festival that year.

44. Danny Villanueva, "In the Realm of the Senseless," *Movie Flash*, March 4, 1983, p. 37.

45. "Uncut Films Irk Marcos," *Times Journal*, January 28, 1983, p. 6.

46. Mendoza, "Festival of Porno Flicks," 7.

47. Crispina Belen and Rod L. Villa, "Sex Movies Rake in Bulk of 'Take' in First Showing," *Bulletin Today*, January 29, 1983, p. 1.

48. "Bold Movies—Part of Growing Up—FL," *Metro Manila Times*, January 29, 1983, p. 1.

49. Manuel S. Pichel, "First Lady: It's Subjective," *Philippines Daily Express*, January 29, 1983, p. 6.

50. Belen and Villa, "Sex Movies," 1.

51. Cited in Ronald K. Constantino, "Brocka–de Leon Crusade," *Tempo*, March 10, 1983, p. 7.

52. Ruther D. Batuigas, "Will Heads Roll after the MIFF?," *Tempo*, February 10, 1983, p. 5.

53. Villanueva, "Realm of the Senseless," 37.

54. "Cinema's Gains Cited," *Times Journal*, January 25, 1982, pp. 1–2.

55. Pet G. Cleto, "Seven Voices: The Issue of Censorship," *Celebrity*, May 15, 1983, p. 41.

56. Ibid., 41.

57. Jo-Ann Maglipon, "The Brocka Battles," in Hernando, *Lino Brocka*, 123.

58. Cleto, "Seven Voices," 41.

59. David Briscoe, "Marcos Foe and Assassin Killed at Airport, Witnesses Say," AP newswire; reprinted in *Reports of the Fact-Finding Board on the Assassination of Senator Benigno S. Aquino, Jr.*, ed. Eugenia D. Apostol (Manila: Mr. & Ms. Publishing, 1984), 2.

60. G. Sidney Silliman, "The Philippines in 1983," *Asian Survey* 24, no. 2 (February 1984): 154.

61. "United States-Philippine Relations and the New Base and Aid Agreement," Hearings before the Subcommittee on Asian and Pacific Affairs of the Committee on Foreign Affairs, House of Representatives, Ninety-Eighth Congress, First Session, June 17, 23, and 28, 1983 (Washington, DC: U.S. Government Printing Office, 1983), 74–76; cited in Lela Garner Noble, "Politics in the Marcos Era," in Bresnan, *Crisis in the Philippines*, 70.

62. Ken Kashiwahara, "Aquino's Final Journey," *New York Times Sunday Magazine*, October 16, 1983, p. 42.

63. Alfonso P. Policarpio, Jr., *Ninoy: The Willing Martyr* (Manila: Isaiah Books, 1986), 187.

64. Kashiwahara, "Aquino's Final Journey," 61.

65. Cited in ibid., 62.

66. Bonner, *Waltzing with a Dictator,* 352.

67. Reuben R. Canoy, *The Counterfeit Revolution: Martial Law in the Philippines* (Manila: Philippine Editions, 1980), 228–29; Wurfel, "Succession Struggle," 22–23.

68. Kashiwahara, "Aquino's Final Journey," 62.

69. Maximo V. Soliven, "Benigno 'Ninoy' Aquino: In the Eye of Memory," in Apostol, *Fact Finding Board,* 13.

70. Aquino had asked the reporters to accompany him on his flight, thinking that their presence might offer him some protection. They were Kiyoshi Wakamiya of Tokyo Broadcasting System, Sandra Burton of *Time,* Max Vanzi of UPI, and Jim Laurie of ABC. Bonner, *Waltzing with a Dictator,* 344.

71. Doronila, "Media," 201.

72. Felix Bautista, *Cardinal Sin and the Miracle of Asia: A Biography* (Manila: Vera-Reyes, 1987), 125; Carmen Navarro Pedrosa, *Imelda Marcos: The Rise and Fall of One of the World's Most Powerful Women* (New York: St. Martin's, 1987), 196.

73. Ma. Serena I. Diokno, "Unity and Struggle," in Javate de Dios, Daroy, and Kalaw-Tirol, *Dictatorship and Revolution,* 132.

74. Doronila, "Media," 201.

75. "Grief and Anger at Home in Mourning," *South China Morning Post,* August 23, 1983; reprinted in Apostol, *Fact Finding Board,* 3.

76. Pedrosa, *Imelda Marcos: Rise and Fall,* 196.

77. Bonner, *Waltzing with a Dictator,* 345.

78. Policarpio, *Ninoy,* 211; emphasis added.

79. *Mr. & Ms.,* September 9, 1983; cited in Ileto, "Past in the Present Crisis," 9.

80. Thompson, *Anti-Marcos Struggle,* 117.

81. On the "switching of signs," see Ileto, "Past in the Present Crisis," 7–16.

82. Cited in ibid, 13.

83. Apostol, *Fact Finding Board,* 14.

84. Cited in Pineda-Ofreneo, *Manipulated Press,* 166.

85. Doronila, "Media," 196–97.

86. Lauren Berlant sees this as a hallmark of sentimental publicity. See Berlant, *Female Complaint: The Unfinished Business of Sentimentality in American Culture* (Durham: Duke University Press, 2008), 146.

87. Doronila, "Media," 202.

88. Berlant, *Female Complaint,* 146.

89. *Mr. & Ms.,* September 30, 1983; cited in Ileto, "Past in the Present Crisis," 14.

90. R. Contreras in *Malaya,* September 15–18, 1983, n.p.; emphasis added.

91. Ileto, "Past in the Present Crisis," 8, 11, 14, 15.

92. Ibid., 9.

93. I am here drawing on Lauren Berlant's astute reading of the sentimental power of the "dead-to-soon-celebrity," in Berlant, *Female Complaint,* 162; emphasis added.

94. Doronila, "Media," 201.

95. Pineda-Ofreneo, *Manipulated Press,* 150; Paredes, "Martial Law Evils," 156–57; Doronila, "Media," 201.

96. "Malaya Goes Daily," *Business Day,* February 22, 1984; cited in Pineda-Ofreneo, *Manipulated Press,* n.p.

97. Gemma N. Almendral, "The Newspaper Wars," *New Day Magazine,* April 12, 1986, n.p.

98. Pineda-Ofreneo, *Manipulated Press,* 168.

99. Ibid., 167; Paredes, "Martial Law Evils," 158.

100. "Corro Asks Release for Plebiscite Polls," *Bulletin Today,* January 25, 1984; "Newsman Released," *Business Day,* November 9, 1984; cited in Pineda-Ofreneo, *Manipulated Press,* 167.

101. Paredes, "Martial Law Evils," 153–54; see also Pineda-Ofreneo, *Manipulated Press,* 170.

102. The board presented President Marcos with two reports. A majority report by the four members implicated Ver, determined that there was a military conspiracy in the Aquino assassination, and recommended the immediate prosecution of all accused. The "Chairman's Report," while concurring that there was a military conspiracy, presented a "minority opinion" exculpating Ver from the group that had plotted the assassination. Both reports are reprinted in the *Mr. and Ms.* publication Apostol, *Fact Finding Board.*

103. Bautista, *Cardinal Sin,* 136–37; emphasis added.

104. Paredes, "Martial Law Evils," 158.

Chapter 6: The New Politics, Lino Brocka, and People Power

1. Mark Thompson, *The Anti-Marcos Struggle: Personalistic Rule and Democratic Transition in the Philippines* (New Haven: Yale University Press, 1995), 116.

2. Nathan Gilbert Quimpo, *Contested Democracy and the Left in the Philippines after Marcos* (New Haven: Yale Southeast Asia Studies, Monograph 58, 2008), 59.

3. Lauren Berlant compellingly argues that sentimental politics must give way to a discourse of demand and radical critique. This chapter examines the anti-Marcos movement's attempt to do just that. See Berlant, "The Subject of True Feeling: Pain, Privacy, and Politics," in *Cultural Pluralism: Identity, Politics, and the Law,* edited by Austin Sarat and Thomas R. Kearns, 49–84 (Ann Arbor: University of Michigan Press, 2001), 84.

4. Communist Party of the Philippines (CPP), "Statement on the Assassination of Ninoy Aquino," August 24, 1983; cited in Rosenberg, "Communism in the Philippines," *Problems of Communism* (September–October 1984): 26.

5. *Southeast Asia Chronicle,* June 1980, 7; cited in Rosenberg, "Communism in the Philippines," 42.

6. Gregg Jones, *Red Revolution: Inside the Philippine Guerrilla Movement* (Boulder: Westview, 1989), 150.

7. Rosenberg, "Communism in the Philippines," 45. See also Vincent Boudreau, *Resisting Dictatorship: Repression and Protest in Southeast Asia* (Cambridge: Cambridge University Press, 2004), 146.

8. Rosenberg, "Communism in the Philippines," 40.

9. Ibid. See also Jones, *Red Revolution,* 147, 150; Boudreau, *Resisting Dictatorship,* 146.

10. Jones, *Red Revolution,* 147.

11. Walden Bello, "The Dual Crisis of the Philippine Progressive Movement," in *Reexamining and Renewing the Philippine Progressive Vision,* ed. John Gershman and Walden Bello (Quezon City: Forum for Philippine Alternatives, 1993), 13.

12. Quimpo, *Contested Democracy,* 75, 82.

13. Cited in Ma. Serena I Diokno, "Unity and Struggle," in Javate de Dios, Daroy, and Kalaw-Tirol, *Dictatorship and Revolution,* 158.

14. Ibid., 160.

15. Quimpo, *Contested Democracy,* 66; Diokno, "Unity and Struggle," 161.

16. Diokno, "Unity and Struggle," 134.

17. Jo-Ann Maglipon, "The Brocka Battles," in Hernando, *Lino Brocka,* 143.

18. Ibid.

19. Ibid., 132.

20. Ibid., 119.

21. Ibid., 123.

22. Ibid., 118; translation mine.

23. Diokno, "Unity and Struggle," 136–37; emphasis in original.

24. The dog show rally nonetheless represents the protestors' clever appropriation of the radical Left's sobriquet *tuta* (lapdog) for Marcos. The word is meant to capture Marcos's allegedly servile relationship with Washington.

25. Emmanuel de Dios, "The Erosion of the Dictatorship," in Javate de Dios, Daroy, and Kalaw-Tirol, *Dictatorship and Revolution,* 109.

26. Paul D. Hutchcroft, *Booty Capitalism: The Politics of Banking in the Philippines* (Ithaca: Cornell University Press, 1998), 170–84.

27. Guy Sacerdoti, "The Crunch Comes," *Far Eastern Economic Review,* October 20, 1983, p. 66.

28. Maglipon, "Brocka Battles," 118.

29. Jeepney is the vernacular term for the most popular form of public transport in Metro Manila—jitneys made from the repurposed bodies World War II–era military Jeeps.

30. As part of the government's austerity program, Marcos eliminated local fuel subsidies. G. Sidney Silliman, "The Philippines in 1983," *Asian Survey* 24, no. 2 (February 1984): 153.

31. In August 1983 the PDA replaced the PCO as the regime's preferred means of preventive detention. Though detention under the PDA was now limited to one year and was to be channeled through the judiciary, the PDA empowered Marcos to detain anyone "who has committed, is committing, or is *about to commit* insurrection, rebellion, subversion, or conspiracy." Guy Sacerdoti, "Law of the Jungle," *Far Eastern Economic Review,* August 25, 1983, p. 14; emphasis added.

32. Maglipon, "Brocka Battles," 128.

33. Boudreau, *Resisting Dictatorship,* 147; emphasis in original.

34. Maglipon, "Brocka Battles," 130; emphasis added.

35. The screenplay is by Jose F. Lacaba, based on two of his short stories: "Strike" and "The Hostage."

36. Ismael Xavier, *Allegories of Underdevelopment: Aesthetics and Politics in Modern Brazilian Cinema* (Minneapolis: University of Minnesota Press, 1997), 16.

37. Quimpo, *Contested Democracy,* 42.

38. Unless otherwise indicated, all dialogue is in Tagalog. The translations here are mine. Emphasis mine.

39. *Echas* is Tagalog slang for feces.

40. Brocka, press statement; quoted in Agustin L. Sotto, "Filmography," in Hernando, *Lino Brocka,* 281.

41. See, for example, Seth Mydans, "The Philippine Middle Class Turning against Marcos," *New York Times Sunday Magazine,* January 2, 1986, 19–26, 53–60; Fermin Adriano, "Revisiting EDSA 2," *Manila Times,* January 21, 2003; Carl Lande, "The Return of 'People Power' in the Philippines," *Journal of Democracy* 12, no. 2 (2001): 88–102.

42. Quimpo, *Contested Democracy,* 47, 71.

43. See Michael Pinches, "The Urban Poor," in May and Nemenzo, *Philippines after Marcos,* 155, 163. This study's prediction of the crucial role that the urban poor will play in the 1986 popular revolt makes it an illuminating intertext to Brocka's film.

44. Boudreau, *Resisting Dictatorship,* 180–81.

45. Thompson, *Anti-Marcos Struggle,* 127.

46. *Ang bayan,* December 1985; cited in Jones, *Red Revolution,* 156.

47. Cited in Gemma Nemenzo Almendral, "The Fall of the Regime," in Javate de Dios, Daroy, and Kalaw-Tirol, *Dictatorship and Revolution,* 194.

48. "Persevere in Correct Struggles, Boycott the Sham Snap Elections," statement of the Bagong Alyansang Makabayan (New Nationalist Alliance) on the snap presidential elections, Manila, January 1986; reprinted in Javate de Dios, Daroy, and Kalaw-Tirol, *Dictatorship and Revolution,* 685.

49. Almendral, "Fall of the Regime," 196.

50. Quoted in Lucy Komisar, *Corazon Aquino: The Story of a Revolution* (New York: George Braziller, 1987), 78.

51. Thompson, "Anti-Marcos Struggle," 145.

52. Cited in Almendral, "Fall of the Regime," 194.

53. Jones, *Red Revolution,* 155.

54. "Interview with Jose Maria Sison," *National Midweek,* December 1985, extract reprinted in Javate de Dios, Daroy, and Kalaw-Tirol, *Dictatorship and Revolution,* 685–89, at 687. Sison was captured by the military in 1977. At the time of the snap elections, the CPP's acting chairman was Rodolfo Salas.

55. "When a Zigzag Turn Is Shorter than a Straight Route," *Praktika* 1, no. 1 (May 14, 1986): 21–22; cited in Jones, *Red Revolution,* 158–59.

56. For a detailed account of the Reagan-Marcos relationship, see Raymond Bonner, *Waltzing with a Dictator: The Marcoses and the Making of American Policy* (New York: Vintage, 1988), 295–358.

57. Ibid., 408–9, 497.

58. Almendral, "Fall of the Regime," 201–2.

59. Thompson, *Anti-Marcos Struggle,* 150.

60. Bonner, *Waltzing with a Dictator,* 428.

61. Almendral, "Fall of the Regime," 202–3.

62. Francis X. Clines, "30 Computer Aides Say Vote Is Rigged," *New York Times,* February 10, 1986, n.p.

63. Bonner, *Waltzing with a Dictator*, 422.

64. Catholic Bishops' Conference of the Philippines, "CBCP Post-Election Statement," *Pulso* 1, no. 4 (February 14, 1986): 336–37.

65. Discussion Notes of the Advisory Committee for the Civil Disobedience Campaign, Makati, February 14, 1986; reprinted in *Dictatorship and Revolution,* 734–37.

66. Boudreau, *Resisting Dictatorship,* 187; emphasis in original.

67. For a comprehensive account of the military rebellion, see Alfred McCoy, *Closer than Brothers: Manhood at the Philippine Military Academy* (New Haven: Yale University Press, 1999).

68. Almendral, "Fall of the Regime," 211.

69. Carmen Navarro Pedrosa, *Imelda Marcos: The Rise and Fall of One of the World's Most Powerful Women* (New York: St. Martin's, 1987), 215; emphasis added.

70. Alexander Aguirre, *A People's Revolution of Our Time—Philippines, February 22–25, 1986: An Inside Story with Politico-military Analysis* (Quezon City: Pan Service Master Consultants, 1986), 22–24.

71. Bryan Johnson, *The Four Days of Courage: The Untold Story of the People Who Brought Marcos Down* (New York: Free Press, 1987), 83.

72. Ibid., 107.

73. Reverend Bernardo Perez, OSB, quoted in Alfeo G. Nudas, *God with Us: The 1986 Philippine Revolution* (Quezon City: Cardinal Bea Institute, Loyola House of Theology, Ateneo de Manila University, 1986), 33.

74. Pedrosa, *Imelda Marcos: Rise and Fall,* 217.

Conclusion: The Force of National Allegory

1. Ella Shohat and Robert Stam, *Unthinking Eurocentrism: Multiculturalism and the Media* (London: Routledge, 1994), 26.

2. Kevin Hewison and Garry Rodan, "The Ebb and Flow of Civil Society and the Decline of the Left in Southeast Asia," in *Political Oppositions in Industrialising Asia,* ed. Rodan (London: Routledge, 1996), 42–43.

3. Figures are for the year 2000. National Statistical Coordination Board, *2003 Statistical Yearbook* (Manila: National Economic and Development Authority, 2003).

4. Nathan Gilbert Quimpo, *Contested Democracy and the Left in the Philippines after Marcos* (New Haven: Yale Southeast Asia Studies, Monograph 58, 2008), 46, 70.

5. Lauren Berlant, *The Female Complaint: The Unfinished Business of Sentimentality in American Culture* (Durham: Duke University Press, 2008), 75.

6. I am here drawing on Berlant's discussion of the sentimental politico-aesthetic in *Female Complaint*.

7. Ibid., 80.

8. Ibid., 97.

9. Ibid., 105.

10. Ibid., 149.

11. Walden Bello, Herbert Docena, Marissa de Guzman, and Mary Lou Malig, *The Anti-development State: The Political Economy of Permanent Crisis in the Philippines* (Quezon City: Department of Sociology, University of the Philippines / Focus on the Global South, 2004).

12. World Bank, "Combating Corruption in the Philippines," paper prepared by the Philippine Country Management Unit, East Asia and Pacific Region, May 3, 2004, p. 3; cited in Quimpo, *Contested Democracy*, 49.

Glossary

"Ako ay Pilipino" (I am a Filipino; Tagalog). A pop song by George Canseco that was commissioned by Imelda Marcos and performed by Kuh Ledesma; it later was used as the title for the television special celebrating Marcos's 1981 presidential inauguration.

Ama ng tahanan (Head of the household; Tagalog). A series of short educational films by the National Media Production Center on proper household management in the New Society.

Ang bandilyo (Announcement; Cebuano). The newsletter of the Catholic prelature of Bukidnon, in Mindanao.

Ang bayan (The nation; Tagalog). The underground newspaper of the CPP.

Atas. Indigenous Filipinos who live in isolated and mountainous parts of Luzon.

bahay, pera, frente. House, money, front (Tagalog). A phrase used by CPP cadres to refer to their strategy of building alliances with elite and middle-class opposition groups for the purpose of acquiring money and safe houses to be used in the insurgency.

"Bayan ko" (My country; Tagalog). Patriotic song originally written in Spanish by Jose Alejandrino for the zarzuela "Walang sugat" (Unwounded), it was translated into Tagalog thirty years later by poet Jose Corazon de Jesus with music by Constancio de Guzman.

Bildungsroman. A type of novel concerned with the education, development, and maturing of a young protagonist.

bomba. A bomb. Slang for sexually explicit movies. Also used for exposés of political corruption in the media.

Bontocs. Indigenous Filipinos who live in the Mountain Province, northern Luzon. Also, the capital of that province.

cacique. A local political boss (Spanish). Benedict Anderson uses the term "cacique democracy" to refer to the political system in the Philippines, which was dominated by political warlords.

Camp Crame. Short for Camp Rafael C. Crame, headquarters of the Philippine National Police.

carabao. A domestic water buffalo (Tagalog), also the national animal of the Philippines.

Chico River Dam project. An electric-power generation project that was resisted by the Kalinga peoples for three decades because it threatened to flood traditional villages. The project was shelved in 1980 and is now considered a landmark case of ancestral-domain issues in the Philippines.

"Dahil sa iyo" (Because of you). A song by Mike Velarde, Jr., written in 1938 for the movie *Bituing markikit* (Beautiful star) and sung by Rogelio de la Rosa. The song was one of Imelda's favorites and later became her signature piece on the 1965 campaign trail.

EO 640-A. An executive order creating the Filipino Motion Picture Development Board. Signed January 5, 1981.

EO 770. An executive order creating the Experimental Cinema of the Philippines. Signed January 29, 1982.

EO 866. An executive order creating the Board of Review for Motion Pictures, Television, and Live Entertainment. Signed January 2, 1983.

Fort Bonifacio (formerly: Fort McKinley). The headquarters of the Armed Forces of the Philippines. The camp is named after Andres Bonifacio, Filipino revolutionary leader during the Spanish-Philippine revolutionary war.

hacienda. A plantation or a large estate (Spanish).

Himala (Miracle). A 1982 film directed by Ishmael Bernal, written by Ricky Lee, produced by the Experimental Cinema of the Philippines, starring Nora Aunor. It follows the tragic story of a woman who claims to have been visited by a Marian apparition in a small drought-stricken town.

Huk. The communist guerrilla movement formed by the peasant farmers of Central Luzon in the 1940s. Also, a member of that movement (slang: rebel).

Iginuhit ng tadhana (Drawn by destiny; Tagalog). A 1965 Tagalog biopic subtitled *The Ferdinand Marcos Story.* Directed by Jose De Villa, Conrado Conde, and Mar S. Torres. See *tadhana.*

Intramuros. The oldest district and historic core of Manila (Spanish: walled city).

jouissance. Physical and intellectual pleasure (French: ecstasy).

Kalingas. Indigenous Filipinos of the Cordillera region, northern Luzon.

kapit sa patalim. A desperate existence (Tagalog). Derived from the aphorism *Ang taong nagigipit, kahit sa patalim kumakapit* (a desperate person will grip onto a blade).

Macli-ing Dulag. Kalinga leader of the Butbut tribe of the Cordillera; he was assassinated by the military for his activism against the Chico Dam project.

maharlika. The feudal warrior class in ancient Tagalog society in Luzon. Maharlika was Marcos's nom de guerre (Tagalog: noble).

Makibaka! Huwag matakot! The slogan of the dissidents during the First Quarter Storm (Tagalog: Fight! Don't be afraid!).

Malacañang Palace. The official residence and principal workplace of the president of the Philippines; built in 1750 by Don Luis Rocha along the Pasig River.

Malakas at Maganda. The first man and woman, according to the Philippine creation myth.

Naiibang hayop (A different kind of animal). A 1983 film directed and written by Artemio Marquez, starring Irma Alegre and Mark Gil. It follows the exploits of a young woman who flees an arranged marriage to become an exotic dancer in the big city.

Oro, plata, mata (Gold, silver, death). A 1982 film directed by Peque
  Gallaga, written by Jose Javier Reyes, and produced by the
  Experimental Cinema of the Philippines, starring Joel Torre
  and Sany Andolong. It follows two rich families who escape to
  the jungle during the Japanese invasion of the Philippines in
  World War II.

Pagta ti bodong. Many pacts bind Kalinga and Bontoc relations, but
  the pagta ti bodong was a historical agreement to unite their
  villages against the government (Kalinga: peace pact).

PCO. Presidential Commitment Order. A presidential issuance (Letter
  of Instruction No. 1211) allowing the "preventive detention"
  of persons for crimes mentioned in Presidential Decree 2045
  "lifting" martial law.

PD 1737. A presidential decree outlining the president's preventive
  detention powers; signed September 12, 1980.

PD 1834. A presidential decree increasing the penalties for rebellion,
  conspiracy, sedition, and inciting to sedition from twenty to
  forty years in prison to death. Signed January 16, 1981.

Php. Philippine peso.

Proclamation 1081. The declaration of martial law in the Philippines.
  Enacted September 21, 1973; signed September 23, 1973.

pulis. The police (Tagalog).

pulitika. Politics (Tagalog). Reynaldo Ileto contrasts pulitika, or
  the "official" politics of the elite, with the more personal
  understanding of politics by the popular classes.

putting pagmamahal. White love (Tagalog). Vicente Rafael uses the term
  to refer to the U.S. policy of benevolent assimilation.

Sagrado Corazon Señor. A religious cult that started in Cebu, in
  the Visayas. With 150,000 members all over the country,
  the paramilitary organization waged a holy war against
  communism in the early 1980s.

sakada. A migrant worker (Negrense).

sama ng loob. Hurt feelings (Tagalog).

tadhana. Destiny (Tagalog). A concept dear to Marcos, who titled his multivolume history of the Philippines *Tadhana,* and whose 1965 campaign biopic was titled *Iginuhit ng tadhana.* See *Inginuhit ng tadhana.*

tadtad. To chop (Tagalog). Slang name for quasi-religious cults targeting Communists and Muslims. They are known for hacking their victims to death so that they would not gain a second life.

taliba. A sentinel (Tagalog). A popular name for newspapers; for example, the tabloid *People's Taliba* and *Taliba ng bayan* (People's guardian), a militant newspaper during the dictatorship.

terno. Matching (Spanish); a traditional costume worn by women for formal occasions. Consists of a one-piece gown with butterfly sleeves.

Waray. An ethnic group in the Visayas. See *Waray-Waray.*

Waray-Waray. The primary language of the *Waray.* Also, a 1954 musical comedy from LVN studios starring Nida Blanca and Nestor de Villa. The eponymous hit song from the movie was among the songs Imelda Marcos performed on the 1965 campaign trail.

zarzuela. Spanish lyric-dramatic genre alternating between spoken and sung scenes. A Philippine version (*sarswela*) was popular at the turn of the century, supplying story lines for the fledgling indigenous film industry.

Bibliography

Abueva, Jose Veloso. "Ideology and Practice in the 'New Society.'" In Rosenberg, *Marcos and Martial Law,* 32–84.

———. "The Philippines: Tradition and Change." *Asian Survey* 10, no. 1 (1970): 56–64.

Agrava, Corazon Juliano. "The Chairman's Report." In Apostol, *Assassination of Benigno Aquino,* 385–420.

Aguirre, Alexander. *A People's Revolution of Our Time—Philippines, February 22–25, 1986: An Inside Story with Politico-military Analysis.* Quezon City: Pan-Service Master Consultants, 1986.

Almario, Manuel F. "How Ferdinand Marcos Woos Reelection." *Graphic,* September 10, 1969.

Almendral, Gemma Nemenzo. "The Fall of the Regime." In Javate de Dios, Daroy, and Kalaw-Tirol, *Dictatorship and Revolution,* 176–220.

Amnesty International, USA. *"Disappearances": A Workbook.* New York: Amnesty International, 1981.

Anderson, Benedict. *The Spectre of Comparisons: Nationalism, Southeast Asia and the World.* London: Verso, 1998.

Anker, Elisabeth. "Villains, Victims and Heroes: Melodrama, Media and September 11." *Journal of Communication* 55, no. 1 (2005): 22–37.

Apostol, Eugenia D., ed. *Reports of the Fact-Finding Board on the Assassination of Senator Benigno S. Aquino, Jr.* Manila: Mr. & Ms. Publishing, 1984.

Aragon, Albert. "The Controversial, Complicated, Celebrated ECP: Two Views." *WHO,* October 6, 1982.

ASEAN. Committee on Culture and Information. Working Group on Film. "The Film Industry in the Philippines." In *ASEAN Country Reports on Film,* 23–30. Manila: Office of Media Affairs, National Media Production Center, 1983.

Baudrillard, Jean. *Simulacra and Simulation.* Ann Arbor: University of Michigan Press, 1994.

Bautista, Felix. *Cardinal Sin and the Miracle of Asia: A Biography.* Manila: Vera-Reyes, 1987.

Belen, Crispina, and Rod L. Villa. "Sex Movies Rake in Bulk of 'Take' in First Showing." *Bulletin Today,* January 29, 1983.

Bello, Walden, Herbert Docena, Marissa de Guzman, and Mary Lou Malig. *The Anti-development State: The Political Economy of Permanent Crisis in the Philippines.* Quezon City: Department of Sociology, University of the Philippines, and Focus on the Global South, 2004.

Bello, Walden, David Kinley, and Elaine Elinson. *Development Debacle: The World Bank in the Philippines.* San Francisco: Institute for Food and Development Policy, 1982.

Benesa, Leonidas V. "Do We Have a Cultural Policy?" Paper presented at the Symposium on Cultural Policy of the Philippines, Manila, Cultural Center of the Philippines, December 11, 1972.

Bennett, Tony. *The Birth of the Museum: History, Theory, Politics.* London: Routledge, 1995.

———. *Culture: A Reformer's Science.* London: Sage, 1998.

Berlant, Lauren. *The Anatomy of National Fantasy: Hawthorne, Utopia, and Everyday Life.* Chicago: University of Chicago Press, 1991.

———. "The Epistemology of State Emotion." In *Dissent in Dangerous Times,* edited by Austin Sarat, 46–78. Ann Arbor: University of Michigan Press, 2005.

———. *The Female Complaint: The Unfinished Business of Sentimentality in American Culture.* Durham: Duke University Press, 2008.

———. "The Subject of True Feeling: Pain, Privacy, and Politics," in *Cultural Pluralism: Identity, Politics, and the Law,* edited by Austin Sarat and Thomas R. Kearns, 49–84. Ann Arbor: University of Michigan Press, 2001.

Berlant, Lauren, and Michael Warner. "Sex in Public." *Critical Inquiry* 24, no. 2, Intimacy (special issue, Winter 1998): 547–66.

Blackburn, Robin. "The Philippines: Rebirth of the Revolution." *Nation* 211 (1970): 582–87.

Bonner, Raymond. *Waltzing with a Dictator: The Marcoses and the Making of American Policy.* New York: Vintage, 1988.

Boorstin, Daniel J. *The Image; or, What Happened to the American Dream.* New York: Atheneum, 1962.

Boudreau, Vincent. *Resisting Dictatorship: Repression and Protest in Southeast Asia.* Cambridge: Cambridge University Press, 2004.

Bresnan, John, ed. *Crisis in the Philippines: The Marcos Era and Beyond.* Princeton: Princeton University Press, 1986.

Brooks, Peter. "The Melodramatic Imagination." In Landy, *Imitations of Life,* 50–67.

Buckley, Matthew. "Introduction." *Modern Drama* 55 no. 4 (Winter 2012): 429–36.

———. "Refugee Theater: Melodrama and Modernity's Crisis." *Theatre Journal* 61, no. 2 (2009): 175–90.

Campbell, Alex. "The Lawless and Corrupt Philippines." *New Republic* 160 (1969): 15–17.

Canoy, Reuben R. *The Counterfeit Revolution: Martial Law in the Philippines.* Manila: Philippine Editions, 1980.

Cleto, Pet G. "Seven Voices: The Issue of Censorship." *Celebrity,* May 15, 1983, n.p.

Constantino, Renato. *The State of the Philippine Press: Report of the National Press Club Seminar Committee.* Manila: Foundation for Nationalist Studies, 1983.

Dacanay, Julian E. "The State of Research on Cultural Development in the Philippines." Unpublished manuscript prepared for UNESCO Division for Cultural Development, Institute of Philippine Culture, Ateneo de Manila University, 1973.

David, Joel. *The National Pastime: Contemporary Philippine Cinema.* Manila: Anvil, 1990.

de Dios, Emmanuel. "The Erosion of the Dictatorship." In Javate de Dios, Daroy, and Kalaw-Tirol, *Dictatorship and Revolution,* 70–131.

del Carmen, Cristina P. "The Cultural Edifice Turns into a Tombstone." *WHO,* January 9, 1982.

del Mundo, Clodualdo. "Philippine Cinema: An Historical Overview." *Asian Cinema* 10, no. 2 (Spring/Summer, 1999): 29–66.

De Vega, Guillermo C. *Film and Freedom: Movie Censorship in the Philippines.* Manila: Board of Censors for Motion Pictures, 1975.

———. "A Look at Film Censorship." *Fookien Times Yearbook* (1974): 338–44.

Diokno, Ma. Serena I. "Unity and Struggle." In Javate de Dios, Daroy, and Kalaw-Tirol, *Dictatorship and Revolution,* 132–75.

Donzelot, Jacques. *The Policing of Families.* Translated by Robert Hurley. New York: Pantheon, 1979.

Doronila, Amando. "The Media." In May and Nemenzo, *Philippines after Marcos,* 194–206.

Doyo, Ma. Ceres. "Was Magli-ing Killed Because He Damned the Chico Dam?" In *The Philippine Press—Under Siege,* vol. 2, edited by National Press Club, 13–19. Manila: National Press Club, Committee to Protect Writers, 1985.

Dubsky, Roman. "The Institutionalizing of Social Conduct and the New Society of the Philippines." *Philippine Journal of Public Administration* 18, no. 2 (1974): 127–45.

Durdin, Tillman. "Philippine Communism." *Problems of Communism* (May–June 1976): 40–49.

Espiritu, Talitha. "The Marcos Romance and the Cultural Center of the Philippines: The Melodrama of a Therapeutic Cultural Policy." *Journal of Narrative Theory* 45, no. 1 (Winter 2015): 141–62.

———. "Native Subjects on Display: Reviving the Colonial Exposition in Marcos' Philippines." *Social Identities* 18, no. 6 (Fall 2012): 729–44.

———. "Performing Native Identities: Human Displays and Indigenous Activism in Marcos' Philippines." In *The Routledge Companion to Global Popular Culture,* edited by Toby Miller, 417–25. New York: Routledge, 2015.

Fanon, Frantz. *The Wretched of the Earth.* Translated by Constance Farrington. New York: Grove Press, 1963.

Flor, Lina. "Problems of the Philippine Movie Industry." *Fookien Times Yearbook,* 1961, 223, 231.

Foucault, Michael. "Governmentality." In *The Foucault Effect: Studies in Governmentality,* edited by Graham Burchell, Colin Gordon, and Peter Miller, 87–104. London: Harvester Wheatsheaf, 1991.

Francia, Luis. "Philippine Cinema: The Struggle against Repression." In *Film and Politics in the Third World,* edited by John D. H. Downing, 209–218. New York: Praeger, 1987.

Francisco, Luzviminda. "The Philippine-American War." In *The Philippines Reader: A History of Colonialism, Neocolonialism, Dictatorship and Resistance,* edited by Daniel B. Schirmer and Stephen Rosskam Shalom, 8–19. Boston: South End Press, 1987.

Golay, Frank. *The Philippines: Public Policy and National Economic Development.* Ithaca: Cornell University Press, 1961.

Gould, Deborah. "On Affect and Protest." In *Political Emotions: New Agendas in Communication,* edited by Janet Staiger, Ann Cvetkovich, and Ann Reynolds, 18–44. New York: Routledge, 2010.

Guerrero, Amado [pseud. for Jose Maria Sison]. *Philippine Society and Revolution.* 4th ed. Hayward, CA: Philippine Information Network Service, 1996.

Haggard, Stephan. "The Political Economy of the Philippine Debt Crisis." In *Economic Crisis and Policy Choice,* edited by Joan M. Nelson, 215–55. Princeton: Princeton University Press, 1990.

Hawes, Gary. *The Philippine State and the Marcos Regime: The Politics of Export.* Ithaca: Cornell University Press, 1987.

Hernando, Mario. "Lino Brocka: Director in Control, Blending Popular Entertainment, Realism and Social Comment." In Hernando, *Lino Brocka,* 38–48.

———, ed. *Lino Brocka: The Artist and His Times.* Manila: Cultural Center of the Philippines, 1993.

Hoberman, J. *The Dream Life: Movies, Media, and the Mythology of the Sixties.* New York: New Press, 2003.

Huntington, Samuel P. *Political Order in Changing Societies.* New Haven: Yale University Press, 1968.

Hutchcroft, Paul D. *Booty Capitalism: The Politics of Banking in the Philippines.* Ithaca: Cornell University Press, 1998.

———. "Oligarchs and Cronies in the Philippine State: The Politics of Patrimonial Plunder." *World Politics* 43, no. 3 (1991): 414–50.

Ileto, Reynaldo. "The Past in the Present Crisis." In May and Nemenzo, *Philippines after Marcos,* 7–16.

Ingles, Jose D. "The Cultural Policy of the New Society." Paper presented at the Symposium on Cultural Policy of the Philippines, Manila, December 11, 1972.

Javate de Dios, Aurora, Petronilo Bn. Daroy, and Lorna Kalaw-Tirol, eds. *Dictatorship and Revolution: Roots of People's Power.* Manila: Conspectus, 1988.

Johnson, Bryan. *The Four Days of Courage: The Untold Story of the People Who Brought Marcos Down.* New York: Free Press, 1987.

Jones, Gregg. *Red Revolution: Inside the Philippine Guerrilla Movement.* Boulder: Westview, 1989.

Kasilag, Lucrecia R. "The Cultural Center of the Philippines: Its Role in the Development of National Culture." Paper presented at the National Conference on Enhancing the Development of Our National Culture, National Library, Manila, April 7–9, 1980.

Kessler, Richard. *Rebellion and Repression in the Philippines.* New Haven: Yale University Press, 1989.

Komisar, Lucy. *Corazon Aquino: The Story of a Revolution.* New York: George Braziller, 1987.

Kramer, Paul A. "The Pragmatic Empire: U.S. Anthropology and Colonial Politics in the Occupied Philippines, 1898–1916." PhD dissertation, Princeton University, 1998.

Lacaba, Jose F. *Days of Disquiet, Nights of Rage: The First Quarter Storm and Related Events.* Manila: Salinlahi Publishing House, 1982.

Lachica, Eduardo. *The Huks: Philippine Agrarian Society in Revolt.* New York: Praeger, 1971.

Lande, Carl H. "The Political Crisis." In Bresnan, *Crisis in the Philippines,* 114–44.

Landy, Marcia. *Imitations of Life: A Reader on Film and Television Melodrama.* Detroit: Wayne State University Press, 1991.

Latham, Michael E. *Modernization as Ideology: American Social Science and "Nation Building" in the Kennedy Era.* Chapel Hill: University of North Carolina Press, 2001.

Lent, John A. *The Asian Film Industry.* Austin: University of Texas Press, 1990.

———. *Broadcasting in Asia and the Pacific: A Continental Survey of Radio and Television.* Philadelphia: Temple University Press, 1983.

Lico, Gerardo. *Edifice Complex: Power, Myth and Marcos State Architecture.* Manila: Ateneo de Manila University Press, 2003.

Lopez, Ana. "The Melodrama in Latin America: Films, Telenovelas, and the Currency of a Popular Form." In Landy, *Imitations of Life,* 596–606.

Lumbera, Bienvenido. *Pelikula: An Essay on Philippine Film, 1961–1992.* Manila: Cultural Center of the Philippines, 1992.

———. "Problems in Philippine Film History." In *Readings in Philippine Cinema,* edited by Rafael Ma. Guerrero, 67–78. Manila: Experimental Cinema of the Philippines, 1983.

Machado, Kit G. "The Philippines in 1978: Authoritarian Consolidation Continues." *Asian Survey* 19, no. 2 (February 1979): 131–40.

Maglipon, Jo-Anne. "The Brocka Battles." In Hernando, *Lino Brocka,* 118–54.

Manapat, Ricardo. *Some Are Smarter Than Others: The History of Marcos' Crony Capitalism.* New York: Aletheia Publications, 1991.

Maramag, Ilenea. *Official Primer of the Cultural Center of the Philippines.* Souvenir program. Manila: Cultural Center of the Philippines, 1969.

Maravilla, J. "Upsurge of Anti-Imperialist Movement in the Philippines." *World Marxist Review* 8, no. 11 (November 1965): 58–64.

Marcos, Ferdinand E. *The Democratic Revolution in the Philippines.* 2nd ed. Englewood Cliffs, NJ: Prentice-Hall International, 1979.

———. *Five Years of the New Society.* Manila: Marcos Foundation, 1978.

———. *An Ideology for Filipinos.* Manila: Marcos Foundation, 1980.

———. *In Search of Alternatives: The Third World in an Age of Crisis.* Manila: Marcos Foundation, 1980.

———. *Notes on the New Society of the Philippines.* Manila: Marcos Foundation, 1973.

———. *Progress and Martial Law.* Manila: Marcos Foundation, 1981.

Marcos, Imelda Romualdez. "Film as Art." In *The Compassionate Society and Other Selected Speeches,* edited by Ileana Maramag, 58–59. Manila: National Media Production Center, 1975.

May, R. J., and Francisco Nemenzo, eds. *The Philippines after Marcos.* London: Croom Helm, 1985.

McCoy, Alfred W. *An Anarchy of Families: State and Family in the Philippines,* edited by McCoy. Manila: Ateneo de Manila University Press, 1998.

———. "An Anarchy of Families: The Historiography of State and Family in the Philippines." In McCoy, *Anarchy of Families*, 1–32.

———. *Closer than Brothers: Manhood at the Philippine Military Academy.* New Haven: Yale University Press, 1999.

Mendoza, Al. S. "A Festival of Porno Flicks." *Philippine Panorama,* February 13, 1983.

Miller, Toby. *The Well-Tempered Self: Citizenship, Culture, and the Postmodern Subject.* Baltimore: Johns Hopkins University Press, 1993.

Miller, Toby, and George Yúdice. *Cultural Policy.* London: Sage, 2002.

Neher, Clark D. "The Philippines in 1980: The Gathering Storm." *Asian Survey* 21, no. 2 (1981): 261–73.

Noble, Lela Garner. "Politics in the Marcos Era." In Bresnan, *Crisis in the Philippines,* 70–113.

Ocampo, Sheilah. "Breaching a Dam of Despair." *Far Eastern Economic Review,* June 13, 1980.

———. "Marcos Wins on All Fronts." *Far Eastern Economic Review,* February 15, 1980.

Paredes, Joel C. "Martial Law Evils Still Dominate Local Media." In *Philippine Mass Media: A Book of Readings,* edited by Clodualdo del Mundo, 153–59. Manila: Communication Foundation for Asia, 1986.

Pedrosa, Carmen Navarro. *Imelda Marcos: The Rise and Fall of One of the World's Most Powerful Women.* New York: St. Martin's, 1987.

———. *The Untold Story of Imelda Marcos.* Manila: Bookmark, 1969.

Philippines National Media Production Center. *Annual Report, 1981.* Manila: National Media Production Center, 1981.

Pineda-Ofreneo, Rosalinda. *The Manipulated Press: A History of Philippine Journalism since 1945.* Manila: Solar, 1986.

Policarpio, Alfonso P., Jr. *Ninoy: The Willing Martyr.* Manila: Isaiah Books, 1986.

Polotan, Kerima. *Imelda Romualdez Marcos.* New York: World Publishing, 1969.

Pomeroy, William. *American Neo-colonialism: Its Emergence in the Philippines and Asia.* New York: International Publishers, 1970.

———. *The Philippines: Colonialism, Collaboration, and Resistance.* New York: International Publishers, 1992.

Quimpo, Nathan Gilbert. *Contested Democracy and the Left in the Philippines after Marcos.* New Haven: Yale Southeast Asia Studies, Monograph 58, 2008.

Rafael, Vicente. "Patronage and Pornography: Ideology and Spectatorship in the Early Marcos Years." *Comparative Studies in Society and History* 32, no. 2 (1990): 282–304.

————. *White Love and Other Events in Filipino History.* Manila: Ateneo de Manila University Press, 2000.

Rempel, William C. *Delusions of a Dictator: The Mind of Marcos as Revealed in His Secret Diaries.* Boston: Little, Brown, 1993.

Riley, Denise. *Am I That Name? Feminism and the Category of "Women" in History.* London: Macmillan, 1988.

Rocamora, Joel. "The Political Uses of PANAMIN." *Southeast Asia Chronicle* 67 (October 1979): 11–21.

Rogin, Michael. "'Make My Day!': Spectacle as Amnesia in Imperial Politics." *Representations* 29 (Winter 1990): 99–123.

————. *Ronald Reagan, The Movie, and Other Episodes of Political Demonology.* Berkeley: University of California Press, 1987.

Rosenberg, David. "Communism in the Philippines." *Problems of Communism* (September–October 1984): 24–45.

————. "Liberty versus Loyalty: The Transformation of the Philippine News Media under Martial Law." In Rosenberg, *Marcos and Martial Law,* 145–79.

————, ed. *Marcos and Martial Law in the Philippines.* Ithaca: Cornell University Press, 1979.

Shohat, Ella, and Robert Stam. *Unthinking Eurocentrism: Multiculturalism and the Media.* London: Routledge, 1994.

Silliman, G. Sidney. "The Philippines in 1983." *Asian Survey* 24, no. 2 (February 1984): 149–58.

Singer, Ben. *Melodrama and Modernity: Early Sensational Cinema and Its Contexts.* New York: Columbia University Press, 2001.

Slotkin, Richard. *Gunfighter Nation: The Myth of the Frontier in Twentieth-Century America.* New York: Atheneum, 1992.

Soliven, Maximo V. "Benigno 'Ninoy' Aquino: In the Eye of Memory." In Apostol, *Assassination of Benigno Aquino,* 6–13.

Soriano, Marcelo B. *The Quiet Revolt of the Philippine Press.* Manila: WE Forum, 1981.

Sotto, Agustin L. "Filmography." In Hernando, *Lino Brocka,* 245–308.

Spence, Hartzell. *For Every Tear a Victory: The Story of Ferdinand E. Marcos.* New York: McGraw-Hill, 1964.

————. *Marcos of the Philippines.* New York: World Publishing, 1982.

Tasker, Rodney. "A Political Star Is Reborn." *Far Eastern Economic Review,* March 24, 1978.

Thompson, Mark. *The Anti-Marcos Struggle: Personalistic Rule and Democratic Transition in the Philippines.* New Haven: Yale University Press, 1995.

Tiglao, Rigoberto D. "The Consolidation of the Dictatorship." In Javate de Dios, Daroy, and Kalaw-Tirol, *Dictatorship and Revolution*, 26–69. Manila: Conspectus, 1988.

Tiongson, Nicanor. "The Filipino Film Industry." *East-West Film Journal* 6, no. 2 (1992): 23–61.

———. "The Filipino Film in the Decade of the 1980s." In *The Urian Anthology, 1980–1989*, edited by Tiongson, xvi–xxxv. Manila: Antonio P. Tuvera, 2001.

UNESCO. National Commission of the Philippines. *Cultural Policy in the Philippines: A Study Prepared under the Auspices of the UNESCO National Commission of the Philippines*. Paris: UNESCO, 1973.

Urlanda, Randy V., and A. C. Lee. "It's Alarming to Think What the Next MIFF Might Bring." *Philippine Panorama*, February 13, 1983.

Van der Kroef, Justus M. "Philippine Communist Theory and Strategy: A New Departure?" *Pacific Affairs* 48, no. 1 (1975): 181–98.

———. "The Philippine Maoists." *Orbis* 16, no. 4 (1973): 892–926.

Villanueva, Danny. "In the Realm of the Senseless." *Movie Flash*, March 4, 1982.

Vokey, Richard. "Assault on the Peaks of Power." *Far Eastern Economic Review*, June 13, 1980.

Wideman, Bernard. "Cracking Down on Dissent" *Far Eastern Economic Review*, February 6, 1976.

———. "The Philippines' Tough Line on Strikes." *Far Eastern Economic Review*, November 14, 1975.

Williams, Linda. "Mega-melodrama! Vertical and Horizontal Suspensions of the 'Classical.'" *Modern Drama* 55, no. 4 (2012): 523–43.

Winnacker, Martha. "The Battle to Stop the Chico Dams." *Southeast Asia Chronicle* 67 (October 1979): 22–29.

Wurfel, David. *Filipino Politics: Development and Decay*. Ithaca: Cornell University Press, 1988.

———. "The Succession Struggle." In May and Nemenzo, *Philippines after Marcos*, 17–44.

Xavier, Ismail. *Allegories of Underdevelopment: Aesthetics and Politics in Modern Brazilian Cinema*. Minneapolis: University of Minnesota Press, 1997.

Youngblood, Robert L. "Government-Media Relations in the Philippines." *Asian Survey* 21, no. 7 (1981): 710–28.

———. *Marcos against the Church: Economic Development and Political Repression in the Philippines*. Ithaca: Cornell University Press, 1990.

Index

Abaya, Marilou (née Diaz): *Brutal* and
  Moral, 236n70; *Karnal,* 112
ABS-CBN (television network), 23,
  123, 147
Agrava Fact-Finding Board, 170,
  247n102
"Ako ay Pilipino" (TV special), 144
Alejandrino, Noe, 170
Almendral, Gemma, 199
alternative press: emergence of, 165–70;
  national allegories of, 166–67; and
  people power, 19; sentimental pub-
  licity of, 166–68, 180, 214–15
Amatong, Jacobo, 170
American Society of Travel Agents
  (ASTA), convention bombing
  (1980), 140–41, 219
Amnesty International, 133, 142
Anderson, Benedict, 117
anti-Marcos movement, 11, 15–18,
  171–75, 194, 203, 215
Apostol, Eugenia D., 149, 169
April Sixth Liberation Movement
  (A6LM), 140, 219
Aquino, Aurora, 164
Aquino, Benigno, Jr.: and April 6th
  Liberation Movement, 140; arrest
  and detention of, 51, 135; assassination of, 18, 160–65, 213, 246n70;
  coverage by alternative press, 166–
  70; funeral of, 165–66; LABAN
  campaign, 135–36; Light a Fire
  Movement, participation in, 138–39;
  and national reconciliation, 161;
  opposition to the Cultural Center
  of the Philippines, 78; rivalry with
  Marcos, 1, 118; senate speech on
  student deaths during First Quarter

Storm, 95–97; U.S. exile, 139; as
  "willing martyr," 162, 167
Aquino, Corazon C., 164, 194–96,
  199–200, 214, 237n5
Armed Forces of the Philippines
  (AFP), 42–43, 61, 118, 200, 219,
  227n76, 254
Arnold, Matthew, 72, 75
Arriola, Joyce, 3
Arroyo, Gloria (née Macapagal), 217
Association of Major Religious Superiors of the Philippines (AMRSP),
  238n16; on human rights violations,
  133 (*see also* Task Force Detainees
  of the Philippines (TFDP)); *Icthys*
  (newsletter), 166; on Negros sugar
  workers, 120–24; on consciousness
  raising, 124, 239n29; *Signs of the
  Times* (weekly bulletin), 143

Babst, Arlene, 149–50
Bagatsing, Ramon, 157
Bagong Alyansang Makabayan
  (BAYAN), 173–74, 194–95, 219
bakya, 86
Bansang Nagkaisa sa Diwa at Layunin
  (BANDILA), 174, 194, 219
Basic Christian Communities (BCCs),
  132, 219
Bautista, Felix, 170
Bayan, Ang (CPP-NPA news organ),
  43, 166, 194
Bayan Ko (protest song), 137
Bayan Ko: Kapit sa Patalim (Brocka),
  19, 181–94, 202, 214, 216
Beams, Dovie, 93–95, 234n30, 234n33,
  235n35
Benedicto, Roberto, 121–22

melodrama: affective conditioning, of, 9, 210–16; and cultural policy, 7–11, 65–66, 209, 211; and First Quarter Storm, 32, 210; and Marcos's political rise, 33, 210; and national allegory, 4, 7–11, 17–19, 214–16
Menzi, Hans, 123, 144–47
Metro Manila, creation of, 146, 242n6
Metro Manila Film Festival, 114, 237n77, 244n32
Mijares, Primitivo, 151; *The Conjugal Dictatorship of Ferdinand and Imelda Marcos*, 151
militarization, 141–43, 148–49
military: interrogation of journalists, 149–50; killings of journalists, 151–52, 170; and people power, 200–201
Miller, Toby, 66; and Yúdice, George (on cultural policy), 70, 73
Ministry of Human Settlements, 146, 159
modernization, 17, 35, 52–62, 72, 79, 80–81, 209
Montes, Sylvia P., 159
Morales, Horacio, Jr., 134
Morato, Manuel, 178
Movement for a Free Philippines (MFP), 139
Movie Workers Welfare Fund (MOW-ELFUND), 114, 237n78
Mr. &Ms., 165–69, 214
Mulvey, Laura, 69

Nacionalista Party, 117
Naiibang Hayop (Marquez), 155–58
national allegory, 1, 4–7, 13, 19, 26, 65–66, 95, 110–12, 167, 192–93, 204, 204–18
National Citizen's Movement for Free Elections (NAMFREL), 198, 206
National Democrats, 127, 174–77, 188–89, 195–99, 208, 215, 217
National Democratic Front (NDF), 122; and Aquino, Corazon, 195; and command demonstrations, 181; post-1986, 217; vangaurdism of, 171–74
national discipline, 53, 63, 205, 209
national family, 68, 83, 98–99, 119, 145–47, 162, 210

national grief, 18, 165–68, 215
National Press Club (NPC), 151, 169–70, 208, 215–17, 220
national reconciliation, 161
national sentimentality, 11–18
national sexuality, 17, 95–99, 103, 110, 157, 209
national symbolic, the, 4, 99, 111
Negros (island), 120
New Cinema, the: auteurs of, 113–14, 160, 236 n70; auteurs and Imelda Marcos, 112–14; and Brocka, Lino, 107; cinematic activism of, 106–14, 160, 210–12; emergence under dictatorship, 18, 83, 106; influence of radical youth politics on, 103–6, 210; and Manila International Film Festival, 158–59; national allegories of, 212
new politics, 2, 19, 171, 175, 182; in *Bayan Ko: Kapit sa Patalim*, 182–95; and elections, 194; and people power, 195–203; post-1986, 217
New Republic, the, 141: disappearances and summary executions in, 142, 170; media coverage of, 144–46; media repression in, 148–52, 170
New Society, the: heritage culture in, 80–83; human rights abuses in, 133; and the internal revolution, 65, 82–83, 100, 209 ; land reform in, 119; and the Marcos romance, 211; media repression in, 143; and modernization, 35, 52, 60; and the New Filipino, 17, 60, 74, 76–79, 82, 100–101, 144; and the quiet revolt of the press, 144–45; regimentation of social conduct in, 52–53, 61–64, 65, 83, 208
Nieva, Antonio, 151, 244n26
Notes on the New Society of the Philippines (Marcos), 53, 57, 64
Nuyda, Doris, 149

Olaguer, Eduardo, 138
oligarchy, 116–18; controlled-media (before martial law), 22, 43, 54, 147; post-1986, 216. *See also* elite politics
Olivares, Ninez (née Cacho), 149, 164

Olivas, Prospero (general), 158
Orcullo, Alex, 170
Oro, Plata, Mata (Gallaga), 156–67,
    236n70, 256
Osmeña, Sergio, Jr., 92

Panorama (Manila), 144–52
*Partido Demokratiko-Sosyalista ng Pili-
    pinas* (PDSP), 137–38
patron-client relations, 119; portrayal
    in *Bayan Ko: Kapit sa Patalim*,
    182–87. *See also* elite politics
Pedrosa, Carmen (née Navarro):
    *Imelda Marcos, the Rise and Fall
    of One of the World's Most Power-
    ful Women*, 73, 94, 202; on people
    power, 202; *The Untold Story of
    Imelda Marcos*, 69
people power, 1–2; elite and middle-
    class agitation in, 19, 193; and
    LABAN campaign, 136; popular
    classes and, 19, 193, 202
People's Victory Rally, 200
Philippine-American War, 58, 229n18
Philippine Motion Picture Producers
    Association (PMPPA), 154
Philippines Free Press (Manila), 16, 25,
    34, 94, 208
Philippine Society and Revolution (Si-
    son), 125
Philippines Times (Manila), 165–69
Pinches, Michael, 193
Plaza Miranda bombing, 44–45
political arrests (during martial law),
    133
political demonology, 16, 39–41, 46–49,
    53, 58, 150, 216
political emotion, 1–3, 105–6, 207–17
political spectacle, 1, 16, 46, 188, 208, 210
political succession struggle, 146, 162
political violence (during elections),
    90–91, 136, 140, 198
Polotan, Kerima, 72, 123
popular classes: activism of (*see* democ-
    racy from below); and alternative
    press, 168; and anti-Marcos move-
    ment, 19; and Aquino, Corazon,
    195–96; *Bayan Ko: Kapit Sa Patalim*,
    portrayal in, 182–94; and business

class, 179–80; and Communist Party
    of the Philippines (CPP-NPA), 122,
    176, 180, 203; and Cultural Center of
    the Philippines, 77–78; and cultural
    policy, 65–67, 81, 209; double repre-
    sentation of (as abject and politically
    volatile), 15–19, 184, 193, 202–3;
    and human rights abuses, 133; and
    melodrama, 10, 195; and patronage
    politics, 174, 217; and people power,
    19, 193, 198–99, 203, 215; sentimental
    portrayal in Marcos romance, 70–75;
    and snap elections, 194, 198
Presidential Assistant on National Mi-
    norities (PANAMIN), 130–31
Presidential Commitment Order
    (PCO), 142, 249n31
Preventive Detention Action (PDA),
    180, 249n31
Project Public Justice, 139
Psinakis, Steve, 138

Quimpo, Nathan Gilbert, 18, 183, 193

Radio Philippines Network (RPN), 123
Radio Veritas, 163–64, 198, 201
Rafael, Vicente: on *puting magmamahal*
    (white love), 58–60, 209; on youth
    politics of the First Quarter Storm,
    28–29,103–4
Ramos, Fidel V., 200
Reagan, Ronald, 199, 250n56
Reform the Armed Forces Movement
    (RAM), 200; coup plot, 201
Rogin, Michael, 38–40, 44–49, 51
Romero, Eddie: *Ganito kami noon,
    paano kayo ngayon?*, 236n70
Romualdez, Benjamin, 123

Sagrado Corazon Señor (Sacred Heart
    of the Lord), 142
Sakada (Cervantes), 18, 122–30, 180,
    213, 215
Salonga, Jovito, 134
Salvador, Leroy: *The Victim*, 155–58
salvagings (summary executions), 142,
    151–52, 170, 176
Sanjuan, Epifanio, Jr., 196–97
sentimental aesthetic, 13, 211–12

www.ingramcontent.com/pod-product-compliance
Lightning Source LLC
Chambersburg PA
CBHW021855020426
42334CB00013B/335